PROACTIVE PARENTING

PROACTIVE PARENTING

GUIDING YOUR CHILD FROM TWO TO SIX

FACULTY OF TUFTS UNIVERSITY'S
ELIOT-PEARSON DEPARTMENT OF CHILD
DEVELOPMENT

Foreword by David Elkind

BERKLEY BOOKS, NEW YORK

A Berkley Book
Published by The Berkley Publishing Group
A division of Penguin Putnam Inc.
375 Hudson Street
New York, New York 10014

Every effort has been made to ensure that the information contained in this book is complete and accurate. However, neither the publisher nor the authors are engaged in rendering professional advice or services to the individual reader. The ideas, procedures, and suggestions contained in this book are not intended as a substitute for consulting with your physician. All matters regarding your child's health require medical supervision. Neither the authors nor the publisher shall be liable or responsible for any loss, injury, or damage allegedly arising from any information or suggestion in this book. The opinions expressed in this book represent the personal views of the authors and not of the publisher.

Excerpt on pages 28–29 from *The Only Child*, from *The Fascinating Stranger* by Booth Tarkington (New York, Doubleday, Page and Co., 1923).

First edition: February 2003

Visit our website at
www.penguinputnam.com

Library of Congress Cataloging-in-Publication Data

Proactive parenting : guiding your child from two to six / faculty of Tufts University's Eliot-Pearson Department of Child Development.
p. cm.
Includes bibliographical references and index.
ISBN 0-425-18837-X
1. Child rearing. 2. Parenting. 3. Parent and child. I. Tufts University. Eliot-Pearson Dept. of Child Development.

HQ769 .P8294 2003
649'.1—dc21   2002038568

PRINTED IN THE UNITED STATES OF AMERICA

10   9   8   7   6   5   4   3   2   1

CONTENTS

Children and Parents in Relationships

Children and Parents as Learners

FOREWORD

What is really going on when your three-year-old starts bossing around her playmates, or your four-year-old "plays doctor" with the child next door? How should you respond when your frightened preschooler wants to sleep in your bed, or your toddler grabs a friend's toy? It's at times like these that it's useful to understand why your child is behaving this way, and how these behaviors reflect the child's unique understanding of the world.

That is where this book can help. It's a collaborative effort from my colleagues at the Eliot-Pearson Department of Child Development at Tufts University, one of the world's premier centers for the study of how children grow and learn, and how best to apply that knowledge to children in the real world. The book's authors have a tremendous amount of combined experience in hands-on work with children of all kinds, as well as in research and teaching. This book distills their experience into key information that parents need to know to help their young children grow up healthy and ready for success in today's world.

The Eliot-Pearson philosophy holds that early childhood is a unique period of life that has to be seen as important in its own right, not just as preparation for the next phase. Young children are not in the wings of life, waiting to perform; they are already on life's stage and are actively playing their parts. Our core values flow from this basic tenet:

- Respect for the young child as a unique person deserving of respect, thoughtfulness, and unconditional acceptance—even when that child needs firm guidance to change negative behavior. Also, while young children have ways of seeing the world different from ours, these perspectives are not wrong; they are simply different, and natural to their ages.

- Commitment to the active development of partnerships and community, including partnerships between parents and schools. We recognize the need to work at building connections and caring relationships—especially in today's mobile society—and wish to model that behavior for children.

- Celebration of diversity and respect for individual and cultural variation. We appreciate the things we can learn from and share with each other, and try to develop connections across our differences. This book includes examples from a number of different cultures and perspectives.

- Belief in the importance of humility and humor. We acknowledge and accept our own and others' fallibility, and try not to take ourselves too seriously.

Finally, it's important to recognize that parents are people, too, and that child rearing is best seen as people relating to people. It is this conception of parents as people, rather than as therapists, trainers, or disciplinarians, that makes this book different from so many other parenting books. The book is different in other respects as well. Rather than simply describing strategies and techniques, the authors anchor them to development research and theory. The research and theory, however, are presented in accessible language, in such ways that the parenting practices flow naturally from them, and are illustrated with examples drawn from the department's laboratory schools. It is this unique melding of child development theory and research with practical parenting advice that makes this book so different from other parenting books and manuals.

The book is divided into two parts. The first section, Children and Parents in Relationships, looks at ideas and issues that are embedded in how parents, children, and families interact. The first chapter, Improving the Parent-Child Match, sets the stage for the interactional and context-based approach to child rearing that is the hallmark of this book. This chapter explains the ways in which the presence of a child has a profound and long-lasting influence on you, the parent. It reviews the factors, from temperament to cognitive style to personality, that make your child the unique individual that she is, and how those factors affect the way a parent responds to her child. Finally, it looks at practical ways to improve the "goodness of fit" between parent and child.

The second chapter, Conflicts and Routines, focuses on ways that the interactions of family members—between parent and child, between siblings, and between parents—can promote or reduce conflict. It stresses the fact that living together effectively requires continual negotiation and balancing of needs and interests, and that creating routines is one good way to reduce tensions and promote harmony. The third chapter, Proactive Parenting for Behavior Problems, extends the theme of the previous chapter in showing how behavior problems reflect a child's attempts to adapt to his world. Discipline, then, is not a matter of stamping out "bad" behaviors but of helping children learn more effective coping strategies. The chapter discusses how to encourage your child to behave appropriately in the short term (or, when necessary, immediately!) while also teaching lessons for the long term.

Despite the comfort with sexually explicit material suggested by our media, sexuality and physical affection are still difficult topics for parents to deal with. The chapter on "Touchy" Issues: Physical Closeness and Affection deals with these issues in a sensitive and supportive way. It emphasizes the importance of closeness, and looks at how different families and cultures express it. It also stresses a nonjudgmental, informed acceptance of the young child's natural curiosity about her own and others' bodies, and the need to provide appropriate guidance about physical exploration and sexuality.

Certainly one of the most important indices of healthy development is the ability to interact positively with peers. The Importance of Friendship looks at children's understanding of friendships, and how those friendships evolve from parallel play to shared fantasy play. There are also helpful suggestions on how parents can help their children develop age-appropriate friendships, and teach their children to handle those inevitable conflicts with peers. The last chapter in this section, Transition, Change, and Crisis, looks at how children try to adapt to and make sense of change. It gives example-based advice on ways to help children negotiate the many kinds of change that life presents to us, from benign (a new baby) to serious (illness or death).

The second half of the book, Children and Parents as Learners, deals with another facet of the "parents as people" approach to child rearing. Learning is often thought of in the narrow sense, as something that goes on in school. At Eliot-Pearson, learning is viewed more broadly as a life-long activity that goes on naturally all of the time. Children learn from a walk in the woods, a visit to grandparents in another part of the country, or a stop at the post office. This theme is elaborated in many different ways in this part of the book.

Frederich Froebel, who created the kindergarten, was among the first to recognize the parents' role as teachers and the home as the first school. This theme is elaborated in the chapter Home as the First School, which stresses that what most prepares a child for school is not teaching the alphabet, but instead promoting curiosity, a love of learning, and the confidence to take age-appropriate risks. This includes discovering and nurturing a child's various interests, abilities, and talents. There are helpful hints about providing age-appropriate creative materials in the home and making the most of excursions outside the home.

Perhaps one of the most misunderstood concepts with respect to young children is that of play. Montessori's unfortunate identification of "play as the child's work" is one reason. The confusion of play with competitive sports is another. The chapter on Supporting Your Child's Play does much to clarify how children use play to make sense of their world. It looks at how play evolves over time, and what this reveals about the child's thinking and stage of development. Along with helpful suggestions on ways to support healthy play, this chapter reassures parents about what's "normal"—including play with themes of war or death— and gives examples of how to redirect overly aggressive play.

Certainly one of the most exciting and challenging aspects of young children's development is their progressive mastery of language. The Child as Communicator deals with many of the concerns that parents have about the development of their children's growing communicative capacities. In a sensitive, supportive way, it helps parents understand children's linguistic "mistakes," the value of baby talk, and when to be concerned about issues such as language delays. This chapter also untangles much of the confusion about bilingualism and gives many helpful examples for building a child's language skills. Closely related to the child's developing verbal skills is the attainment of literacy. The next chapter, Learning to Write and Read, helps parents understand how children make sense of the mysteries of written language, and why some children have difficulty despite the efforts of parents and teachers. It also emphasizes the fact that not all children learn to read in the same way, and that parents and teachers have to be flexible in their approach. At the same time, it emphasizes that adults reading to children—and providing them with a rich language environment—is helpful to all children.

One of the ways in which the contemporary environment is unique for today's children is the pervasiveness of the media. Children today, unlike those of the past, spend a great deal of their waking time in front of screens: movie screens, television screens, and computer screens. Electronic Media in Young Children's Lives provides a balanced and reassuring assessment of the effects of the time and attention spent watching screens. In addition to calming fears about the harm done to children by the media, it makes a case for helping children develop "media literacy": to become critical consumers of media fare.

Another way in which the contemporary environment is different from the past is the number of young children who are enrolled in early childhood programs. It is estimated that more that 60 percent of mothers with young children are in the workforce full- or part-time, and make use of some form of early childhood education. This requires parents to become informed consumers of early childhood programs. Becoming informed consumers is the best response to the natural anxiety many parents feel when thinking about out-of-home care for their young child. Parents' anxiety is based upon fears that out-of-home care won't be good for their child. Happily, the reality is that there are many wonderful early childhood programs where young children don't just adjust, they thrive. It's important, then, to know how to find them and how to find the best match for your child. The chapter on Sending Your Child to School: The Home/School Partnership seeks to help parents choose wisely and well. Here the authors offer not only a checklist of things to look for but also guidance in finding the best match for program and child, and for working with the school in partnership.

Now that I have summarized the major topics and themes of the book, it is appropriate to say something about it in general. Books written by different authors often lack consistency and coherence. That is not the case with this book. The theme of child rearing as "people dealing with people" is the common thread that provides unity and consistency across all chapters. Another thread is the sympathetic approach to parents—an understanding of their normal and reasonable concerns and anxieties. Last but not least is the thread of deep-seated respect and concern for children. For all of these reasons, I do not see this book as a guide or handbook for parents, but rather as a kind of portable mentor. That is, it's the empathetic tone and sympathetic style of the book, as much as its content, that should make parents regard it as a trusted friend whose advice they feel confident and comfortable about putting into practice.

—David Elkind, Ph.D.,
author of *The Hurried Child*

ACKNOWLEDGMENTS

This book is the product of a group of faculty and collaborators at the Eliot-Pearson Department of Child Development at Tufts University. It was inspired by the children whom we see on our playgrounds, in our hallways, and outside our windows (at the Eliot-Pearson Children's School and the Tufts Educational Day Care Center, our two laboratory schools) and by their families. The joy, courage, dedication, and good humor with which they meet the challenges of growing up and raising children put meaning to the written word of this book.

To get a group of faculty to articulate a unified vision, to come to consensus, to speak in a singular voice rather than multiples, is a monumental, some might say impossible, task. This challenge was made easier by the fact that Eliot-Pearson, as an institution, shares a singular vision and mission that has unified our disparate voices throughout its eighty-year history. That mission is to study and serve children and families and to promote their positive development. In doing so, we recognize the importance of those who work on behalf of these goals, both by creating and exploring theory about how children develop and by working directly with children and families. This commitment undoubtedly sustained us throughout the process of conceptualizing and writing this volume.

The process of writing this book had many phases, just like childhood. The initial spark came from Gareth Esersky and Carol Mann of the

Carol Mann Agency. We thank them for providing the "seeds of imagination"—that Eliot-Pearson was the right place to develop such a book for and about children and parents—and for providing expert guidance along the way.

At the outset of the project, Susan Ernst, dean of arts and sciences at Tufts University, provided both the emotional support needed to encourage our group to undertake such a task, unusual in a university setting, as well as the financial support to make it possible. Francine Jacobs, then chair of the department, engaged faculty in the project and shepherded the initial phase of the writing process. Sylvia Feinburg, our beloved professor emeritus, lent her wisdom to initial discussions of how best to conceive of and design this book.

Two faculty members, George Scarlett and Fred Rothbaum, embraced the "book project" with particular energy and vision. They assumed special responsibility for coordinating the writing of the chapters and working with the editors and publishers, bringing the book forward to completion.

The help of several consultants resulted in a book that draws upon the expertise of Eliot-Pearson and makes it accessible to parents. Jennifer Kapuscik lent her considerable editing skills to help fashion the initial book proposal. Larry Kutner provided helpful advice and encouragement, and Mindy Werner worked to help us find the right model for shaping different chapters to make a harmonious whole. Toward the end of the writing process, Cheryl Olson spent several months working her "editorial magic" in order to take the group's many voices and writing styles and create the one common voice and style that makes the book so readable.

Finally, the entire faculty of Eliot-Pearson contributed to this book by reading and commenting on versions of chapters and by agreeing to the Eliot-Pearson signature.

—Ann Easterbrooks
chair, Eliot-Pearson Department of Child Development

Photo by Shirley Scarlett

Children and Parents in Relationships

C H A P T E R   O N E

"Easy," "Difficult," or Unique?
Improving the Parent-Child Match

Richard M. Lerner

When his son was born, Mitch had imagined tossing a giggling Jordan up in the air and teaching him to kick a ball—just as his dad had done with him. He pictured young Jordan coming in sweaty and streaked with dirt, with some new discovery to show off.

But three-year-old Jordan gets upset when Mitch tries to roughhouse with him. He hangs back in new situations instead of jumping in. He'd rather sit down and listen to a story than run around outside. Jordan is so different from the rambunctious boy Mitch expected that he worries, **"Are we doing something wrong?"**

In our fondest fantasies, we imagine that our children will combine the best traits of both parents: Mom's easy laugh and gift with words, Dad's patience and dexterous hands—and maybe Uncle Gil's talent for finance.

We recall phrases such as "like father, like son" and "the apple doesn't fall far from the tree."

Wouldn't it be great if the combination of your genes and your child rearing brought forth a delightful child who shared all of your interests and talents, and never woke you up at night? Unfortunately, reality is much more complicated than that. Now that your baby has grown into a toddler or preschooler, he's made it his business to let you know that he's a distinct individual. And, if you've had more than one child, you know what different results similar genes and environments can create.

Like Mitch, many parents feel surprised or frustrated—even worried or guilty—when their child behaves contrary to expectations, or unlike other children in the family or neighborhood. But there is a lot parents can do to enable their hopes to be fulfilled. The key is *understanding the factors that make your child an individual.*

Your child is partly a product of who you are and what you do. But no two children, not even identical twins, are completely alike. Your child is unique in her combination of talents, interests and attitudes; her physical abilities, looks, or medical problems; her intellect and learning style; and the way she reacts to and behaves toward you and the rest of her family.

Your child's behavior is also influenced by many sources that lie outside the family. Kids exist in a complex ecology of human development—including peers, the neighborhood, the larger culture (and perhaps subcultures), and the historical time in which you live. These forces and more all affect your child's development.

The best way to change a child's behavior is not through pestering or punishing; by knowing what to expect from him, you can create an emotional and physical environment that will bring out the best in your child—and in you. Your child may meet, or miss, some of the original expectations and hopes you had—but he may also surpass your dreams, perhaps in unexpected ways.

In this chapter, we'll look at:

- How your child's individuality affects you as a parent

- Understanding your child's temperament (including the "difficult" child)

- Cognitive style, personality, and other ways your child is unique

- Understanding "goodness of fit" between child and parent

- Ways to improve the match between parent and child

- Ways to improve the match between child and home environment

How Your Child Influences You

Deirdre's first child, Kirk, was an easygoing little boy. She and her husband often took him to restaurants and out shopping. As long as he wasn't hungry or overtired, he was usually in a cheerful mood, and would play happily next to his mom or dad in a playpen in the office of their family business. As Kirk grew older, he'd color or watch favorite videos (about fire trucks and construction sites) in the back of the office after preschool.

With their second child, Kaitlin, it was a completely different story. She had medical problems that needed monitoring, so there was extra worry from the start. But she was also squirmy and hard to comfort and calm. As she grew older, she was very sensitive to small irritations, from sunlight in her eyes to labels in clothing; haircuts were a particular trial, since she hated getting any hair down her neck. Deirdre confided to a friend that if Kaitlin had been her first child, she'd have thought long and hard before having a second.

From the moment you realize "I'm going to be a parent!" your behavior begins to change. The mere idea of a baby alters what the prospective mother eats and drinks. It changes the adult partnership into which the baby will be born, as the future parents rethink who they are and who they want to be. It changes the home where the baby will live and develop as parents buy gear, prepare a space, and move breakable or dangerous objects. The physical reality of a new child has an even greater effect on parents' behavior and psychology, as you miss sleep, face strong feelings of love and anger, and worry about your competence and your child's future.

It's clear that not only do parents influence their child's development, but in turn, the presence of a child has a profound and long-lasting influence on how her parents think and act. Think of the many ways being a parent makes you different than you'd be if you were childless. For example:

- You make friends with other parents; conversations often shift to the topic of children and child rearing. (What did you used to talk about?)

- You search for experiences that will enrich your child's life: preschool programs, playdates with other children, or trips to zoos or amusement parks. You go to many places you'd never otherwise visit.

- You may seek advice from your own parents—who now, as grandparents, represent a significant source of support and (to their delight) wisdom.

- You seek ways to enrich your knowledge and skills as a parent, perhaps through taking a parent education course, or (as you're now doing) reading a book about parenting.

The mere fact that you now have a child for whom you are responsible changes your behavior, thoughts, and feelings. But that doesn't even consider your child as a person—the effects of his specific health, physical, behavioral, and cognitive characteristics on your behavior. Just as your behavior shapes the parent-child relationship, your child's does, too. In a sense, your child rears *you* as much as you rear *him*.

The specific and often special characteristics of a particular child influence her parents in unique ways. How we behave toward our children depends quite a lot on how they influence us to behave. Think of the effects these scenarios would have on you as a parent (and on your relationship with your spouse or partner):

- Your child has a chronic or acute medical condition or physical disability.

- Your child is extremely active and restless, resistant to changes in eating or sleeping routines, and reacts dramatically when upset (behavior problems).

- Your child has a short attention span, is highly distractible, and has trouble with speech or reading (learning problems).

Researchers who study child development have a name for the way a child's unique characteristics influence his parents: they call this *child effects*. Through child effects, children influence the parents who are influencing them. Children are then shaping a key source of their own development: their family. In this sense, children are producers of their own development. Of course, this bidirectional relationship continues when the child is an adolescent and an adult. And corresponding relationships exist between the child and his siblings, friends, teachers—and indeed, all other significant people in his life. (For simplicity's sake, we focus here on effects on parents, though the examples may apply to other relationships as well.)

CHILD EFFECTS: HOW THE CYCLE WORKS

1. *Each child is a unique individual*, with distinctive physical, behavioral, and psychological characteristics. As a simple illustration, let's look at two toddlers. David is a cuddly child who has a predictable nap each

day and sleeps pretty much all night. Cole can be delightful at times, but doesn't like a lot of physical closeness; he naps irregularly (often not at all) and sometimes wakes up early in the morning.

2. As a result of their individuality, *children show different behavior and give different feedback to their parents*. David, who often reaches out for hugs, and naps with little complaint, creates a different experience for his parents than Cole does for his.

3. *Because of different ways their children behave, parents will behave, think, and feel differently*. One obvious example is that David's parents will be better rested, which should positively affect their mood!

4. *Parents are individuals*, too, and their unique combination of characteristics will *affect the feedback they give to their children*—thus completing the circle of child effects. For example, if Cole's father likes lots of physical roughhousing and affection, he will be bothered by Cole's tense reaction to touch. The father may withdraw, feeling rejected, and wonder what's wrong with Cole—or what he himself is doing wrong. On the other hand, if Cole's mother likes to have more personal space, she'll enjoy having him sit near her while she reads, rather than on her lap—and may read to him more often.

The individuality of these parents' reactions underscores the idea that parents are as individually distinct as are their children. Not all parents of, let's say, a stubborn, clingy child who's a picky eater will react with concern or frustration. Similarly, some parents will be stressed by even the most regular, predictable, and positive child. You may be surprised when your child's behavior makes you react in ways that you didn't anticipate, and may not like. Such parental individuality makes child effects more complicated to study. However, at the same time, parental individuality is part of the unique nature of each child's world.

Differences in Temperament

The fact that no two children are exactly alike is the key to understanding the role of your child in your behavior as a parent. To understand the importance of child individuality, let's first look at children's temperaments.

> "Dee was such an *easy* baby; we could take her anywhere."
>
> "Sidney can be so *difficult* at times—especially at bedtime!"
>
> "Give him time; Diego's just *slow to warm up*."

In the 1950s, the assumption of many "experts" was that if a child had behavior problems, it was his mother's fault. But some observers noticed that emotionally disturbed mothers sometimes had healthy kids, and some mothers who seemed to "do everything right" had very problematic children. Concerns like these led to the start of a famous study of temperament, the New York Longitudinal Study, by Stella Chess, Alexander Thomas, and Herbert Birch.

Temperament (behavioral style) is a way of describing *how* children do whatever they do, though not *what* or *why* they do it. For instance, all children eat and sleep. These are instances of what children do. Temperament is the *style* of eating or sleeping shown by a child: if he gets hungry at the same times each day, and tends to eat the same amount at every meal, then this child has (at least, as concerns eating) a regular, or rhythmic, temperament. A child who gets hungry at different times of the day, or who may unpredictably eat a lot or a little, would have an arrhythmic temperament.

As the babies in the study grew into children and teens, it became clear that children's temperaments can vary along a number of dimensions:

Categories of Temperament

(Chess and Thomas)

Activity level: One child can sit still at the table for half an hour, while another is squirming in his chair within minutes.

Distractibility: One child can listen to you read a story despite the road construction outside; another is easily diverted by the noise or movements.

Attention span and persistence: One child focuses intently for a long time on building a wall (perhaps to the point of stubbornness when asked to move on); another quickly grows bored and seeks a new activity.

Adaptability: One child adjusts fairly quickly to a new routine, and recovers from a stubbed toe after a brief fuss; another needs extra support and time to feel comfortable in a new place, and cries longer over a hurt.

Approach or withdrawal: One child is shy and hangs back when meeting new kids, and is reluctant to try new foods; another jumps in quickly.

Intensity of reaction: One child expresses dramatic highs and lows, while another is usually even-tempered and is more likely to whimper than cry loudly.

Regularity (rhythmicity): One child has fairly predictable naptimes and hungry times; another sleeps erratically, and is ravenous one day, picky the next.

Sensory threshold: One child is sensitive to rough clothing and loud noises, and sometimes stiffens when touched; another is easygoing about these, and requires a lot of stimulation to provoke a reaction.

Mood: One child wakes up with a smile most days; another is often cranky and hard to cheer up.

Of course, not all children are at one extreme or the other; many are "middling" in most temperament categories. Each child will express her individual combination of these traits. Both genes and environment shape temperament, and as a result, brothers and sisters, and even twins, can have quite different temperaments.

Another thing the researchers noticed was that in some (but not all) children, these traits seemed to cluster into patterns: an "easy" child had regular routines, a generally positive and undramatic mood, and adjusted well to new people and situations. Another pattern could be called "slow to warm up": children who hang back and need time to adjust to new people and environments. A smaller number of kids were "difficult": they had variable eating and sleeping routines, were often irritable, had more intense moods, and were slow to adjust to changes.

Is "Difficult" Bad?

When we look more closely at "difficult" children, we see that whether their behavior is a problem or not depends in part on the situation.

One study in Africa looked at "easy" and "difficult" small children among the Masai during a time of famine. When the researchers returned a year later, they found that many of the children were no longer alive—and that most of the dead were from the "easy" temperament group. Why? The difficult kids demanded more attention, food, and water. The easy kids adapted to scarcity, complained less . . . and died. In some situations, the old saying applies: "the squeaky wheel gets the grease."

In most U.S. homes, the demands, moods, and erratic schedules of "difficult" children are not a good fit. However, this also depends on the parents' interpretation of the children's behavior. Some days, exhausted parents can feel that an oppositional or grumpy child is "out to get them." By contrast, in one survey, many moms pointed to their "difficult" child with pride—as someone who "wouldn't take crap from anybody."

Instead of labeling or judging a child based on temperament, it makes more sense to look at the relationship between a child's *characteristics* and the *context* he's in. If a child refuses to share or trade a toy, it may be partly due to his nondistractible, persistent temperament (as well as his age, of course); it doesn't mean that he'll grow up to be selfish. A child's arrhythmic sleeping patterns can be a plus if a parent's work requires changing shifts and he wants to spend time with his child. An intense child is hard to take when she's upset, but can be delightful when she dramatically and affectionately expresses her happiness. Also, intense children often have lots of energy, which can be a plus *if* that energy is constructively directed.

Differences in Cognitive Style

> Looking down at the vegetable on his plate, five-year-old Ricky says, "I don't like that."
>
> "Ricky, I know you didn't like the broccoli," his dad says reasonably.
>
> "But these are peas. They taste completely different."
>
> "No. I don't like green food."

Another way children show their individuality is through their cognitive style. People differ in the way they think about objects or events. Some people like to group things, and tend to look for similarities: we call them "levelers." Others, the "sharpeners," tend to focus on differences. Ricky is a classic leveler: since he doesn't like broccoli, and it's a green vegetable, he figures he won't like asparagus, green beans, or peas.

A child who's a sharpener might say to himself, "Well, broccoli looks like a spiky flower and it tastes yucky. But peas are small and round—I can try those." If you know your child is a leveler, you may need to find ways to reward him in some situations for noticing differences. "Okay, I'll tell him that flowery things taste different from round things—and not mention the green part." Or, you might mix the peas in with something that will help disguise the color.

Another example: A young child tends to want to hear the same book over and over, which can drive a parent crazy—especially if you didn't care for it much the first time. A sharpener in particular might say, "No, I just want *that* book." Try to find out what he particularly likes about that book: perhaps the colors, drawings, size, texture, rhymes, or some aspect of the characters or plot. If you know he likes the Donald Duck book, you can say, "Well, both Donald Duck and Bugs Bunny do funny things. Let's see if we can find something in the Bugs book that's funny like the Donald Duck book."

As with temperament, context is key. Both leveling and sharpening have good points, depending on the situation. A leveler will listen when you say, "Never go home with someone after preschool except Mom, Dad, or your brother." In other words, "Treat anyone who's not us the same way."

But a six-year-old sharpener could handle this request better: "We always want you to tell people the truth. If you're not going to eat something, we want you to be polite and say 'No thanks, I'm not hungry.' That is, except if you're at Grandma's—she makes cookies especially for you. She'll be hurt if you don't take a cookie. So if you're not hungry, tell Grandma, 'Thanks for the cookie; I'm going to save it for later.' "

Other Ways Children Can Be Different

Temperament and cognitive style are just two of the many aspects of your child's individuality. Children also differ in personality. Your child may be a reckless daredevil or very cautious. Some children are gregarious and make friends easily, while others like to have one best friend and don't care to play in groups. Some children learn and adapt to rules well, while others may learn the rules but not adapt well.

Children also differ in their interests and potential abilities (we say more about interests and "intelligences" in chapter 7). While parents can shape interests by exposing children to different things, children will naturally find certain subjects more appealing. They also vary in their physical appearance and their motor skills; if your child resembles a beloved relative, or has trouble holding on to a ball, it can definitely affect how you respond to her.

Finally, children differ in their rates of growth and development; this can worry parents, especially if they don't realize that the "norms" on the pediatrician's charts are merely averages, and have little meaning for individual kids. (Often, *when* a child passes a milestone [such as toilet training] matters far less than *whether* he eventually does pass it—though this is small comfort to a parent who's tired of diapers, or who needs her child to be fully trained to enter a preschool.)

All of these aspects of your child's individuality affect you as a parent—but not all of them are things you are responsible for creating. Also, many aspects will change with time and maturation. So, for most of these small annoyances of child rearing, don't feel too guilty, and don't worry too much.

For each of these aspects of individuality, parents and others who care for a child have to be aware of what can be changed about the *child,* the *adult,* or the *context* to achieve a better fit. Because all of these areas interact, it's a highly complex undertaking.

Parent-Child "Goodness of Fit"

When the New York Longitudinal Study began, one assumption was that children's temperaments would strongly affect how those children "turned out" psychologically. But the researchers found that a better predictor of healthy psychological functioning was how well a child's abilities, personality, and temperament matched her environment, and the expectations and demands she faced from her parents and other important adults. This idea came to be called *goodness of fit.*

> Darya was a little terror. At age three, she was generally in a bad mood and couldn't be "jollied" out of it. She expressed her highs and lows with great intensity, and there was no discernible pattern to when or how long she would sleep or be hungry.
>
> Her siblings were the dutiful, high-achieving kind, fitting the expecta-

tions of her parents. Her father was a successful entrepreneur in the arts. He, in particular, found Darya so contrary to his image of what a smart, cute little girl should be that they were constantly in conflict. He sometimes took his anger out on Darya's mother: "Why aren't you being a better parent? This child is a devil; she's destroying the family." In turn, when she was old enough to express it, Darya said her dad was mean and never liked anything she did.

This continued as Darya started elementary school. Then one evening, everything changed. Her dad had some leading musicians over for a business-related party. Some had come straight from practice, bringing their instruments along in cases.

When Darya wandered in, her dad said, "Stay out of the way!" Darya had shown no interest in music up to now (perhaps because her dad loved it). She picked up an instrument and blew into it. Her dad moved to grab her, but its owner said, "Let her play." Within a few minutes, Darya had figured out how to use it and was making up music. Soon she moved on to another instrument and did the same thing.

Suddenly her father reinterpreted not only Darya's current behavior, but all of her past. "My daughter may be temperamental, but she's an artist. We have to bend a bit to accommodate creative genius!"

The two went on to develop a very good relationship. Darya became a successful musician, and viewed her father as loving and supportive.

This story, based on a real child in the New York Longitudinal Study, may be unusual, but it does illustrate the importance of how a parent *interprets* his child's behavior, and how he then *behaves* toward her based on that interpretation plus his expectations of how the child ought to behave.

(This also shows that "difficult" children can turn out very well. In fact, the child with the "easiest" temperament in the NYLS—a warm, cheerful, and attractive girl, with predictable habits and an easygoing approach to life—eventually had an emotional breakdown. The point is not to make premature assumptions and judgments about your child's behavior and what it might mean.)

Parents and children can even share a temperamental characteristic and still not have a good match. For example, you may dislike seeing your own stubbornness in your child, or you may both have irregular sleeping patterns, but you still hate it when your child wakes you at odd hours.

So, a good fit is not a matter of your temperament versus your child's, but of the *demands* placed on your child. By "demand," we mean something the child must do either to meet her parents' expectations, or to adjust to the rules or characteristics of the family. Just as children bring their individual traits to their relationships with parents, parents and the homes they provide place social and physical demands on their children. Demands may take the form of:

- *Attitudes or values the parents may have* about, for instance, child obedience to family rules, or about the extent to which the child's own desires or opinions are appropriate to consider in family decisions;

- *Behavioral characteristics or needs of the parents,* for instance, in regard to the needs of a parent with a very busy work schedule to have the child go to bed at a fixed time; or finally

- *Physical characteristics of the home,* for instance, in a home with several other siblings, pets, and two busy parents, noise and activity levels may be high; an easily distractible child with a short attention span might not find it easy to accomplish her chores or do her homework in such a setting.

In sum, goodness of fit concerns a match between behaviors, attitudes, and values and the physical characteristics of a place. A simple example is that of a parent who really wants extra sleep on the weekend. If she has a very active child and lives in a small apartment, this goal will be constantly frustrated.

Because children differ in their physical and behavioral characteristics, they may not be equally able to meet the attitudinal, behavioral, or physical demands of their parents or families. *Differences in meeting these demands provide a basis for the specific feedback the child gets from parents and from the family in general.*

For example, consider demands associated with attitudes and values. Parents might wish their children to be moderately distractible when, for example, they need them to move from watching television to dinner or to bed. A child whose temperament is generally very distractible, will meet that "go to bed" demand differently from a child who is hard to distract. If the parents see the "hard to distract" behavior as stubbornness or deliberate disobedience, tense parent-child relations might develop as a consequence of a child's lack of match—or a lack of goodness of fit—with the demand.

Researchers at Eliot-Pearson and elsewhere have found that if a child's individual characteristics provide a good fit (or match) with the demands of parents and the home, then healthy and positive child development will result. In turn, if those characteristics fit poorly or are mismatched, children show problems in their development.

For instance, attributes of temperament that create "difficulty" for caregiving—that don't match with, or fit, the parents' demands—are often associated with negative parental and family relations. We talked earlier about children whom parents often find "difficult": they are moody and arrhythmic, they don't fit with the attitudes, preferences, or behavioral expectations of parents, and they often get into more "trouble" with their parents or siblings than do children with "easy" temperaments (children who are rhythmic, have a positive mood, and who fit more with parent preferences or expectations).

Understandably, mothers of difficult children often use intrusive, controlling techniques to keep them out of trouble. Not surprisingly, these children resist their mothers' attempts at control—and the result is a relationship marked by conflict. If a parent can't figure out what her child needs, or what to do about it ("Why is this kid always so negative?" "He's constantly wearing me out!"), she'll feel ineffective and frustrated. If a parent finds, over and over, that she can't create a warm, positive interaction with her child, it's hard for her not to respond with anger, avoidance, or worse. Indeed, some research has found that mothers of difficult children interact less with them and are less responsive to them than are mothers of easy children.

In short, through the goodness of fit that exists between the child's characteristics of individuality, and the demands placed upon the child by the parents' own characteristics and by the home they provide, a circle of positive or negative feedback is created. Thus, characteristics of child individuality, be they physical or behavioral, can influence the parent-child relationship and the entire family. The question is, How can you use this knowledge about the influence of your child's individuality on your behavior to create a healthy home setting—one that promotes positive child (and parent) development?

Child Effects and Your Family: Predicting Areas of Conflict

Many guides for parents do a superb job of explaining the general characteristics of infancy, childhood, and adolescence. This is important—in fact invaluable—information because in some respects, all children are like all other children (in their sequence of physical growth, or in their stages of cognitive development). In addition, *all* children are like *some* other children in some respects (e.g., they may share with other children of their gender, race, or ethnicity specific physical attributes and cultural heritages). However, each child is also like *no* other child. And here, in respect to this distinctiveness, no general guide for parents can tell you all the precise ways in which your specific child is an individual.

General information on child effects—that your child can affect your own behavior and development—will not help you figure out just what specific effects exist in your relationship with your son or daughter. How, then, do you learn about the specific child effects present in your family? In addition to learning your child's characteristics of individuality, you need to know something about the characteristics of each person in the family (including your own) if you want to improve the fit between your child, you, and the other members of his family.

Useful questions to assess child effects include:

• What attitudes and emotional or behavioral reactions exist in your family regarding your child's physical, cognitive, and temperamental characteristics?

Examples: You were hoping for a big kid who could play football, or a small flexible one for gymnastics. You like to relax and read on weekends, and your active child bugs you to run around with her outside.

• Do you or other members of the family feel that your child's behavior is violating family rules, traditions, or preferences?

Examples: You like to sit and talk with your spouse for a half hour to reconnect after work, and your child wants to eat and run immediately. Good manners means sitting quietly at holiday dinners, and your child's up tearing around after five minutes.

• Are you easily upset if your child refuses food, or if he can't be calmed when in the midst of a tantrum?

Examples: Your child refuses to try your aunt's spinach quiche. You believe that giving a hug is calming and loving, but your child pushes you away when he's upset.

• Do you feel annoyed if it takes a long time to get your child to sleep?

Example: It's eight o'clock and you want some adult private time, or need time to work; your child can't seem to settle down without your physical presence.

• Does your toddler's high activity level wear you down, or do you worry that he might outrun you and get hurt? Who in the family can best handle this kind of energy level?

• Who will help your child get back to sleep, especially when there are repeated needs for such caregiving?

• Who in the family is particularly disturbed if the child cries loudly, plays loud music, or is otherwise noisy? Who can more easily adjust to this?

Answering questions such as these will help you start finding areas
where you need to create a better fit. By finding creative ways to change
yourself, your child, other family members, and the home, you can create
a happier environment for all of you. (Note that temperament also affects
sibling fights; preschoolers with different temperaments tend to have
more conflicts, especially if at least one child is highly active, with high
emotional intensity and low persistence.)

With some of the above, there is limited room for change; you can't
control your child's size, only your attitude toward it. Other areas give
more room for adjustment.

Examples of Ways to Improve the Parent-Child Fit

When Molly was a child, her family made a point of having dinner
together as a way to touch base each day. It's important to her to continue this tradition; she likes to have dinner on the table every night at six.
While her husband and older daughter enjoy this time as well, her young
son, Pete, often pushes his plate away, saying, "I'm not hungry." This really
bothers Molly, who works hard to arrange her schedule so she can cook
healthy meals.

If your child is hungry at unpredictable times, and you like the family to sit down to dinner every night at six, you can expect to have a series
of bad interactions at dinner. In the example, there's also the perceived
challenge to Molly's values (and an insult to her cooking), although Pete
is not doing this on purpose.

To create a better fit, a parent in this situation can try several things:
Change the child's lunch or snack routines to increase the odds that he'll
be hungry at dinner. Eat a late snack yourself, and delay dinner until six-
thirty or seven. Or, continue with the current schedule; if the child's not
hungry, say, "Okay. Sit here and talk with us. I'll give you a banana and
cereal in an hour." This at least forms a habit of sitting down to dinner

together; in time, your child may develop a more predictable eating schedule.

With planning, parents can usually improve the fit with their child's particular brand of individuality. There are relatively easy changes that parents can make in their own behavior (such as giving their child extra warning before a transition) or by working with the child's teacher on simple changes at preschool (such as reducing distractions at naptime). When this works, it provides a wonderful feeling of competence (and relief!) to know that you've found an effective way to meet your beloved child's needs.

With the child who rejects spinach, you can try to develop ways to make it more palatable (perhaps combining it with favorite foods). You may also decide some battles (i.e., green vegetables versus your five-year-old) aren't worth fighting, and simply say, "Andy doesn't do green." As he grows, his tastes will change. With an intense and moody child who throws a tantrum, keep the focus on safety; once you're sure your child won't hurt himself, find ways to deal with the behavior that are less upsetting to your confidence as a parent or to the customs of the family.

You can also use *rules* to create a better fit. With a highly active child who may run ahead of you, one strategy is getting her to exercise cognitive control over her emotions and her body. Practice saying and acting out the rule: "When you come to the street, say to yourself, 'Is anybody coming left? Is anybody coming right? Does the signal say I can cross?' Then wait and hold a grown-up's hand.") And make sure when she's under the care of other adults that they also know the rules.

Another way to enhance fit is to change the *physical environment*. Let's say that as part of your temperament, you have a "sensory threshold" problem with loud noises or music, and that your child likes to turn up the volume. You might place decorative quilt hangings on the wall of your child's room to absorb excess noise. You can move the music player to a part of the house least likely to disturb people (such as a basement family room). Or, give the child headphones (making sure that she doesn't set the volume too high).

In sum, look for openings where you can influence your child's individual *characteristics,* the *context* they are being expressed in, the *demands* being placed on your child, and your (and your partner's) own individual traits. This is a complicated undertaking, especially at first. Eventually, though, you'll find this happens as reflexively as driving or typing.

In the back of your mind, you'll be thinking, "We want to go out with friends to a nice restaurant. Perry is biologically rhythmic, so I know what time he'll be hungry. He has a fairly short attention span, so I'll bring several activities in my purse; if he has something to do, I know he can sit still for an hour. He's bothered by noise, so we'll choose a quiet restaurant or go when it's less busy."

> Sei-Lai was at her wit's end with her two-year-old son, Yeng Leng, who was very difficult to get to sleep. She had little time to herself at night, and his irregular sleep meant that she was always tired at work.

The unpredictability of sleep is a major problem for parents. Sometimes a child has trouble settling down at night because of temperament, especially if she needs more time to make transitions, is distractible, or has been playing active physical games before bed. It's important to remember that the child isn't doing this to be pesky; it's just his nature. Develop a strategy to suit the child's temperament. Start the settling process earlier, with a predictable series of steps. Keep the child's room quiet and free of distractions. Avoid wrestling-type games and overstimulating TV shows and videos near bedtime.

If the problem is an irregular sleep pattern, parents may need to try a variety of strategies. Sei-Lai might try shortening or cutting out her son's nap, keeping him up until he's very tired (instead of sending him off, still perky, to bed), or taking a walk with him an hour before bed. She might also try waking him earlier in the morning in hopes that he'll be more tired at night. A problem like this may need time to improve; she may be able to gradually extend the time her son sleeps so that the time he starts kindergarten, he's on a reasonable rhythm. (See chapter 4 for more on sleep problems.)

IMPROVING THE MATCH BETWEEN TEMPERAMENT AND CONTEXT

Adianes, a physician, had to be at the hospital early in the morning to see patients. Her son had been cared for by a nanny at home, but now that Pablo was three, it seemed time for him to get out and socialize with other children. His parents enrolled him in a local preschool. They had the schedule planned: Adianes would drop off Pablo in the morning, and his dad, Felipe, would pick him up in the afternoon.

But when Adianes dropped off Pablo on the first day, she found to her surprise that he was very upset by the new grown-ups and strange kids, and threw a prolonged tantrum. Hoping Pablo would settle in, as kids often do, his mother rushed off to work—but she soon received a call from the school, saying, "We just can't keep Pablo here today; he's disrupting the rest of the class." Adianes hastily canceled appointments and came back.

The same thing happened the next day. So, on the third day, Adianes cleared her schedule. She brought Pablo to school, and stayed. He clung to her for the first hour, then slowly moved into the classroom (as if wading into a cold lake), dragging his mom along to see another child or explore an interesting toy. Two weeks later, his mom still stayed for an hour each morning, but within that time he'd forget that she was there. Within two months, Pablo was tearing out of the car and rushing into his preschool activities.

It turned out that Pablo was a slow-to-warm-up child, and needed lots of support with new people and new environments. His parents had no opportunity to learn this about him until he enrolled in preschool, and so were not prepared. For Pablo to adjust to the new social situation his parents wanted for him, his mother had to adapt her behavior to Pablo's temperament. Not all parents have the luxury of making schedule changes; if Adianes couldn't make these arrangements, she'd have had to give up on preschool for a while—which might have just postponed the problem until kindergarten.

When parents introduce significant changes to a child's usual context, they may see characteristics of individuality come out that they hadn't noticed before. This means that trying to adjust the situation, your behavior, or the child's behavior for a better fit is not a onetime effort, but requires many "tweaks" over time.

Context has a big effect on distractibility. Kids differ in how distracted they are by what's going on around them. (This does not mean that they have an attention deficit, just that their focus is easily diverted.) Children need to focus when they are reading or trying to concentrate on a project. At home, parents can create a better fit for a distractible child by reducing competition for her attention: not keeping the television on in the background, and making sure siblings don't interrupt.

At school, it's more difficult, because even if the teacher calls for "quiet time," the child may be easily distracted by the twenty other kids in the room. The parent may have to work with the teacher to find ways to reduce distractions, such as putting the child in a part of the room with kids who have high attention spans and low distractibility, and who are therefore more likely to stay on task and less likely to move him off course. In the same way, where the child's naptime mat is placed at preschool would also be important.

A child's sensory threshold (also called threshold of responsivity) is simply how much stimulation you need to give to get her to react. With some kids, a pin dropping gets them to react; with others, you need to drop a brick—they can seem to have selective deafness. This can be a problem at either extreme. If you need to get your child to pay attention to you, or come to dinner or go to bed, a high threshold is a problem, because you have to scream to get her attention. A child with a low threshold will focus on you more easily, but will also wake up when the door slams.

A child who combines low distractibility with a high sensory threshold will be very task-oriented; he'll be engrossed in that LEGO tower and won't notice the teacher calling him. With another child, one who has a low sensory threshold, the teacher can say, "Put your things away; it's time to sit on the mat for story time," and he'll hear her and act on it. If the teacher is aware of the first child's temperament, she can arrange to tap him on the shoulder and give extra time for the transition; if not, he may be labeled a problem.

A child with a positive mood and low sensory threshold will react to something new in a pleasant way: "Oh, let's investigate." A child with an initial negative mood and low threshold may react to something new with alarm, crying, or withdrawal. These children obviously require different parenting approaches when introduced to new situations. However, one temperament is not necessarily better than another. If the new thing is dangerous, the latter reaction is useful; the "positive" child might plunge into danger and hurt himself. But if there's no danger, the positive child may dive into an interesting situation and learn something new.

If you know your child tends to be negative, you can prepare her in advance for those situations likely to bring out a bad mood or withdrawal. For example, if you've noticed that traveling upsets her, try to prepare her mentally. If she can anticipate that a trip may make her feel nervous or afraid, the two of you can talk about it, and you can link it with something she likes. If she says, "I don't want to sit so long in the car to go to Grandma's," you can say, "We have a new Etch A Sketch" (or other portable toy that appeals to her interests). "We'll let you play with it all the way to Grandma's."

> Six-year-old Justin walked with his parents next to the velvet rope that separated museum goers from the art. As they paused in front of a well-known painting by an old Dutch master, Justin was fascinated by its color and texture—and darted under the rope to touch the painting. Several uniformed guards raced over to remove him: "What are you doing, little boy? Don't touch that!"

To his parents' embarrassment, this was clearly a context where a highly distractible child was a problem. Fortunately, Justin generally had an upbeat mood, and recovered quickly from his adventure. And this enthusiasm served him well later, showing up as a passion for new books when he started to read.

Sometimes, a persistent parent can create a better fit by changing his child's attitudes and interests. Another parent who took his five-year-old son to a museum found that Jarrett made a great show of boredom, saying, "I want to get a hamburger. I wouldn't give you a penny for all these paintings!" This family set a high value on art and creativity, and wanted their son to share their enthusiasm. Seven years later, that same child asked for a book on art history for Hanukkah.

How did this happen? Through continuing to gradually expose Jarrett to different kinds of art, as well as valuing his own attempts at art and letting him know what was interesting and important about them. This method doesn't always work, of course. And sometimes it can work in reverse; your child's enthusiasm for Egyptian mummies, swimming, or shiny rocks may spark a new interest in you.

Some Final Words

Your child is a person: she was born with a host of physical, medical, and behavioral characteristics that make her a distinct individual. Your child is not a carbon copy of you. She may look and behave in ways you did not anticipate and may find challenging. *The most important step you can take as a parent is to get to know this individual and all of the ways she is special.* By understanding how your child is affecting you, how she is influencing you as an adult and, especially, as a parent, you can improve your ability to help your child grow in healthy ways. Your goal is to create positive parent-child interactions that lead to healthy development—and a lot of good memories.

Parenting, then, is not just a matter of child rearing. It is also in large measure a matter of being "reared" by your child. As you come to know him over time, his characteristics of individuality will continue to engage you in the joy—and the challenge—of being an effective and a loving parent.

Suggestions for Further Reading

William Carey and the Children's Hospital of Philadelphia. *Understanding Your Child's Temperament.* Hungry Minds, Inc., 1999.

Stella Chess and Alexander Thomas. *Temperament in Clinical Practice.* Guilford Press, 1995.

Stanley Greenspan. *The Challenging Child: Understanding, Raising, and Enjoying the Five "Difficult" Types of Children.* Perseus Press, 1996.

Ward Swallow. *The Shy Child.* Warner Books, 2000.

Stanley Turecki. *The Difficult Child.* Bantam Doubleday Dell, 2000.

Photo by Shirley Scarlett

C H A P T E R T W O

Conflicts and Routines:
A Family System Approach

Fred Rothbaum

The little boy was afraid to go into the dark room on the other side of the hall.

"Aren't you ashamed of yourself, Ludlum Thomas?" the father called . . . "You walk straight into that dining room, turn on the light, and get what you want."

. . . Ludlum disregarded this speech. "Mamma," he called plaintively. "I want you to come turn on the light for me. *Please,* mamma! . . . Won't you please come get my bow-and-arry for me?"

"Didn't you hear what I said?"

"Yes, sir," the boy replied, with eyes still pleading upon his mother.

. . . Mrs. Thomas intervened cheerfully. "Don't be afraid, dearie," she said. "Your papa thinks you ought to begin to learn how to be manly . . ."

Suddenly, he made a scene. Having started it, he went in for all he was worth and made it a big one . . . The end of it was, that when Ludlum retired (to bed) he was accompanied by both his parents, his father carrying him, and Mrs. Thomas following close behind with the bow-and-arry.

—Booth Tarkington, *The Only Child* (1923)

Ludlum's fears, including his fear of the dark, bring out very different reactions from his parents. His mother empathizes and tries to reassure him, giving in to his pleas for help. His father, by contrast, wants him to be tough and to overcome his fears on his own. He believes his wife is overindulging Ludlum and making him "soft." The more the mother responds to her son's fears, the more angry and harsh the father becomes—and the more protective the mother becomes. Each parent is aware of what the other parent is doing that's harmful to the child, but neither seems aware of the larger problem: their conflicting messages and lack of unity. Ludlum's fears are made worse by his parents' inability to work through their differences.

In this chapter, we'll look at what's behind family conflicts, such as arguments between parents and siblings, as well as ways to reduce those conflicts. One approach to these problems involves looking at your family as a system. The idea is that you can't fully understand your family by looking at just your own behavior, your partner's, and your child's in isolation. You must also consider the *interactions* between family members, and the *influences surrounding* your relationship with your child. By orchestrating these influences, you can promote family harmony, and subtly shape your child's healthy development. Throughout this chapter, we'll return to the theme of parents as conductors of, as well as players in, their family's symphony.

Influences on the parent-child relationship include: (1) parents' relationship with each other, (2) children's sibling relationships, (3) family routines, (4) people close to but outside the immediate family (relatives and friends), and (5) larger cultural factors that both endanger your child (drugs or violence) and protect your child (religious and ethnic affiliations). Parents who don't understand these influences are often too quick to blame themselves for their children's problems. (We have devoted separate chapters to influences such as school and electronic media—as well as the critical role of temperament in parent-child conflict.)

From the family systems perspective, *the whole is more than the sum of the parts,* because the whole includes *interactions* among the parts. To illustrate this, think of a family car trip. If Mom likes cool air, she might roll down her window to let in a breeze. But when you open a car window, it actually blows more air on the person opposite you. If Dad (who likes it warmer) feels cold and closes his window, it affects Mom more than it does him. This opening and closing of windows also warms and chills the children in the backseat, which affects how they behave.

Parents are constantly influencing each other and, in the process, influencing their children. Parents' ability to understand and communicate about how they influence each other has profound effects on their family and their children. To create change in the family system, it's much easier for you to alter your own behavior and reactions than to change anyone else's.

The bottom line is that your control is limited. To paraphrase the Alcoholics Anonymous motto, your goal is to find the strength to change the things you can control, the serenity to accept the things you can't, and the wisdom to tell these apart. In this chapter, we'll explore changes you *can* make to create a more harmonious family life. The chapter is divided into four sections:

- *When parents (or other adult caregivers) disagree:* disagreeing in front of the children; constructive vs. destructive arguing; effects of destructive arguing on children; and getting past destructive conflict.

- *Sibling conflicts:* children's fights; "bullies" and "victims"; competition for your attention; and jealousy.

- *Conflict prevention: reducing tension with structure and routines*: getting going in the morning; returning from work and school; managing mealtime; and reconnecting at bedtime.

- *Extended family and friends:* handling differences and finding support.

When Parents Disagree

ARGUING IN FRONT OF THE CHILDREN

It is 6:15 P.M. at the Brown-Smith home. Carol and Deena arrive home within ten minutes of each other. Carol stopped to pick up their three-year-old son, Brian, from his family day care, then the two of them stopped by the drugstore. Brian was happy at first, but the line was long at the cash register and he was tired and hungry. He fussed and cried for the ten minutes it took to drive home.

They walk into the house to find Deena changed out of her work clothes and on the phone with a friend. Carol notices that there are no signs of dinner preparations. She dumps Brian's backpack, her briefcase, purse, and the bag from the drugstore on the kitchen counter. Brian states that he is hungry and he wants something to eat right *now.* Carol looks pleadingly at Deena, who smiles and signals that she will be two more minutes on the phone.

Carol grabs a cup and slams it down on the counter. She pours some apple juice and hands it to Brian. She stands and watches Deena as she talks on the phone. Deena sighs and tells her friend that she will have to call back later.

Deena asks, "What's wrong?" Carol replies with irritation, "I don't mind picking Brian up and picking up the things at the store, but can't you at least start dinner when you get home first?" Deena answers with equal irritation, "I got home ten minutes ago. I changed my clothes and answered the telephone. Is that a problem?" Their voices grow louder as they continue to argue about responsibilities.

Brian is drinking his juice quietly at the table, and suddenly he asks for more juice, before he has finished the first cup. Deena and Carol stop their argument and Deena hugs Brian and says, "I didn't even say hello

to you. Hi, Brian. I'm glad to see you. I'll get you some juice." The two
women postpone the rest of the conversation until later. They smile at
each other and at Brian, deciding they will all make dinner together.
Brian hugs them each in turn and runs to the refrigerator to get some
food.

(In this book, we repeatedly refer to your partner and to your marriage. However, the points we are making apply to all adults—you, your
spouse, a grandparent, a trusted aunt, a child-care provider—with whom
you share important parenting responsibilities. For parents who do not
have spouses, try to keep in mind these other partners.)

Many parents wonder, "Is it okay if my partner and I argue in front of
the kids?" Let's take a step back and first ask, "Is the goal to disagree as
little as possible?" In the children's interest, many of us try to paper over
our differences. In an effort to model restraint and control, we try to hide
our disagreements from both the children and each other. But this
approach is neither practical nor helpful to our children.

Disagreements are part of everyday life, especially everyday family
life. We have different preferences, needs, and perspectives that make disagreements inevitable. Rather than pretend they're not there, it's far easier
to try to work them out. While it makes sense to prioritize our disagreements, paying most attention to those that cause real problems, that's a
different matter from trying to make disagreements as rare as possible.

Equally important, it is not helpful to children to eliminate disagreements between parents. In our society, we value standing up for what we
believe and working out our differences in fair and respectful ways.
When parents hide disagreements, children lose the opportunity to learn
constructive ways of resolving them.

It is a rainy Saturday afternoon. Two-year-old Scott and his four-year-old
brother, Damon, have been playing happily for most of the day. Their
parents, Giorlys and Garrett, have been taking turns doing errands and
exercising.

When Giorlys gets home, the floor is a sea of blocks, trucks, and stuffed animals. She's overwhelmed by the chaos that she finds in every room. She erupts at her husband: "I can't believe this mess! Couldn't you clean up a little along the way? I suppose you expect *me* to clean all this up. The boys aren't babies, you know. They can actually put toys back into containers."

Garrett is furious. "We've been having a great time, and then you come in and spoil it. Who cares if the toys get put away? They're just going to take them all out again anyway. Why do you have to make such a big deal of everything?"

Giorlys storms around the room picking up toys and yelling, "I like to have a little order in the house, and maybe be able to walk around without tripping over things. Anyway, don't you want the boys to learn to take responsibility for their things? How do you think that's going to happen if we don't set an example and expect something of them?"

Garrett shouts back, "I didn't say they should never clean up. You just ruined a perfectly fine afternoon by caring more about how clean the house is than about having fun." He leaves the room, slamming the door.

The two don't speak to each other for the rest of the day, but they manage to interact with the boys in a fairly normal way.

Earlier we said that disagreeing is inevitable and healthy, but what about this fight between Giorlys and Garrett? It feels different from the one between Deena and Carol. Below we consider why.

Constructive vs. Destructive Arguing

Keeping in mind the two examples above, let's go back to our original question: Is it okay to argue in front of children? In both examples, that's what happened. But the second argument felt more damaging than the first. That argument went on longer, but that's not the most important difference. There are four other qualities that distinguish constructive arguments from destructive ones:

- the *way* in which you argue

- the *topic* about which you argue

- the *resolution* of the argument, and

- the *emotional climate* in the home between disagreements

The argument between Deena and Carol is not a freewheeling, no-holds-barred contest. The two followed implicit *rules* for fair fighting: no "hitting below the belt," no swearing or character assassination ("You are a no-good, lying . . ."), no screaming—and above all, no physical threats or actions. Giorlys and Garrett's argument is less constructive in that they display more intense negative emotions, with accusations, sarcasm, and door slamming.

Deena and Carol's argument is about differences between the *parents*—not about the *children* or about their child rearing. When children witness their parents arguing about them, they feel much more threatened and distressed, because the parents are in effect saying that they don't know how to deal with their children. Arguments about the children also tend to make the kids feel guilty. Despite reassurances to the contrary, the fact remains that the argument is, in some sense, due to them. The content of the argument between Giorlys and Garrett is more difficult for their boys, because the argument is about them.

Perhaps most important is the fact that Deena and Carol are able to postpone their discussion in order to respond to their son. Research has shown that how parents *resolve* their arguments has the greatest effect on children. Although Deena and Carol don't work out their differences at that moment, they're able to put the conflict aside for now—for the sake of the child and the family—and to work together. In so doing, they've taught their child an invaluable lesson: when people disagree, they can get past it, and still be loving and giving.

By contrast, there is no resolution to the argument between Garrett and Giorlys. The parents have emotionally separated themselves and are not speaking. While it's comforting to imagine that children won't notice this "silent treatment" between parents, it's actually quite distressing to kids. If Giorlys and Garrett had acknowledged their different priorities ("I'm really glad you had a great time with the boys; the mess just gets to me sometimes") and negotiated what they might do about them ("I'm sorry things got out of hand; let's talk this over later tonight"), the boys could have benefited from seeing their parents' differences.

Closely associated with parents' ability to resolve conflict is the *atmosphere* they create in the home at times when there is no conflict. Immediately after calling their truce, Deena and Carol are able to hug their child, to be sensitive to his needs, and most impressive of all, to smile at each other and to work on dinner together. There's no sign that Giorlys and Garrett can re-create a positive mood in their home.

We can't overemphasize the *value of positive emotion* in the home. Arguments that are constructive for parents, and good models for children, most often happen against a generally positive emotional background. This can be brought out by *humor,* as well as by positive comments. These grease the wheels of interaction and make everything easier, whether it be enforcing a rule with your child or making up with your partner. Most important, they take the edge off conflicts.

Thinking back to Garrett and Giorlys, there are a number of ways they might have created a more positive mood in the home. Since tolerance for mess created by children is a common source of tension between parents, this was probably not their first argument about it. If either parent had used humor to defuse the situation, their fight might have never happened. Garrett could have anticipated his wife's reaction to the mess and said when she returned home, "I know it looks like a tornado came through here, but it was just the three men in your life. We're not just a wrecking crew, we can clean, too." This would help Giorlys relax.

On the other hand, Giorlys could have come in and said, "Hurricane Scott/Damon has hit. Help!" Laughing together, they could move on to dealing with the mess. Humor is a great gift in family life. It can be used so well at these moments when parents know where problems lie, acknowledge them through humor, and then move on to resolution.

EFFECTS OF DESTRUCTIVE ARGUING ON KIDS

It's breakfast time at Gordy and Adele's house. Five-year-old Jimmy has been crabby since they woke him up twenty minutes ago. Gordy's already running late when Adele mentions that she'd like him to speak to Jimmy's teacher for a minute after he drops the boy off at kindergarten.

"I'm sure it can wait until tomorrow," he says.

"Can't you take a few minutes for your son?" she asks with a sarcastic edge to her voice.

"I'm already taking him to school. If it's so important, why don't you just call her?"

By this point, Jimmy has stopped eating and is watching his parents. As their argument grows, he reaches out, grabs his glass of milk, and throws it to the floor. Immediately his father picks up the fallen glass and his mother grabs some paper towels to wipe up the spill. They're both angry at him. But Jimmy is smiling.

Earlier we said that parents' destructive arguing can have negative effects on their children. These effects can range from withdrawal to acting out and aggression, sometimes even bullying. Particularly common consequences of enduring conflict are children's fearfulness (including fears that a parent will leave) and physical complaints (such as headaches and stomachaches) that result from emotional stress. (Of course, these problems can be caused by other things, and not all children who are distressed by arguments will show such problems.)

And then there are the children like Jimmy, who have discovered that while acting out may result in a punishment, it's a small price to pay for being able to stop his parents from arguing. Paradoxically, he feels more stress when they're angry at each other than when they're angry at him.

We have talked with many teenagers about what it was like growing up in a home where parents argued a lot. They tell us consistently that the key was whether their parents presented a *united front:* whether they were able to get their act together when it came to child rearing. This harkens back to the importance of not arguing about the children, and of working to resolve conflicts. If parents can't present a united front, they are open to manipulation. Many older teens tell us how, even at young ages, they were able to undermine a reasonable limit that one parent enforced by appealing to the other parent.

An even more important reason for a united front is that it allows your child to forge close relations with both parents. When parents are openly in conflict, children feel forced to choose sides. They can only be loyal to one parent, and they suffer from the stress that this choice creates. There is evidence that boys suffer to a greater degree from such conflict, perhaps because of their greater identification with their fathers.

To find out if your arguments with your partner are hurting (or helping) your child, look at:

• What the child *does* during, and immediately after, the conflict.

• What the child *says* (directly or indirectly) about the conflict.

In the case of Deena and Carol above, we know that Brian was a bit uncomfortable hearing his parents upset with each other, because he interrupted the argument by making a request (in this case, for juice). While Brian's request was a gentle interruption, sometimes a child will misbehave, and escalate that misbehavior, as a way of stopping an argument. Or he might emotionally withdraw, becoming frightened or feeling sick—again, to distract his parents from their anger and to reassure himself that he isn't being forgotten.

That's why Jimmy threw his glass of milk on the floor, and then smiled when his parents became upset. A child knows that if he does something he shouldn't, his parents will have to stop to deal with it. Over time, the child learns to use acting out, fears, or illness as a strategy for dealing with conflict or stress. Thus a major warning sign is if your child repeatedly displays increased misbehavior, fearfulness, or illnesses *during* or *soon after* an argument with your partner.

Children have many ways of telling you about how you are affecting them. Some children tell you directly: "Daddy, I feel scared when you and Mommy yell." Much more often, they tell you indirectly. You might see the child playing with dolls or imaginary friends, reenacting elements of your argument with your spouse. While you might not think your child's characterization of your or your partner's behavior is accurate, you can be confident that it is how your child experiences it. Or the child might tell you how she feels by describing her fears: "I can't fall back asleep because I had a bad dream that two giants were biting off each other's head." If you listen closely to your children, they will often tell you how you affect them.

GETTING PAST DESTRUCTIVE ARGUING

John likes it when his four-year-old daughter Danielle wants to climb to the top of the jungle gym. He views her risk taking as something she'll need in order to succeed in a competitive world. But when Martie looks at their daughter climbing eight feet in the air, she immediately imagines what might happen if the girl fell. "Be careful, dear," she cries. While she keeps a watchful eye on Danielle, she lets the girl continue.

John and Martie used to argue about how much to encourage or hold back their daughter's risk taking. While they still disagree, they've acknowledged to each other that each of them has a point. And so they've worked out ahead of time what might be acceptable risks for Danielle to take at her age. Yes, she can climb to the top of the jungle gym at the playground; no, she can't cross the street unless she's holding an adult's hand.

In well-functioning families, the parents often learn to regard their differences as strengths. For example, parents who are locked in a battle of "she is too permissive" and "he is too controlling and rigid" can learn to respect and even appreciate what each partner brings to the table. The father might come to view his wife's "giving in" as expressions of empathy and emotional support rather than signs that she's overindulgent or weak. The mother may see that her husband's insistence on certain behaviors and limits are meant to provide structure and promote independence—and not as rigid power plays. Of course, these positive attributions work equally well when the mother is the strict one and the father is more lax. Once Mom and Dad understand that they're both working (in their own ways) to help their child, they can coordinate their different approaches, and turn them from points of contention into strengths.

Since it's not possible to force your partner to take a parenting role he (or she) finds uncomfortable and alien, you need to learn how to support each other's child-rearing styles. If you believe your partner's behavior is not in your child's best interest, you can work toward change by giving each other feedback that is encouraging rather than critical.

A particular skill of some parents is what we call *positive framing*: finding positive motives for the things that most upset you about your partner. If your partner yells at your child, frame it as a desire to help the child pay attention and focus. It's much easier for your partner to listen to you, and accept the notion that his (or her) behavior is misguided if you have already acknowledged that his behavior is well intentioned and that interventions are needed: "I know you yell because you're very concerned about this. I'm concerned, too. But I think there's a more effective way of getting Julio to pay attention."

If your partner is unwilling or unable to change his behavior despite your repeated efforts, repeated criticism from you won't help. This calls for intervention by a third party whom both of you can trust, such as an impartial family member or a professional therapist. Too many parents endure prolonged suffering before they finally decide to seek outside help.

We strongly recommend counseling if you're caught in a cycle of ongoing destructive conflicts or considering divorce. Problems parents have in resolving conflicts don't end with divorce. The content of the conflicts may change, but they don't go away. While you may have less contact with each other, the meetings you have are often more strained because of hurt and anger. Since you still share responsibility for the children, many issues will require calm discussion and compromise. For their sake, it's still critical that you learn ways to resolve your conflicts.

Talk to your physician or community mental health center to find a qualified therapist with training and expertise in family counseling.

Conflicts Between Siblings

In this section we focus on your children's relations with their siblings, but many of the points pertain to their relations with playmates as well (see chapter 5 for more on children's friendships). Siblings provide a sort of testing ground for working out disagreements: lessons that can be applied later to negotiating differences with peers. While there are things parents can do to help children learn to work out their differences, we'll first look at when and how much you should get involved.

SIBLING FIGHTS: SHOULD PARENTS INTERVENE?

> Preschoolers Sallie and Jenna are in the backseat of their dad's car, on their way to swimming lessons.
> Suddenly he hears, "Sallie hit me!"
> "Well, she kicked me first!"
> He takes a deep breath through gritted teeth because he knows exactly where the rest of this conversation is going. What should he do?

The best answer here is, let them settle it themselves. It's important for children to learn how to work out their differences; they can't do this when parents get involved. Even if you have great ideas about how your kids can solve their problem, your ideas deprive them of the chance to come up with their own. Even seemingly trivial interventions ("Sallie, listen to what Jenna is saying. And Jenna, you listen to Sallie.") change the nature of their interaction and shift the attention to you. Children are very alert to what you think, particularly when negotiating with their siblings, and anything you say is likely to change their focus to gaining your approval.

Of course, this doesn't mean that you should *never* get involved. If there's an issue of physical safety, you need to intervene. If the issue centers on you—for example, if the children are upset about your alleged preferential treatment of one of them—then you have to stay involved.

So how do you respond if, in the middle of a conflict, one of the children tries to drag you into it? Often the younger or more submissive child will turn to you, as a way to even the playing field with her older or more dominant sibling. Although it's hard to refuse these pleas for assistance, we encourage parents to try to stay on the sidelines. It's usually better to help your child think of ways *she* can negotiate the situation than to take over negotiations yourself. We say more about this later.

WHEN ONE CHILD IS ALWAYS THE VICTIM

Three-and-a-half-year-old Simon has been struggling to learn to use the toilet. His five-year-old sister, Trisha, is very aware of the fact that she learned to use the toilet when she was two and a half. She seizes every chance to remind Simon of this. This afternoon, the children have been sorting outgrown clothes with their mother to pass on to their cousins.

Trisha looks at each item and announces, "This is what I wore when I was a baby and wore diapers. I guess it would be good for you, Simon."

Simon protests, "I am not a baby. I used the toilet two times today."

Trisha quickly counters with, "Yeah, but you wet your pants today, too, baby!"

Their mother is exasperated by this constant teasing. "Trisha, you stop teasing your brother or you can't help us anymore!"

Trisha is quiet for a few minutes, until her mother leaves the room to get some bags. Then she immediately begins taunting Simon. "Baby, baby, baby Simon. Baby, baby . . ." Simon begins to cry and looks alarmed as he realizes that he has wet his pants. Trisha bursts out laughing and cries, "See, I told you. You're a big baby! Even Mommy will say you're a baby now."

Their mother returns to find Simon lying on the floor wailing, Trisha
laughing and saying, "Look, Mommy, I told you Simon was a baby. He
wet his pants again. I never wet my pants when I was three and a half."

It's much harder not to intervene when one child consistently domi-
nates and "wins" and the other child submits and "loses." But if you try
to make things right for the "loser," it often makes matters worse. In the
biblical tale of Cain and Abel, it was the parent's favoritism toward one
brother (by showing a preference for his gift) that caused the other
brother's jealousy and rage. The more a parent intervenes on behalf of the
victimized child, the more the parent inadvertently strengthens the
aggressive sibling's conviction that the other child is favored. Your children are competing for the same pool of resources: your love and affection. You can't stop it because you didn't create it; it's built into the
relationship. The older sibling often feels, "Things were pretty good
around here until *he* came along."

Simon's toileting troubles have taken a lot of time and attention from
his parents. Trisha has been looking for any way she can to divert some of
that attention to herself. Since toilet training is an emotional issue, it's
particularly challenging for parents to stay calm and keep out of things.

The children's mother could point out both that Trisha was very successful learning to use the toilet, and that she has complete confidence
that Simon will be very successful, too, when he is ready. She can remind
them both that she is very proud of them. She might also address Trisha's
underlying jealousy and fear of losing her mother's attention by arrang-
ing to spend some "special time" alone with her each day. This will help
Trisha feel that she doesn't always have to compete with her brother to
get the attention she craves.

Families tend to repeat patterns from one generation to the next.
Certain aspects of sibling rivalry seem to be handed down from generation to generation. It's hard not to be upset by one of your children bullying another when it stirs up memories of your own childhood conflicts.
It's also disturbing to think that your children are repeating a family pattern, whether you feel guilty for having been the bully or resentment

about being the victim. In these cases, one of the best ways to alter the pattern is come to terms with the negative feelings from your childhood by reexamining old relationships and making peace with the past. This will make it easier for you to intervene in constructive ways with your children.

Consistent with our theme of parents as conductors of their family orchestra, we emphasize two less direct ways in which you can influence your children's conflicts. First, you can talk with your children (individually or together) in a setting removed from the conflict. Then talk about the problems you once had with your siblings, rather than your child's current difficulties. ("Once, when I was your age, I was so angry at my brother that I broke one of our toys and then told my mom that he did it.") While your children may not be ready at this stage to benefit from your specific suggestions (and perhaps not until they have kids of their own), they will benefit immediately from your empathy and emotional support.

Second, you can model good ways to resolve conflicts when you handle your own disagreements with others, particularly with your partner. But here again, you should not expect short-term effects, nor should you judge your effectiveness by the presence or absence of conflicts between your children. There are many parents who are extremely thoughtful and constructive in how they resolve conflicts, whose children frequently bicker.

COMPETITION FOR LOVE AND ATTENTION

Ben and Megan's mother, Gwen, is cooking their favorite noodles for lunch, with the two of them watching closely. They stand at the counter, next to their bowls, waiting anxiously to be served. They are not keeping watch because they are ravenously hungry, but rather because they want to make sure they get the exact same amount, or better yet, more noodles than their sibling.

Gwen drains the noodles, looking wearily at her children as she anticipates the fuss they will make over their servings. She carefully spoons out the noodles, doing her best to make the portions even. Immediately Ben and Megan erupt into shouts of "You gave him/her more!" and "I want that bowl, not this one."

Gwen tries to reassure them that they have the same amount and finally shouts back at them to "sit down and eat what I gave you or nobody will have noodles."

Short of counting out the noodles, trying to convince siblings that you've treated them evenhandedly is generally futile. There are several approaches to try here. The issue is not really the amount of noodles, but that each child wants to feel recognized and cared for. This is frustrating for parents to accept, when their whole day has been devoted to precisely this goal. Unfortunately, each child is focused on the myriad little ways that his sibling got more attention. Despite parents' best efforts, they can't treat two very different human beings exactly the same.

One way Ben and Megan's mother could have responded is by saying, "You two must be really hungry. I'm going to make sure you both get plenty of food for lunch." This reassures them that she'll take care of both of their needs, shifting attention from the competition they've created.

Gwen could also use humor and say, "Well, the only way we'll know for sure who has the most is to count each and every noodle. We better dump them out on the counter and start counting." Most likely, the children would start to laugh and the crisis would be over. If they instead started arguing about long versus short noodles, Gwen would do better to incorporate noodle length into the game than to blow up at the persistence of their rivalry.

In fact, humor is one of the most effective ways to cope with sibling competition. The very qualities that make the rivalry so exasperating and outrageous also make it comical. One five-year-old explained to his classmates, "I know something about baby brothers: you can't hit, bite, or kick them, but you can hug them until they cry." Children's comments about their contempt for their siblings are often very funny, if you can manage to get a little psychological distance from the endless conflicts.

As that last example shows, children often have profound feelings of ambivalence about their brothers or sisters. This makes it that much harder for parents (and children) to sort out sibling conflicts. Trying to help her child understand his mixed feelings, one parent said, "It's like one hand wants to hug your brother and the other wants to hit him." The child replied, "No, Mom, both my hands want to hit him!" As parents understand sibling competition, see it as normal, and practice dealing with it through a combination of humor and respect for children's needs, the conflicts become easier to defuse.

HE SAID, SHE SAID . . .

Six-year-old Lisa is totally engrossed in building with plastic bricks. Her three-year-old sister, Romy, has been trying to engage her in playing with her stuffed animals. Lisa has shown no interest in Romy's game and is getting irritated by her constant interruptions.

Romy watches Lisa building for a few minutes and notices she is collecting all the yellow blocks for one section of her building. Quietly, Romy begins to take as many yellow blocks as she can find and puts them behind her.

Lisa soon notices that her supply of yellow blocks is disappearing and asks Romy where she put them. Romy feigns innocence, so Lisa stands up and looks behind her, discovering the pile of blocks. She pushes Romy and tells her, "Get out of the room. You're not allowed to be in here anymore."

Romy begins to cry and soon their father, Gerry, appears. He is clearly angry and asks, "Now what did you do to her, Lisa?"

Romy is the first to speak and tells her father that Lisa pushed her. Lisa angrily tells him, "I did not! Romy stole my blocks and wrecked my building." Romy's crying has become louder and she has climbed onto Gerry's lap.

He says, "Lisa, I don't care what she did to you. Don't push your little sister." Lisa protests, telling her father again that Romy stole her blocks. He says, "How many times do I have to tell you! Leave your sister alone!" Lisa storms out of the room while Romy snuggles with her father.

Lisa and Romy's father walked in on a situation where he didn't see what happened, and where the younger child was in tears. Gerry makes it clear that he thinks Lisa is to blame as he asks her what she's done to cause the problem. He knows that in past fights, she's usually been the aggressor.

This is a particularly tough situation for parents. If you decide to intervene, here are steps to follow in handling this kind of sibling conflict.

First, *resist assigning roles* of victims or bullies to children. When a caregiver has not witnessed the events leading up to a confrontation, he must resist the temptation to respond to the most dramatic or even the most vulnerable child. Even if there's good evidence from the past supporting such assignments, this evidence is from a brief period in the child's life; labeling a child increases the odds that the role will evolve into a lifelong pattern.

Second, *listen to both sides of the story*. Often parents feel they know how the fight began or even who's to blame, based on past patterns or on partial knowledge of the facts. Also, children's reporting of events in these situations is often based more on emotion than on fact. In this situation, for example, Lisa denied pushing her sister when, in fact, she did push her.

Even if the current situation is a carbon copy of its predecessors (which it never is), and even if parents have all the facts (which you never do), we cannot overemphasize the value of listening to both sides of the story. This not only teaches children about fairness and respect, it also decreases the odds that one child will feel picked on by the parent. Moreover, knowledge of the facts is not the same as understanding the feelings and thoughts of each child. You need that understanding if you're going to be helpful to your children.

Third, it's critical to *acknowledge the feelings* of both siblings. This is hard, particularly if you've just watched one child assault another. Wait until you've had a chance to process your own anger before you talk to your children. If you are very angry, you probably cannot listen and you almost certainly can't acknowledge each child's feelings. Also, you can't engage in healthy discussion in the midst of pandemonium. If either child is still very upset, the conversation must be postponed until all parties calm down.

It's also important to keep clear the distinction between acknowledging feelings and accepting behavior. Telling your vengeful child you understand that she is angry, and that you see how what happened made her want to hurt her sister, in no way gives the child permission to physically act on that anger and hit her sister. In fact, if children's feelings are expressed and acknowledged, not only do they feel better (because they see themselves as less bad and less isolated), but they then have the opportunity to explore with you alternative (nonviolent) ways to handle the conflict. If your child does not lay his issues and resentments on the table, you can't address them together, and he can't benefit from your guidance.

Fourth, *let the children know that they've been heard*. Whenever possible, ask both children to tell you what happened. At first, listen without commenting, and don't let the other child interrupt. In Lisa and Romy's situation, their father could have said, "Lisa, it sounds like you were angry that Romy interrupted your building and took the blocks you really needed. Romy, you really wanted to play a different game with Lisa, so you tried to stop the game she was playing." In this way, each child feels that she has been heard and understood.

Finally, their father could go on to *remind them of the rules* of the house. He could say, "I did not see what happened, but I am going to remind you both of our rules. There is no pushing or hurting each other. There is no taking each other's toys without asking." In this way he avoids the argument of who did what, but he has gotten his point across to both of them. By treating the situation objectively, he has set a tone of fairness and empathy for the whole family.

SIBLING JEALOUSIES

Six-year-old Sophie hears the mail come through the slot and races for the door. "What's in the mail today?" her mother, Mariel, asks. Sophie tries unsuccessfully to hide a small envelope addressed to her four-year-old brother, James. It is a birthday party invitation from a neighborhood friend. Mariel leaves the room, saying she will call the friend to accept the invitation.

Sophie is scowling at James as he jumps around excitedly exclaiming, "I was invited to Tom's party and you weren't!" Sophie is clearly hurt at being excluded, and upset by his teasing.

She shouts, "I hate Tom and I would never go to his stupid party. It will be boring and only stupid people go to his parties!"

James, unperturbed, says, "Tom likes me and he hates you. He only plays with you because Mommy makes him when he's here."

Sophie runs over to James and knocks him down, yelling, "Well, I hate *you*. I will never play with you or talk to you again if you go to Tom's party. I'll take back the dog I gave you for your birthday, too, 'cause you're too stupid to have him."

James jumps up and kicks Sophie repeatedly. He shouts, "You can't take a present back. That dog is mine, you butthead!"

They wrestle and shout until their mother appears. She roughly pulls them apart, saying, "Now what's wrong with you two?" The children talk at the same time, continuing to punch and kick at each other. Mariel shouts with exasperation, "I don't care what happened, just leave each other alone. Both of you go to your rooms until I say you can come out!"

Often, rivalry is caused by real differences in your children's ability levels. Here, James is a more sociable personality than his sister, who tends to be moody. The more the children directly compete with each other, the more apparent these differences become and the more the rivalry intensifies. Realizing this, some children avoid competing in the same realms: a child may focus on drawing or hockey if her sibling's a star gymnast. Sophie may start to shy away from social situations, in part because she realizes that James is naturally better at making and keeping friends.

There are things that Mariel can do to help Sophie and James with their rivalry over social issues. Clearly, based on Mariel's reaction to the argument, these children fight often and are competitive, like many siblings. Therefore, she might have anticipated problems when the invitation arrived. It is not surprising that Sophie would feel left out and jealous that her brother was invited to a party and she was not.

To help Sophie cope with her feelings, Mariel could also frame the situation differently. She might say, "James was invited to Tom's party. It must be a party for four-year-olds. That might be a good time for you and me to go get the new jacket you need." She then could wait and see what Sophie's reaction is—and if necessary, empathize with her about how hard it is when a brother or sister is invited to a party. She could recall times in her own childhood when she felt left out, and what she did to feel better. She could also remind Sophie of times when she had invitations or activities and James was not included.

The other major issue for Mariel to address is the behavior during the argument. The children were physically aggressive with each other, and used hurtful and insulting language. Because she was so frustrated by their repeated fighting, Mariel modeled behavior that she would probably not accept from her children. She pushed them, and didn't listen to what they had to say.

It's definitely not easy when feelings are running high, but the more often parents can handle such problems firmly but politely, the more powerful the example they set for their children. The combination of anticipating problems between siblings, remaining available to talk things out when children's feelings are hurt, and calmly and firmly enforcing "no hitting, pushing, or insults in this house" will greatly help this situation. While this approach won't end all conflicts, it will make conflict less frequent and intense. It also makes use of the "teachable moment." Siblings learn that they can have negative feelings toward each other, but still work things out.

Knowing that the comparisons in ability will intensify with age, should you as the parent discourage one child from an activity in which another child is clearly superior? In most cases, no. If the rivalry is intense and if the difference in ability is profound, then your child might benefit from being encouraged to find alternatives—but even in this case, don't allow one child to "corner the market" on any talents, characteristics, or interests. While children clearly benefit from finding their niche (the funny one, the one who's good at math) and cultivating their own special qualities, actively steering a child away from soccer or drama sends the wrong message. Rather than avoiding rivalry at all costs, encourage children to explore a variety of interests, and help them cope with competitive feelings as they arise.

In cases of unequal ability and intense rivalry, parents need to recognize and deal with their own biases. All of us are more knowledgeable about and attracted to some activities versus others (e.g., sports or the arts, fencing or football). For instance, if one child shows promise in her father's favorite sport, it's hard not to favor her over a sibling who draws wonderful cartoons—especially when Dad doesn't feel competent in art. It's all right for Dad to mentor one child more closely in an area he knows and enjoys, as long as this alignment with her skill doesn't evolve into an emotional alignment with the child that shuts out her siblings.

Reducing Conflict with Routines and Structure

Because we tend to focus on the *people* in our family, it's easy to miss the importance of the family *context*. Routines (or their absence) are a critical element of the context of family life. They greatly influence how family members get along. In this section we consider four situations where routines are especially useful:

- the morning

- coming home after work and school

- dinnertime, and

- bedtime

Routines make your life much easier. The more you're struggling with the situations above, the less you will enjoy them, and the less time and energy you'll have for playing with or teaching your children.

Note that the amount of time you spend with your child is not the best indicator of how well that child will do. More important are your availability when your child needs you—either emotionally or behaviorally—and your management of the home. If a parent's availability or management is compromised by emotional problems (such as depression) or by life circumstances (such as traveling extensively for work, or living in another city as a result of divorce), then that can have substantial adverse effects on children. When you can't be physically present, it's important to ensure that all caregivers in your child's life are emotionally supportive, and able to manage the child's environment and routines. (We'll say more about other caregivers at the end of this section.)

Why Do Children Need Routines?

Routines are the foundation of a child's day. The order and predictability that stems from routines and rituals make children feel safe and secure. Creation of routines and rituals are among the most important *proactive* strategies available to you; unlike even the best strategies for *reacting* to problems, they help prevent problems in the first place. Once created, routines take on a life of their own within the family culture: all family members know how they operate and are involved in their execution. The best routines—those that are enjoyable and meet the needs of the family—are easy to maintain, because everyone is invested in keeping them going. Children especially depend on rituals and routines to help them handle everyday transitions, which are potential sources of stress.

Getting Going in the Morning

Four-year-old Luke is an early riser and eats with his dad at 6:15. His six-year-old sister, Kayla, is slow to wake up.

With their father out the door, their mother, Rae, rushes into Kayla's room at seven, calling, "Time to get up. It's a school day. Wake up!" Rae then hurries to the kitchen to make lunches. Luke loudly complains about everything going into his lunch box. Rae ignores him, looks at the clock, and shouts, "Kayla, are you up yet? Don't make me come in there again. Get up."

Luke announces that he's hungry again. Rae hands him a banana and says, "I've got to take a shower. Be right back." When she emerges from the shower, it's 7:30, which leaves just fifteen minutes before the school bus arrives. She glances into Kayla's room and finds her sound asleep. Rae yells, "Get up right now!" and yanks back the covers. Kayla is startled, although this scene is repeated three or four mornings a week.

Pulling clothes from Kayla's drawers, Rae shouts, "Get dressed and get down for breakfast *now*." She stops to grab Luke's clothes and returns to the kitchen to get him dressed, and get a yogurt into Kayla.

The tension continues until 7:45 when the two children rush out to the school bus, waving good-bye to their exhausted mother.

Getting children out in the morning can be one of the most stressful parts of the day. Each family member has her own morning style and issues. Rather than continue the anger and frustration, this is an ideal time to try proactive strategies to make things go more smoothly. Set aside a quiet, nonstressful time with your partner to identify bottlenecks and irritants in your routine, and brainstorm ideas for improvements.

In this example, there are several problem areas. Rae doesn't have enough time to accomplish what she needs to do (get herself ready, plus feed and dress children and make their lunches). She also has one early, hungry riser and one procrastinator to deal with each morning. To improve the morning flow, she first needs to consider her own style. Is it easier for Rae to get up thirty minutes earlier to shower and make lunches, or would she (or her spouse) rather pack lunches and lay out clothes the night before so she can sleep as late as possible? Doing lunches ahead of time also avoids Luke's complaints.

To get her procrastinator moving, she could wake up Kayla ten or fifteen minutes earlier, so she could doze a bit but still have time to get ready. Rae can leave fruit or dry cereal out for Luke in case he gets last-minute hunger pangs. By setting up a routine that is predictable and reduces stress for everyone, the family will have a chance to enjoy one another as they start their day.

RETURNING HOME: UNWINDING AND REGROUPING

Doriane is a single mother of three children: Ethan, who is six, and three-year-old twins, Lara and Lilit. They all arrive home around 5:30 after a long day of work, school, and day care. Doriane sees the light on her answering machine blinking and the mail by the door, but she resists the urge to go to them. Instead she takes off her shoes, deposits her purse and the children's backpacks by the door, and heads straight for the couch. The four of them spend the next fifteen minutes talking and looking at books together. Then she feels ready to tackle making dinner, usually with helpers and nibblers close by.

Doriane has set a positive tone for her family's evening. By resisting the temptation to deal with messages, mail, and an immediate dinner, she has made reconnecting with her children her first priority. The rest of the evening will likely go much more smoothly because of this small investment of time.

When Rose, an active, curious three-year-old, comes home from the park with her father, Vincente, she sits down by the door and takes off her boots before entering the house. She has a bagful of shiny rocks and pretty leaves that she found at the park. She begins to empty the bag on the living-room rug, but her father reminds her, "Those things belong on your table."

Rose runs over to a small table and chair in the corner of the kitchen. She examines her treasures and then tells her father that she is thirsty. He pours her a cup of milk and brings it to the dining-room table. She takes it and starts to walk away from the table. He tells her, "Drink at the table, please," and she protests, "I want to look at my things." He repeats his request and adds, "I'll sit with you." He gently guides her to the table.

Vincente has set up several simple and reasonable systems to avoid problems. Rose always removes her boots upon arriving home. He has a place set up for Rose's messy things, and has a rule that drinks are consumed at a table. Each family will have different priorities and different tolerance for mess, noise, and such. Aside from safety, the details of one family's system versus another's don't matter much. What's critical is setting up systems and routines for the things your family finds important.

MANAGING MEALTIME CHAOS

It's dinnertime at the Johnson home. Ron, the father, works the early shift and picks up his three children from their family day care around four o'clock. His wife, Sherrie, works a later shift and gets home around seven. After some experimenting, he's found that feeding the children at five, then eating with his wife once the kids are in bed, is the least stressful routine for their family.

The children help set the table while Ron works on dinner. Sherrie is in charge of grocery shopping, and clearly has been unable to get to the store. Checking the cupboard, he finds one last box of pasta.

Today, six-year-old Jamal and five-year-old Ruby start to squabble over who puts the cups on the table and who does the silverware. Ron gives each child half of the silverware and cups, and they proceed with their jobs. Two-and-a-half-year-old Malcolm, in charge of napkins, has climbed onto the table to better arrange them. Ron scoops him off the table with a light reminder that boys belong on the floor and napkins belong on the table.

As the water boils for dinner, Ron sits down with the children to read a book to them. When the meal is ready, they all move to the table. As Ron begins to ask about the day's events, Ruby and Jamal both start talking at once—and then the phone rings. As Ron talks with his brother on the phone, Ruby and Jamal's argument escalates to yelling and pushing.

Ron gets off the phone and returns to the table. "I want to hear from both of you, but it has to be one at a time. Jamal, buddy, could you please help Malcolm with his juice cup while Ruby tells me about the park. Then I want to hear what you and Malcolm did today." The meal goes on.

The Johnson family has a few important routines in place to help mealtime be a pleasurable experience. The children have jobs appropriate for their ages. Ron reconnects with the kids by reading to them while dinner is cooking. This extra effort when he's undoubtedly tired is well worth it, since it sets a positive tone for the whole evening. He has found a way to be with all three of them without conflict.

Ron quickly responds to signs of problems, which could easily escalate with three young children. He uses mealtime as an opportunity to talk with his kids, which teaches social skills and mutual respect, and helps keep them occupied and seated at the table. He also tries to postpone phone calls to later hours when possible, since the children clearly need his presence and attention during mealtime.

Reconnecting at Bedtime

It is 7:30 P.M. in the Schreiber household, and the bedtime routine for three-year-old Hallie is under way. She is in the tub playing with her mother, Claire, seated nearby; her father, Kent, is in the kitchen washing dinner dishes. Claire announces, "It's time to get out of the tub," and begins to lift Hallie out. Hallie arches her back and screams, "No! I'm not done!" Hallie slips out of her mother's hands and falls back into the tub. She bursts into tears.

Claire tries to soothe her, saying, "I'm sorry, Hallie. It is time to get out. Daddy will tell you your favorite story tonight. Come on out, okay?" Hallie continues to cry and says, "No, no, no!"

Claire gets the towel, and they struggle through drying off and getting into pajamas. Claire is increasingly frustrated by Hallie's behavior, warning, "If you don't stop this nonsense and brush your teeth, you won't have any story tonight!" This threat seems to have the desired effect (since Hallie's mom usually backs up words with action).

> Claire brushes Hallie's teeth and escorts her into the kitchen. There Hallie's behavior inexplicably takes a turn for the worse. Her mother says a stern good night and hands the now screaming Hallie to her father. Kent carries her up the stairs, trying to calm her down by starting her favorite story about when he was a boy. Hallie's crying continues; her father tells her he can't tell her the story until she is quiet.
>
> Kent leaves the room for several minutes in hopes that she will quiet down. When he returns, she's crying harder than ever and now clearly exhausted. Her mother comes in the room, feeling calmer after getting a few minutes to herself. She gently rubs Hallie's back and her father starts the story. Hallie finally is quiet and grabs her beloved stuffed bear and listens to the story. They are all relieved when Hallie falls asleep.

The Schreibers have developed a predictable series of events for Hallie, but they ran into trouble on this night. Young children often have difficulty moving from one activity to another, especially at bedtime. Claire's abrupt announcement that bathtime was over did not give Hallie the time she needed to make that transition. If her mother had told her to choose one more thing to do before she got out, or told her two minutes until bathtime is over, Hallie might have been able to make the transition smoothly.

Once Hallie was upset, Claire promised her favorite story. But by saying, "Come on out, okay?" she in effect *asked* Hallie to come out of the tub instead of *telling* her what was expected. Adding the word "okay" gave Hallie a chance to say no. Her mother might have asked, "Do you want to climb out of the tub yourself, or would you rather be picked up?" That offers Hallie a bit of control, and either choice achieves the desired result.

Claire also, in frustration, threatened Hallie with the loss of her bedtime story. Parents need to be sure that they're willing to follow through with what they say. Taking away a central part of the bedtime routine, like stories or books, may make bedtime even more difficult, since children rely on their routine to help them relax and go to sleep. It's often more effective to shorten a step than to eliminate it. The particular events of a bedtime routine are not key (books, songs, stories, bath, etc.) but rather their consistent predictability, which signal to a child that bedtime and sleep are coming. The Schreibers have the routine; they just need to help Hallie move through the transitions more smoothly.

Bedtime is a chance to unwind and gain closure to the day. But more important, it's a time to reconnect with your child, when many parents and children have their best conversations and greatest physical closeness. Because they are relaxed, children open up about experiences and feelings that they rarely, if ever, share during the day. This exchange of love is important for the long term well-being of your child, but it also helps your child through the long transition until the morning. Most of the world's children sleep near or with their parents; we suspect that children are "wired" to seek this kind of closeness. Because Americans usually opt for separate sleeping arrangements, it's all the more important to connect with our kids emotionally and physically at this critical time.

MAINTAINING ROUTINES WHEN YOU'RE AWAY

Of course, the oil that makes family routines run smoothly is how they are implemented. All rituals are helped along by a combination of the structure and emotional support you provide for your child.

Structure:
- preparing the child for what's coming next

- explanations that are tailored to the child's level of understanding

- firmness in implementing limits

Support:
- following the child's lead

- flexibility—willingness to adapt to needs

- positive tone and praise

What happens, then, if work, illness, or other factors make it impossible for you to participate in the routines? The key is selecting caregivers who have the necessary child care skills to provide that structure and support. In keeping with the theme of this chapter—that parents are the critical *conductors* of family life—it is important that you communicate with caregivers about routines you follow in the home and routines they follow when they are with the children. You also need to observe and assess the quality of caregiving your children receive from the other key adults in their lives.

While the routines do not need to be carbon copies of one another, each caregiver should be aware of those routines that are particularly important and helpful. The goal is to identify the times of the day and the situations that are most difficult for your children, and to make the most use of whatever works for them. For example, if a child has trouble "winding down" before bedtime, one caregiver might read the child a familiar story as a way of helping with that transition. Another caregiver might offer a few minutes of "cuddle time" on the couch to help prepare the child for bed. Both approaches address the child's need for a quiet, calming activity before going to sleep.

The Influence of Extended Family and Friends

GRANDPARENTS

While her mother puts the baby down for a nap, three-year-old Shannon and her grandmother Cora have gone for a walk around the block. They stop every few feet to smell, observe, pick up, or place all kinds of things in the "treasure pail" (rocks, dandelions, feathers, leaves, acorns, and coins). As they return home, it occurs to Cora that they both were smiling or laughing for the whole thirty minutes it took to walk the quarter of a mile.

There often is a special bond between grandparents and preschoolers. A preschooler's world is filled with discovery and joy in everyday occurrences. The knowledge, acceptance, and serenity that a grandparent can bring to a child gives that child a sense of comfort and security to explore the world. Also, Cora had set aside the morning to be with Shannon. She did not have work, household responsibilities, or other children to distract her. She had the luxury of giving Shannon her undivided attention and as much time as she wanted to walk around the block, something that is often difficult for parents to do. Children's awe of the world and grandparents' devotion to them are a wonderful combination for both.

Grandparents are special in many ways. They pass along family history, giving children a sense of belonging to something that has been around a long time. Grandparents provide children a new group of people, events, and traditions in which they can take pride. They also provide a history of a child's parents, which helps even young children to begin to see their parents in a different way. Stories of parents as children are powerful and often beloved, as children hear about and imagine their parents with the same struggles, joys, and troubles as they have.

If the grandparents do not act as primary caregivers, they can offer unconditional love just as parents do, but without spending time setting limits and enforcing rules. They have been through all those struggles with their own children, and are free simply to love and enjoy their grandchildren. The depth of their love and connection to their grandchildren often means they indulge them in a way that no one else will.

Five-year-old Madelyn and her three-year-old sister, Jackie, are spending the day at home with their grandparents. The girls are both very aware of the house rules when their parents are at home. However, with their parents out, they ask for a second video, to eat ice cream as a morning snack, and to use Play-Doh in the living room. All of these are against house rules, which the girls normally abide by without much protest.

Their grandfather, who is their mother's stepfather, would like to indulge them. He tells his wife, "It won't hurt anything if they watch another movie or eat some ice cream. They're children; let them enjoy themselves." His wife disagrees, but is reluctant to make an issue of this;

she's only been remarried for two years and wants her husband to feel like a real "grandpa."

She says in a gentle way: "I know their parents don't allow them to do those things. Maybe we should try to respect the house rules. What do you think?" They compromise and let the girls watch another movie and eat popcorn.

The grandparents here represent two common viewpoints: supporting their children's rules versus indulging their grandchildren. Ideally, grandparents and their children should discuss such issues before they arise. It's generally best to abide by the parents' rules as much as possible. However, parents and grandparents may negotiate certain areas where grandparents can indulge their grandchildren without confusing them.

Even young children are able to understand that there are different rules about candy (or television or running in the house) in different places: Grampa keeps a lollipop in his pocket for them, but parents never do that. They can also understand that Grampa and Granma each focus on different rules. As long as the important adults in the child's life are aware of and respect one another's ways, children can accommodate to their differences. While parents may have to put up with some unrealistic requests and complaining after a visit to Grampa's, usually consistent home rules are soon accepted again.

But relationships with grandparents, like all close relationships, can be complicated. Parents sometimes witness interactions between their parents and their children that remind them of patterns that bothered them when they were younger, and that they have not been able to successfully address or resolve with their parents. When these patterns are repeated with their own children, they are understandably upset.

If you have ongoing unresolved conflicts with your parents about your children, and if the issues are important enough to you, you may need to *draw boundaries* around the amount of your children's contact with their grandparents. Consider the following example, in which Sara's mother has some serious concerns about her parents' behavior:

One afternoon, Sara and her grandparents go to a playground near Sara's home. It is very crowded and Sara is waiting her turn on the swing as her mother, Ruth, approaches. Ruth and Sara overhear Sara's grandfather saying quite loudly to his wife, "If that n___ kid doesn't get off the swing in one minute, I'm going to yank him off it." His wife replies, "Don't get upset, Sara has only been waiting a couple minutes."

Ruth is horrified that Sara has heard her grandfather use racist language, and worries that the child on the swing may also have heard him. His statement and impatience bring back memories from Ruth's own childhood and she is unsure what to say to Sara or to her own parents. She simply says, "It's time to go home for lunch."

We are often at a loss about what to do when our children are exposed to behaviors that violate our values. If the behavior is that of a relative or close friend, it's that much harder to know how to respond. The important thing to keep in mind is that scenes that are offensive are also great opportunities for teaching values. Ideally Ruth would be able to let her father know, firmly but as respectfully as possible, that such language is not acceptable around Sara. Without causing humiliation, she needs to let her child and her father know how she feels. If Sara's mother addressed this with her father in private, it would be important that she let Sara know the gist of what she said.

Sometimes, grandparents' ill health prevents them from establishing the kind of relationship that they would otherwise want with their grandchildren. Limiting the length of visits so as not to tax the grandparent's patience (which illness always reduces), and limiting the amount of time your child needs to sit still can help. Also look for ways to redirect your child toward less boisterous activities during visits, by bringing books, videos, or other props (art materials, games, etc.) conducive to quiet activity. And, once again, you can turn a difficult situation into an important learning experience by explaining to your children why their grandparent is not responding as they would like.

It is relatively easy for young children to understand physical limitations, especially if the grandparent is bedridden or visibly disabled; it is much harder for them to understand emotional distress due to illness. Gentle reminders such as "Remember how you felt when you had the flu?" and positive messages such as "Your grandma loves you and she would love to see the picture you made" can help redirect children's attention away from limitations and toward things they can understand and ways they can connect with their grandparents.

RELATIVES AND CLOSE FRIENDS

Three-year-old Troy is getting up three or four times a night. When his mother, Irene, talks to her sister about this problem, the sister is immediately concerned about Irene's exhaustion and doesn't ask for much detail about the problem. She advises her to be very firm with Troy.

When Irene discusses the same problem with a friend whose daughter is a close friend of Troy's, she gets an entirely different response. Her friend mentions similar problems she has with her child. She asks a lot of questions about what happens when Troy wakes up, how long he stays up, what he needs to get back to sleep, and what his mother thinks is going on with him.

The sister was primarily concerned about Irene, while the friend was able to step back a bit and help her friend solve the problem.

At times, these roles may be reversed. That is, the relative may be the one who asks the questions about the child and helps the mother examine the child's sleep problem, and the friend may show greater concern regarding the mother's well-being. Which kind of support is most appreciated will depend on your needs at the moment: Do you mainly want ideas for dealing with the problem, or do you need emotional support for yourself? The key point is that friends often provide different kinds of assistance than relatives provide. Indeed, we might unconsciously select friends who fulfill needs not already met by relatives.

Close friends can be a wonderful resource for parents of young children. They often know the whole family, yet they are a little more objective than a family member might be. Because they don't share your family history, they don't carry the baggage of the past—at least not the baggage of your particular family. Long-standing friendships are particularly valuable because they can remind you of important things from the past and help you discern patterns. For example, a friend may note a similarity between your treatment of your daughter and your mother's treatment of you. Friends are chosen, families are not; so it's easier to choose when and how to involve friends in your lives.

> Three-year-old Anna will not stay at the table for a family dinner with her five-year-old brother and parents. She wants to come and go from the table, grabbing something from her plate and then returning to play with her toys. Her brother sat happily at the table with his parents at an even younger age, so they cannot understand why Anna has such difficulty doing this.
>
> Her parents both came from families where it was very important that the family sat at the table together for the evening meal. They have talked to their siblings and parents about how to get Anna to the table for a whole meal. Their families wholeheartedly agree with their desire for a family dinner, and have encouraged them to insist that Anna stay at the table.
>
> However, when they talk to friends with children the same age, their friends don't understand the problem. They feel Anna's parents are being much too rigid about mealtime and think they should let Anna wander until she's older and more able to sit with the family.

This is an instance where knowing family history is a definite help in understanding the parents' feelings. It's also one where recognition of individual differences among children, even in the same family, is important. Anna's brother did not have trouble sitting at the table for a meal, but Anna, in fact, does have trouble. The parents can maintain their goal for a family meal, but can change the definition or expectations a bit while Anna is young.

They can pay attention at the next meal to see exactly what goes on:

What kind of chair is Anna sitting in? When is she expected to get to the table (before the meal is served, when the meal is served)? Is she given a warning that she will need to stop playing to have dinner? Can she sit two minutes before getting up, or five minutes? Does she eat most of her food during the first few minutes at the table, or later in the meal? The parents can then use this information to determine realistic expectations for Anna and for the family meal.

Some Final Words

In this chapter we have focused on forces surrounding you and your child: your relationship with your partner, your children's relationship with one another, the routines in your family, and your relatives and friends. Too often we focus on our direct, one-on-one influence on our child and lose sight of the profound effects these other forces exert on both ourselves and on our children.

According to the family systems perspective, you need to be mindful of the many ways in which these outside forces interact with your relationship with your child. These forces are major players in your family orchestra. To the extent that you understand how they function, you will be better able to serve as the conductor of that orchestra.

Suggestions for Further Reading

Couple Relations

Aaron Beck. *Love Is Never Enough: How Couples Can Overcome Misunderstandings, Resolve Conflicts, and Solve Relationship Problems Through Cognitive Therapy.* HarperCollins, 1989.

E. Mark Cummings and Patrick Davies. *Children and Marital Conflict: The Impact of Family Dispute and Resolution.* Guilford Press, 1994.

Harriet Lerner. *The Dance of Connection: How to Talk to Someone When You're Mad, Hurt, Scared, Frustrated, Insulted, Betrayed, or Desperate.* HarperCollins, 2001.

Siblings
Adele Faber and Elaine Mazlish. *Siblings Without Rivalry.* Avon, 1998.

Jane Nelsen, Roslyn Duffy, and Cheryl Erwin. *Positive Discipline for Preschoolers.* Prima Publishing, 1998.

Nancy Samalin. *Loving Each One Best: A Caring and Practical Approach to Raising Siblings.* Bantam Books, 1997.

Grandparents
David Elkind. *Grandparents: Understanding Today's Children.* Scott Foresman, 1990.

Arthur Kornhaber and Kenneth Woodward. *Grandparents/Grandchildren: The Vital Connection.* Transaction Publishers, 1991.

Children's Books
Andrea Cheng. *Grandfather Counts.* Lee & Low, 2000.

Juan Felipe Herrera. *Grandma and Me at the Flea.* (English/Spanish) Clove Publications, Inc., 2002.

Justin Matott. *When Did I Meet You, Grandpa? / When Did I Meet You, Grandma?* Clove Publications, Inc., 2000.

Patricia Polacco. *My Rotten Redheaded Older Brother.* Simon & Schuster, 1994.

Charlotte Zolotow. *Big Sister and Little Sister.* HarperTrophy, 1990.

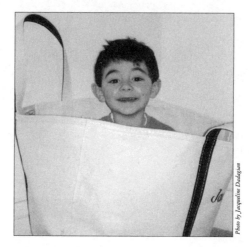

Photo by Jacqueline Dadagian

CHAPTER THREE

Proactive Parenting for Behavior Problems

W. George Scarlett

Three-year-old Margaret has hidden behind the door after seeing her mother take out the hairbrush to brush her hair. Her mother has cut Margaret's hair short to minimize the discomfort, but still Margaret does not like to have her hair brushed. When her mother walks over to where Margaret is hiding and takes her by the hand, Margaret pulls away and screams, "You can't do my hair."

• • •

Sam and Yusef, both age four, have come to the park with their fathers to play on the climbing equipment. Yusef's father asks Sam's father if he will keep an eye on Yusef while he does an errand. A moment later, Sam's father hears Sam yell, "You can't!" and looks up to see Sam hit Yusef and Yusef begin to cry.

Hitting. Whining. Dawdling in the morning rush, or refusing to go to bed. These everyday behavior problems are a constant challenge for parents. When young children are excited, cranky, reckless, angry, obstinate, or just plain annoying, their behavior demands a response. But when you're stressed out, angry, impatient, worried, or tired, your capacity to respond is sorely tested.

Sometimes you need to know what to do to get your child to behave right now. But you also want much more for your child and for yourself. Above all, you want to help your youngster grow into a wonderful older child, and go on to become a happy and successful adolescent and adult.

These two goals define the central dilemma around managing behavior problems: how to get results in the *short term* while also teaching lessons for the *long term*. Sometimes what gets a child to behave *now* isn't always best for her long-term development. Spanking is a prime example (more on that later). But most important, responding to misbehavior in ways that teach life skills (such as self control and problem solving) is the best way to prevent problems down the road. In this chapter, as we explore ways to solve behavior problems now, and make them less frequent over time, we will look at:

- Your parenting philosophy

- *Proactive* parenting

- Tactics for anticipating and responding to behavior problems

- Prevention: tactics for preventing behavior problems

- Guidance: tactics for showing children other ways to behave

- Control: tactics to use when a child must listen now

- Mixing and matching tactics

- Finding openings for change

- The parent-child partnership

As we saw in chapter 1, some children are more difficult to deal with than others—and this depends in part on the temperaments and personalities of the adults who care for them. Before you decide what to do about a child's problem behavior, it's helpful to ask yourself, "For whom is this a problem . . . and why?" Some behaviors are problematic in any situation: for example, ones that endanger a child—such as running into the street—or that hurt other people. Some are problems in certain circumstances, such as dawdling, obstinacy, or whining. And sometimes a behavior (such as jumping on the sofa, or interrupting conversations) bothers a parent or caregiver because it conflicts with his or her values.

In other words, parents need to determine how much their child's behavior is a problem to them, to other significant adults in the child's life, and to the child herself. All children (and adults, too) sometimes act in ways that upset, annoy, or otherwise concern those around them. The fact that we have problems with a child's behavior does not make her a "problem child." That unfairly places blame solely on the child. To keep this distinction between child and behavior in mind, we need to remind ourselves that behavior problems are an inevitable part of childhood.

Your Parenting Philosophy

How can you help your children grow from that impulsive "I want!" state natural to toddlers into more cooperative and self-controlled children ready for elementary school? The way you answer this question reveals your parenting philosophy: how you think children develop, what you think parents' proper roles are, and how you think we ought to respond to problem behaviors. (Parenting experts also have different philosophies.) Let's look at the implications of these different approaches, going from one extreme to the other.

Some parents and professionals say: "We help a child by building or protecting that child's self-esteem." If taken too far, this belief leads to a "permissive" parenting style:

Sam's father has just witnessed his son hit another child and comes running to intervene. Yusef is sitting to the side and wiping away his tears,
and Sam is standing, looking away. Instead of reprimanding the boy,
Sam's father takes his son's hand and says, "You must have felt very
angry."

Sam's father is uncomfortable playing the "heavy" and setting limits
on his son. He may be worried that comforting Yusef or reprimanding
Sam will hurt Sam's feelings and damage his self-esteem. By focusing on
Sam's motivation for hitting, he unintentionally teaches Sam, "It's okay
to hit if you feel angry."

In our experience, too many parents worry that setting limits, reprimanding, and being firm with their children will hurt their children's
self-esteem and undermine their long-term development. As a result,
parents may *undercontrol* by failing to give their children the limits they
really need to feel safe from their own chaotic impulses and to learn how
to exercise self-control.

A different parent or expert might say: "We help a child by setting
limits and enforcing rules for that child's behavior." The assumption here
is that controlling young children will help them form constructive
habits, which lead to cooperation and self-discipline. In this view, children behave as parents wish only through outside control and motivation. If taken to an extreme, this creates an "authoritarian" parenting
style. This style can also have unintended consequences:

Margaret's mother says, "Margaret, you know I have to brush your hair,
so hold still." When Margaret responds, "No!" and tries to run away, her
mother picks her up, presses Margaret's flailing arms to her sides, and
pulls the brush through her screaming daughter's hair. Both Margaret
and her mother are exhausted and bad-tempered by the time the task
is done.

Margaret's mother has established a routine for getting out of the
house. When Margaret is defiant, the routine is carried out through

physical coercion. Since Margaret knows the routine, her mother believes this defiance must be corrected. The message this sends to Margaret: Your feelings are not important.

Of course, sometimes it's necessary to enforce a rule or routine. But the problem with a consistently authoritarian approach is that parents *overcontrol*, making it less likely that children will develop inner self-control—and more likely to "behave" only when their parents are right there. Moreover, parents who believe that their major role is to enforce consistent standards often find themselves drawn into conflicts with their children over little things (such as hair brushing)—conflicts that sap the joy from their relationships with their children.

You can probably guess that our view of parenting falls somewhere between the permissive and authoritarian extremes. But what exactly does this mean? We emphasize the importance of supporting the development of children's inner resources: their capacity to problem-solve in the face of conflict and frustration, and to manage feelings on their own. Supporting development means helping children feel both securely connected to and valued by others, and confident (through experience) that they can make good things happen on their own: the true basis for *self-esteem*.

Supporting development also means helping children develop an understanding and appreciation for limits and rules, an inner morality that works to guide their behavior even when adults are not around: a key to *self-control*. And finally, it means helping children become individuals who can make and maintain good relationships through sharing control, relationships we call *partnerships*.

Let's look again at our examples and imagine a more positive response for each case:

Sam's father has just witnessed his son hit another child and comes running to intervene. Yusef is sitting to the side, wiping away his tears, and Sam is standing, looking away. Sam's father says: "Sam, hitting is not okay. Go sit down on the bench while I make sure Yusef is all right." He then turns to Yusef, puts an arm around him, and asks if he is hurt.

Once he is sure Yusef is okay, he brings him to the bench and, in his presence, asks Sam what happened. "Yusef said he could climb higher than me, so I hit him," says Sam.

Sam's father replies, "I know you felt angry, but hitting is not okay. Can you ask Yusef how he felt when you hit him? Can you think of something you could have said to him instead of hitting?"

• • •

Margaret's mother says, "Margaret, I have to brush your hair before we go. Either you can keep your body still while I do it, or I will have to hold you. You know it is easier for me to brush with both my hands."

When Margaret responds, "No!" and tries to run away, her mother takes her hand and leads her to the chair. She repeats her choices, and when Margaret continues to struggle, she holds her with one arm while she works the brush through her hair.

"I know you don't like this. I guess tomorrow we will have to brush your hair before breakfast so that we aren't late. It's too bad that we're in such a hurry today. I don't like fighting with you before we go to school."

Proactive Parenting

A misbehaving child brings out many emotions in parents: anger, frustration, confusion, depression, even fear. These strong negative feelings can trigger struggles to control that, in turn, lead to more problems—often creating a cycle that undermines both family harmony and children's long-term development.

To avoid this cycle, we offer a parenting philosophy that emphasizes *prevention* and *guidance*. When parents address children's behavior problems in a manner that supports children's overall development, we call it "proactive parenting." Parents adopt this proactive approach to behavior problems when

- they view behavior problems as the *natural* outgrowth of a child's development

- they view children's misbehavior as presenting *opportunities to guide* and help children learn more mature ways to get what they want

- they work to *prevent* behavior problems and the ensuing battles that undermine relationships and harmony in the home (for example, when parents prepare children in advance for new situations, and plan ways to help them cope with probable stress)

Here's an example of this approach, in a child-care center:

> The three-year-olds cluster eagerly around the hot-air popcorn popper, waiting for their snack. The teacher knows the kids won't be able to resist grabbing for the popcorn.
>
> She has the children look at their hands. "Now tell your hands, 'Don't touch! Don't touch!'" With this practice (and distraction), the children make it through the final seconds.

It's natural for young children to be impulsive, and have a low tolerance for frustration. Their teacher gave them an alternative to grabbing that prevented a chaotic mess (and a potential burn danger), and also supported their beginning efforts at self-control.

Another example is preparing to visit a restaurant. Ask young children ahead of time what they want to eat (from two or three choices). If you know your two-and-a-half-year-old can't sit still for long, hold his hand and take him for a walk to the entrance, pointing out interesting sights along the way. Avoid putting children in situations that place too many demands on their emerging abilities to control themselves.

Tactics for Anticipating and Responding to Behavior Problems

Within this proactive parenting framework, the next step is choosing specific tactics for anticipating and responding to behavior problems.

Most people confuse an "approach" (e.g., permissive, authoritarian, positive) with a single tactic or set of tactics for addressing behavior problems. "What is your approach to hitting?" asks one parent, meaning, "What set of tactics do you use when a child hits?" Parents need access not just to one or two but a large collection of tactics if they are to manage behavior problems successfully.

A good tactic will:

- either preserve order and safety for the short-term, or promote long-term development, and

- not undermine one goal (preserving order and safety, or promoting development) while accomplishing the other

It is not necessary for a single tactic to both solve short-term problems and support long-term development; sometimes you need to have your child take a break to preserve order, even though he learns nothing for the long term. It is the *mix* of tactics you use throughout the early childhood years that must serve both short- and long-term goals.

There are three types of behavior management tactics:

- *Prevention tactics* are intended to head off behavior problems and parent-child battles before they get out of hand (or ideally before they begin)—as when you keep paper and crayons in your handbag to occupy a child who has to wait.

- *Guidance tactics* show misbehaving children better ways to act, and teach them lessons that will help prevent or limit problems in the future—as when you help siblings come up with a rule for taking turns.

- *Control tactics* are for controlling children immediately—as when you hold a child who's about to hit another.

With the proactive parenting approach, parents *mix* and *match* tactics from each group to meet anticipated challenges and respond to unexpected problems.

PREVENTION TACTICS

As they say, an ounce of prevention is worth a pound of cure. But prevention is not magic. It takes "tons" of thoughtfulness, energy, and humor to make that ounce of prevention. The good news is that the more you practice prevention, the better you get at it. The better news is that over time your child also gets better at anticipating and avoiding potential problems.

The first step in preventing problems is to develop routines and habits of behavior for ourselves as well as our children that limit the stress, anxiety, and hurry that lead to problems (or that turn small challenges into major conflicts). The second step: carrying out necessary tasks as smoothly and happily as possible. The third: anticipating situations where specific problems tend to happen, and acting to head them off or to limit their bad consequences. Here are a couple of examples.

> Four-year-old Jamie is taking more responsibility for his personal hygiene. Jamie has developed a routine for getting ready. Every night, his father gives him a ten-minute warning. When it is time, Jamie takes his bath (or washes his face and hands) and puts on his pajamas. Then he goes back to the bathroom to his brush his teeth.
>
> To help Jamie do a good job brushing his front teeth, his father says, "Look in the mirror and 'grrr' like a bear." For the back teeth, Jamie's father says, "Now roar like a lion."

Bedtime and washing up are common occasions for parent-child conflicts. Routines help limit possible problems and keep things running smoothly. In this example, Jamie's dad is in control of when bedtime comes, but he gives his son a warning and steps back to let Jamie practice being responsible.

Notice the ingenious specificity of his father's tooth-brushing tactic. He doesn't just say, "Pretend you're an animal." He directs Jamie to act like two specific animals that are likely to impress a power-conscious young boy. What's more, those two animal sounds shape Jamie's mouth perfectly for brushing front and back.

> Three-year-old Justina loves jumping in puddles. Her mother, knowing that this is a fun game for her daughter, chooses a relatively dry route when they have to walk to the grocery store after a big rainstorm. But she also outfits Justina with tall rubber boots.
>
> She tells Justina, "We're getting ready for puddles. But we go *around* the puddles on the way to the store. On the way back, it's time to jump *into* puddles. Then when we get home, I'll change your clothes."

Justina's mother does not object to her daughter jumping in puddles in general, but she is concerned about letting her walk around in wet clothes for a long time. She uses several different prevention tactics. She plans the driest route to the store to reduce puddle-jumping temptations. She dresses her daughter so that, should she step in a puddle, she will be less likely to get soaked. Finally, she tells Justina her plan, and balances her practical need to keep Justina dry with her daughter's desire to play.

Pearls of wisdom and parents' diamonds.

There are some tactics that follow logically from experts' pearls of wisdom: general rules that fit almost any home situation. And there are some tactics ("diamonds") that parents find after mining their own situation and attending to their specific circumstances. Three important pearls of wisdom for preventing behavior problems have to do with transitions, forecasting, and organizing the home so as to promote constructive activity.

A simple and time-tested rule is to *give warnings before transitions*, "Five minutes until teeth brushing," "Ten more minutes and we have to leave." While most parents know this, it's often forgotten as we get caught up in the telephone calls, laundry, and other tasks and distractions of family life. Lack of warning often leads to conflicts and problems that could have been prevented, and that contribute further to our feelings of tension and frustration.

Another general rule is *"forecasting,"* getting children to think ahead about what is to come. On the way to a restaurant, a parent can forecast that there will be waiting, and perhaps have a child decide beforehand what to order. Similarly, on the way to a toy store, a parent can forecast what is to happen: picking out a small treat for the child and a larger birthday gift for the child's friend. Again, parents often ignore this pearl and let children enter restaurants, toy stores, museums or other stimulating environments without preparing them to cope with what's inside or with their own feelings.

A third rule has to do with *organizing settings* to promote constructive activity by giving children playthings that can engage them for long periods of time such as blocks, dollhouses, crayons, or other art materials. Organizing the setting also means providing labeled storage bins so children can initiate play on their own and clean up afterward. Many parents overlook this pearl because they haven't thought about how to organize their home to promote constructive activity. (More about this in chapters 5 and 7.)

Some Prevention Tactics

- Give Warnings for Transitions

- Divert Attention Away from Trouble

- Infuse Humor and Fun into Required Tasks

- Ignore Minor Problems

- "Forecast" to Defuse Potentially Difficult Situations

- Eliminate Factors That Trigger Problems

- Provide Toys and Materials for Constructive Play

- Set Up Good Routines

Parents constantly add to experts' pearls of wisdom by using the knowledge they have of their particular child and home to find and adapt tactics to their own situations. We call these more specific tactics "parents' diamonds." Diamonds are often found when you've analyzed problem-prone situations—getting dressed in the morning, going out to eat, or taking long trips in the car—and thought about your own child's interests, temperament, challenges, and strengths.

At first glance, diamonds appear simple, but they are both thoughtful and specific. Here are some favorites:

- To prevent spilling, a tactful parent offers his proud four-year-old a "commuter cup"—knowing a sippy cup will no longer do.

- A trip to a local fast food restaurant with several small children in tow goes easier when Mom uses the drive-through to order food and then takes the kids inside to eat.

- On cold mornings, young children often balk at getting dressed. A clever parent warms her children's clothes in a dryer or on a radiator.

GUIDANCE TACTICS

Guidance tactics are a central ingredient in a positive parenting approach. We are guiding when we act to increase children's understanding of adults' expectations, when we help them to think about how to pursue their own goals in ways that don't conflict with our expectations, and when we take the time to teach and promote more mature behavior. For very young children, guidance may simply mean redirecting their attention; for older children with more cognitive maturity, it may include a simple discussion of the problem and alternatives for handling it.

Parents who are good at using guidance tactics don't just repeat "I expect you to sit still": they provide children with specific information, models, and options. When a child misbehaves, the guiding caregiver tries to focus on the positive choices that the child can make to fix the problem, rather than (or as well as) on misbehavior itself.

Problem solving. Many guidance tactics stimulate the thinking behind problem solving. Young children are only beginners at problem solving, and find it particularly tough when they are experiencing strong emotions (anger, excitement, frustration). In fact, many times adults forget how to do this themselves. Parents can help by acknowledging the feelings, and talking through the problem solving process to give their child a model to follow.

Consider again the example of taking a walk with your child and coming upon a puddle. What if she's dressed in good shoes, and gears up for a fight when you tell her she can't jump in? What are you to do: Threaten her? Grab her? Drag her away? Attempts to control an excited child may turn into a contest of wills. Here may be a perfect time to guide her by redirecting her attention: "What could you do with this puddle besides jump in it? Here's a stone; what can you do with that? How about this stick?" Such prompts might work to stimulate problem solving. Dropping stones to see them splash or "sailing" sticks to see how far they will go is fun, and keeps the shoes dry.

Control for guidance. Some guidance tactics may start out as ways to control children's behavior, but they reveal their true nature by redirecting the child. When a mother says to her four-year-old, "Do not use those bad words!"—and then, instead of giving him a brief time-out, she works with him to figure out other words that might help him express his feelings, she is using a guidance tactic.

Negative consequences for misbehavior are guidance tactics when their logic is apparent to the child. An example would be taking a toy away from two children who are fighting over it, getting them to understand that the removal of the toy was for their own safety, then saying they can have the toy back when they both have figured out how to share.

Some Guidance Tactics

- Teach Alternative, More Mature Behavior

- Set and Use Logical Consequences for Misbehavior

- Stimulate Problem Solving in the Face of Frustration

- Join with Children to Work Out Alternative Behaviors

Here is an example of a parent teaching young children about logical consequences. Note how this mother uses an extraordinarily powerful tactic without acting as a heavy.

> When Regan, age six, and her younger brother, Emmett, age four, dialed 911, they did so because they thought it was a game. They called, got an operator, then hung up. When the operator called back to see if there was an emergency, their mother was not amused.
>
> Rather than punishing them, she explained why it was wrong to make a game out of calling 911 and helped them write a letter to the operator about what they had learned. Then she led them to the police station, where an officer explained further.

In this example, guidance means more than using words or preaching: it means getting children to act and practice. Notice, too, that the overall tone is positive, in part because the mother is able to control her anger and in part because learning something new makes the experience positive for the children.

CONTROL TACTICS

At certain moments, you may not have the freedom or emotional capacity to be concerned with long-term development. You are only concerned with getting your child to clean up, sit down, or stay safe. In those moments you need to use control tactics to get your child to behave *right now*. Directives, negative consequences, rewards, and physical interventions are some of the different types of control tactics that parents and caregivers use.

Directives such as "Stop running," "Pick up your coat," and "Sit in your chair" control children by telling them what to do and what not to do. The advantages of using directives are clear. They are fast and simple. We need only say what we want or refer to a known rule.

So why not rely solely on directives to manage? One answer is that they don't always work. Directives work best when you've established a climate of cooperation, where your child trusts you to direct her in her best interests as well as your own. Directives also work best when your child knows that, if necessary, you will back them up with more powerful controls. To ensure follow-through, use directives sparingly. We suggest that parents try rephrasing directives to emphasize the need rather than the imperative: "You need to sit down now" may garner cooperation, whereas "Sit down!" invites challenge.

Negative consequences (or threats of negative consequences) are powerful controls. By negative consequences, we mean results children don't want, such as putting a toy away when they can't share it, or going home when they can't be pleasant in public. The removal of a child to a solitary spot for a specified period—sometimes called "time-out"—is a particular type of negative consequence.

From the Classroom: Teachers' Tips on Talking to Kids

Here are some examples of phrases veteran early-childhood teachers use to set limits and guide children in the classroom. Note the concreteness and specific meaning of words used, to make these phrases more understandable to young children.

- It's time to clean up. I'm not going to change my mind.

- That's not okay.

- Use your words.

- You're the boss of your body. (If you can't boss your body, then I have to pick you up and move you.)

- Tell your hands "no touching."

- Thank you for cooperating.

Two-year-old Lera loves to play outside. One sunny day, she and her mother are smelling flowers in the flower boxes in front of their apartment building. Lera grins mischievously and steps off the curb.

Her mother quickly grabs her and carries her back onto the sidewalk. She looks straight into her daughter's eyes and says, "You need to stay on the sidewalk." It is a voice Lera does not hear very often, so she looks closely at her mother.

Her mother continues, "It is not safe to go in the street. If you go in the street again we will have to go inside." Lera goes back to the flowers, but a few minutes later she steps off the curb again. Her mother takes her, crying, into their building. The next time they are out, Lera goes up to the curb and her mother reminds her firmly, "Stay on the sidewalk." She needs no further reminders that day.

Lera's mother needs to control her daughter in a potentially dangerous situation. One repeat of the dangerous behavior is followed by a negative consequence (going inside). The result is that Lera is kept safe in the short run, and is beginning to learn a limit to maintain her safety in the long run.

Rewards (or the promise of rewards) are also powerful controls. Used thoughtfully and systematically, they can help redirect even the strongest-willed child. But since redirection is not the same as supporting the development of children's self-control, they, too, should not be overused. Rewards can be confusing if they are offered in times of conflict. If it appears that children are being rewarded for stopping a particular misbehavior, they may learn to misbehave in order to get a reward. Rewards are more effective when they are linked to positive actions, as opposed to the termination of negative actions, and are planned in advance.

> **Control Tactics**
>
> - Directives Spoken with Firmness
> - Negative Consequences for Misbehavior to Establish Immediate Control
> - Rewards to Shape Behavior over Time
> - Physical Interventions to Prevent Continued Misbehavior or Unsafe Behavior

One of the most powerful rewards is praise, such as, "You did a great job of brushing your teeth. I'm proud of you." Praise works so well because it meets several key criteria: It can be given immediately after the behavior you wish to reinforce. (For young children, immediate praise is more powerful than saying something like, "You'll get a special treat after dinner.") It's always available. Children never get tired of it. Finally, its value is proportional to the behavior you're rewarding.

Physically controlling a child is necessary when there's immediate danger or when matters have truly gotten out of hand. Usually, a parent holds a child to prevent harm or further mischief. While physical interventions are effective, they shouldn't be used alone. That's because they don't give the child a chance to practice exercising self-control and making his own decisions. It is especially important that you avoid intervening physically when you're angry, since you might do things you'll regret.

Taking a Break vs. "Time-Out"

We don't like the term "time-out." While many parents use removal from an activity as a guidance or control tactic, for others, "time-out" has become a punitive response to all types of behavior problems. It may be useful to move a child to a solitary place for a short period to "take a break" after a failed directive or violation of a rule, to help children appreciate the importance of the rule. Taking a break can also help when emotions are high, and children need to calm down and regain some measure of self-control (parents may need these breaks sometimes, too). With young children, these breaks should be kept brief (one or two minutes only) and not used too often. Further, make it clear that moving the child away is a pause in the activity, not a punishment for wrongdoing.

Martin is a precocious five-year-old and his sister, Maura, is three. Maura was born with Down syndrome and her parents have been very involved in supporting her development. One afternoon, Maura begins working on a puzzle and her mother stops reading from Martin's book to watch and praise Maura's progress.

Martin throws his book at Maura and says, "Stop it, that's mine." His mother puts her arms around Martin to keep his hands still and says, "I won't let you hurt Maura." While he struggles, she continues to talk to Maura.

Then she turns back to Martin and says, "You need to go sit in that chair for three minutes and calm down. I'll set the timer."

Negative consequences and physical interventions should not be relied upon too much. Rather, prevention and guidance should be parents' bread and butter, along with firmness in setting limits.

Firmness. Being firm means setting reasonable limits in reasonable ways and backing them up if needed. Being firm means being calm and serious. It does not mean venting anger. Occasional outbursts of anger occur in every family. They rarely cause harm—especially if they are acknowledged openly—so you need not feel guilty or concerned over occasionally getting angry. But you should be concerned if outbursts are common or if chronic anger characterizes parenting in your home.

Being firm also means not giving the impression that your instructions at that moment are open to debate. (If you say, "It's time for bed, okay?" you're implying to your child that she has the option of saying, "No, it's not okay!" Simply say, "It's time for bed.") Being firm means adopting a tone of voice (matter-of-fact and serious), a facial expression (stern, but not angry), and a posture (upright, but not menacing) that communicates, "I mean it!" And being firm means being willing and able to take corrective action if children continue to misbehave.

Over time, if you have consistently been firm when firmness was needed, your child will know when you really "mean it"; your child will learn to read your tone of voice, your facial expression, and your posture and respond appropriately. In fact, in homes where parents do not know how to be firm—either because they overreact (often blow up or display anger) or because they reason too much and often give in—children may not learn how to read adults' behavior, leading to problems for teachers and other caregivers as well as parents.

A Note on Rules

Rules can be used as control tactics, guidance tactics, or prevention tactics—depending on how they are used by adults, and how they are received by children. For control, rules may be repeated as directives telling children what adults expect of them ("The rule is, no running in the street"). For guidance, rules may be the subject of a family meeting where young siblings help come up with a "fair" rule to ensure that toys get picked up after play ("The rule is that everyone who played has to help with cleanup"). For prevention, rules may be the focus of discussions forecasting expectations before entering a restaurant ("Remember, the rule is no getting up from the table and wandering around the restaurant").

Note also that as children mature, the extent to which they "put rules on the inside" changes. Older children can make rules their own and live by them not because they come from adults but because they feel like good and fair rules to live by. Adults can help this process of putting rules on the inside by encouraging children to help make up new rules and by explaining the reasons that make particular rules good or fair.

Rules also can help parents maintain their own perspective when problems arise. In the heat of the moment, rules help parents distinguish between those things that are negotiable and those that are not, making it easier to "choose your battles" and avoid getting caught up in reasoning and debating at inappropriate times.

Also, where parents have not learned how to be firm, small battles often escalate into major confrontations—confrontations in which parents may become angry and lose their tempers. This can be very frightening to a child. It may cause immediate compliance, but it also increases the odds of future outbursts by both parents and children. The goal is to be able to assess situations wisely, to be firm when needed, and to use the least coercive control tactic to meet the need, so that you will not have to resort to tactics such as spanking.

Spanking

Spanking is a hot-button issue, dividing both parents and experts into camps armed with a multitude of arguments, anecdotes, studies, and references.

Social scientists, counselors, and medical practitioners are often unequivocally opposed to spanking because of studies showing connections between spanking and behavior problems. Recent studies show that the majority of American parents spank their children and spank often—even though these same parents say they spank only occasionally. Studies also show that if and when spanking does not work immediately, too many parents become abusive.

Some parents are unequivocally in favor of spanking because they see it as a necessary means of controlling and teaching children. In many cultures, spanking is common practice, either because of religious beliefs, family traditions, or shared values. Some believe it works if not done impulsively or in anger.

While we do not regard all instances of spanking as abusive, we believe that spanking is *not* a good tactic for managing behavior problems. First, we worry about it doing possible harm: not just physical harm, but a more subtle harm, because it increases fear as a factor in children's relationships with their parents.

Second, as a tactic, spanking may work to maintain order and safety in the short term, but it does not work to promote positive development. Because it often yields immediate results, parents who spank say, "It works." But spanking does not help children engage in problem solving. It does not help them internalize parents' values.

And it does not work to curb bad behavior in the long term; in fact, the evidence suggests that spanking may exacerbate some behavior problems and lead to other problems as children grow. After all, if it really were effective you wouldn't have to do it more than once or twice.

Finally, it is our conviction that if you are thoughtful in the ways you prevent and guide, and steadfast and clear when firmness is required, you should not need to spank.

Mixing and Matching Tactics

Mixing. Our *proactive* approach assumes that parents will use a mixture of prevention, guidance, and control in managing children's behavior problems. No one of these will be enough to navigate life with children; no one will be enough to support children's development. We focus not so much on which tactics are best in any one situation, but on learning to use different kinds and to choose among options.

Think of tactics as parts of a recipe, with ingredients from three groups: prevention, guidance, and control. The proportions will differ according to the age, temperament, and personality of each child, as well as the circumstances. They might also differ according to the style and culture of each family. But prevention and guidance will be the dominant flavors.

Matching. Our approach also emphasizes matching tactics not to particular problem behaviors (hitting, whining, or whatever) but to particular circumstances and to the uniqueness of each child. A common and simple example illustrates what we mean by matching:

"Don't look at me!" shouts four-year-old Maria to her older brother, Rey. Rey just rolls his eyes and goes back to his blocks. Maria has been shouting and bothering him for several minutes. She runs to her father and complains, "Rey keeps looking at me and I told him to stop."

Her father recognizes this behavior. Every day, just before dinner, Maria becomes irritable and disruptive. At another time of day, he would remind Maria that there is no shouting in the house. Instead, he realizes he forgot to give her a drink of juice or a piece of fruit to hold her over until dinner. He invites her to join him in making a salad for dinner and gives her a cup of juice. Within a few minutes, her normal good nature is restored.

What if Maria's father used a one-size-fits-all tactic to respond to yelling, such as time-out—without regard for circumstances or Maria's personality? It might do the job and curb the misbehavior, but we doubt it would support development. Here, Maria's father knows that she's affected by hunger, so he deals with that underlying problem rather than focusing on her yelling. The tactic is responsive both to the child and to the situation, and it succeeds in putting a stop to the misbehavior while supporting a positive relationship between Maria and her father.

Take another example of matching, this time matching a tactic to a child's age. Should a four-year-old who has hit another be treated the same way as a two-and-a-half-year-old who has done the same?

Two-and-a-half-year-old Annie is riding her new tricycle. Her friend Tula comes over and holds on to the handlebars. Annie hits Tula's hand and shouts, "Mine!"

Annie's mother quickly comes over and tells Annie, "No hitting."

Annie repeats, "Mine."

Her mother reassures her, "This *is* your tricycle. Tula was just touching it. You can say no if you don't want her to touch it."

Contrast this interaction with one between two four-year-olds.

Janet is riding her new bike. Her friend Alex comes over and holds on to the handlebars. Janet hits her hand and shouts, "You can't touch my new bike."

Janet's mother quickly comes over and asks, "What's going on here? There is no hitting, Janet. Alex, are you okay?"

Janet explains, "Alex was touching my new bike and I don't want her to."

Her mother asks, "How could you have let her know that, Janet?"

Janet says, "I guess I could have told her not to touch it."

Her mother replies, "That sounds like a good way."

Annie's mother responds to her daughter's hitting by using a control tactic, a forceful directive, and by giving her a better option. But because Janet is older, has more self-control, and has a greater capacity to reason, her mother reminds her of a rule and elicits problem solving.

Adjusting over time. Any use of tactics for managing behavior problems has to take into account that both children and conditions are constantly changing. What worked at one time in a child's life may not work at another time.

Celia's mother is a nurse's aide working the evening shift. Every day at 2:30 when her mother leaves for work, Celia's uncle comes over to take care of Celia, give her dinner, and put her to bed. Although three-year-old Celia has been sleeping through the night since she was very young, lately she has begun waking up when she hears her mother come home at 11:30 and crying when her uncle tries to say good-bye. Her mother then has a hard time getting her back to sleep before midnight.

Such scenes are normal in parenting young children. Parents must constantly adjust and try out new tactics when old ones get outworn or outgrown, or when a child's new stage of development or a home's new circumstances present fresh challenges and behavior problems.

Celia's mother decides to try something new. On the next Monday when her uncle puts Celia to bed, he tells her he'll wake her up to say good-bye when her mother comes home. Just before 11:30, he wakes Celia and brings her into the kitchen for a glass of milk while they wait. When her mother arrives he says, "I'll see you tomorrow, Celia," and gives her a kiss good-bye.

Her mother asks Celia about her day while she finishes her milk and goes to the bathroom. At 11:45, her mother says, "Okay, it's time to get back to bed. I'm tired after my long night at work." Celia climbs into her bed, kisses her mother, and lies down to sleep.

This revised routine may not be the ultimate solution for whatever changes Celia is going through, but it is one attempt to disrupt the problem and introduce an alternative. Celia's sleep is broken up, but it appears that she might actually get more sleep with this routine, and she seems to get through the "changing of the guard" more calmly.

Finding Openings for Change

In other books, this chapter might have been called "Proactive Discipline." We have not used the term "discipline" because it is so often associated with the actions parents take after a child has misbehaved. It is *reactive*. Part of proactive parenting is relying on prior experience to anticipate events (when possible) so as to behave more thoughtfully.

This means analyzing problem situations to look for factors that influence your child's behavior. Then, with those factors in mind, you can begin to look for areas open to change, or "points of entry." For example: Is there a way to change the setting or location? To reduce a source of stress or discomfort? To introduce or remove people, animals, or toys? To redirect the child's attention, or your own? At each point of entry, we can choose among many options, drawing from our storehouse of tactics for prevention, guidance, or control.

Many factors might be involved in a particular instance of misbehavior: say, a hungry child, easily upset by crowds and noise, who grabs an expensive stuffed toy at the store. Although some factors can't be changed—such as a child's temperament or interests—once you have identified potential points of entry, you can choose appropriate tactics for changing those things you can. You can also consider temperament and interests when you redirect his attention ("Isn't that other dog the same kind Grandma has?"), or add something to the setting ("Let's get you some juice.").

> Three-year-old Tim and his mother have been home from his morning preschool program for an hour. Tim begins to whine, "Play with me, Mommy. Stop writing."
>
> His mother sighs as she realizes Tim is not content to play alone while she gets things done. When they first got home, she set aside time to play with him, helping him complete the transition from school to home. They read books and worked on a couple of puzzles before she attempted to do some paperwork.
>
> "Let's see what you can build with your blocks," she suggests.
>
> Tim is not interested. "I don't want to use blocks. I want you to play with me."

In this situation, we would certainly understand if Tim's mother chose to give up on her work, or set a limit on Tim's choices to stop his whining. But recognizing that this type of problem is recurring, she begins to analyze the situation and think about a range of possible points of entry.

> Tim's mother tries to figure out exactly what the issue is for Tim. Does he need her attention? Does he just want company? Does he need more opportunities to play with other children? Is he tired? Is he upset about something?

Tim's mother has identified several important considerations: Tim's relationship with her, his desire for company, his interest in play, and his physical or emotional states. She can now focus on points of entry where she might act: change the setting (invite a friend over, set out different playthings), change the interaction between them (stop what she is doing to play with him, involve him in one of her chores), address his physical comfort (offer a snack, suggest a quiet activity), or adjust her own perception of the problem (ignore his whining and leave him to find his own activity). At each point of entry she can choose from a different set of tactics.

Some Points of Entry

Is there unusual stress or tension in the home? If yes, think about how you could reduce overall stress levels for the family by injecting more humor into interactions, planning more downtime, playing together, discussing stressful circumstances, and asking about children's feelings.

Are caregivers in agreement when it comes to dealing with children's needs and problems? If not, work on coordinating your approaches by consulting a trusted third party, reading a book about parenting together, or otherwise changing expectations about different roles and responsibilities.

Do you have good routines set up for your child to follow? If routines have been neglected or have stopped working well, think about how you could introduce or change them to make things more predictable and regular. Are there new family priorities that need attention, or newly developed abilities and challenges that need to be accommodated? Think about how to help children understand routines by talking about them or enlisting their help in the planning.

Have you recently spent one-on-one time playing, reading, or otherwise giving undivided attention to your child? This question is about building up a positive relationship and providing times when a child can get *his* way (have control) so that at other times you can better insist on having *your* way and maintaining control.

Could you do more as far as organizing a good play space and providing materials for constructive play (such as blocks and paper and markers)? Problem behavior between parent and child can sometimes be resolved when children are helped to play constructively on their own.

To maximize your choice of tactics and approach behavior problems positively, always look for multiple points of entry. It may be that you'll need to address several issues simultaneously, or different ones over time, to resolve behavior problems. Parents who focus exclusively on one point of entry or one set of tactics often find they are only intermittently effective. Children change as they grow, and so the options we generate should be evolving as well.

Proactive parenting is something we get better at over time. No parent or professional knows the best response to every problem in all situations. But experience helps: the more you have thought about points of entry with regard to one problem, the more easily you will be able to generate options when a new problem arises. Get into the habit of analyzing situations as they arise or after you have emerged from a crisis. When the voice in your head says, "Oops, I should have said . . ." bringing on feelings of guilt, change it to "Next time I'll say . . ." and add that response to your collection of tactics for the future.

The Parent-Child Partnership

Proactive parenting is not only about responding to behavior problems, but doing so in ways that support a strong positive relationship with your child. The essence of this proactive approach is the development of *partnerships* between parents and children.

Partnership between parent and child does not imply equality or permissiveness. Rather, it means mutual and demonstrable respect of parent for child and child for parent—respect that often comes from parents finding ways to coordinate their own agendas with those of their children. Developing partnerships with children requires, then, finding ways to appropriately *share* control. It means being as committed to, and clever about, the ways you *give away* control as you are about the ways you *assert or retain* control.

With preschoolers and older children this often involves negotiating, discussing family rules and expectations, and planning future events. With younger children, a commitment to partnership involves acknowledging children's feelings, providing avenues for them to pursue their goals, and helping them to do what parents have determined must be done. Redirection, offering limited choices, and making necessary activities enjoyable or inviting are familiar strategies that foster shared control. Here's a school example:

Stopping by the sand table, the kindergarten teacher calls out, "Time to clean up, it's circle time." Dana and Sylvie protest and dawdle. Rather than crack down on them, the teacher asks, "What is the problem?"

"If we put the lid on the sand table, our castles will be squished!"

The teacher asks, "Can you think of a way to clean up without squashing your castles?" After some thought, the children stack up blocks to prop up the lid, then go happily to their meeting.

When a teacher listens to the children's concerns, and gives them limited control, children get practice in problem solving, and the classroom runs more smoothly. Of course, sharing control is not possible all the time. Often adults have to lay down the law or give up in exhaustion. But by giving your child appropriate practice in sharing control, and working together to meet everyone's goals, you'll be doing more than just managing behavior problems; you will be supporting your child's overall development to the benefit of your child, yourself, and your family.

Some Final Words

Behavior problems can undermine relationships. The ties that bind parent to child become frayed when there are too many battles and too much control on either side. Once these ties loosen, it becomes hard to support children's development. The single most important reason for adopting a proactive approach is that it strengthens those ties. But the approach is not always easy. As the great Swiss psychologist Jean Piaget once pointed out, "the best methods are also the most difficult ones."

To minimize behavior problems and guide children takes enormous time, energy, and creativity. A proactive, partnership-oriented approach needs time to bear fruit, and many results aren't seen until later childhood and beyond. To be firm with children in the ways we have described takes enormous patience and self-discipline. The proactive approach advocated here demands a lot from parents. But it can produce children who are strong in character, who don't simply behave themselves but who become caring, fair-minded, and productive adults. The demands of this approach, then, are not too great, given the rewards.

Suggestions for Further Reading

Adults
Laura Davis and Janis Keyser. *Becoming the Parent You Want to Be: A Sourcebook of Strategies for the First Five Years.* Broadway Books, 1997.

Adele Faber and Elaine Mazlish. *How to Talk So Kids Will Listen and Listen So Kids Will Talk.* Avon Books, 1999.

Ross W. Greene. *The Explosive Child: A New Approach for Understanding and Parenting Easily Frustrated, Chronically Inflexible Children.* HarperCollins, 2001.

Jane Nelsen, Cheryl Erwin, and Roslyn Duffy. *Positive Discipline for Preschoolers.* Prima Publishing, 1998.

Nancy Samalin. *Loving Your Child Is Not Enough: Positive Discipline That Works.* Penguin Books, 1998.

W. George Scarlett and Associates. *Trouble in the Classroom: Managing the Behavior Problems of Young Children.* Jossey-Bass, 1997.

Children's Books
John Burningham. *Mr. Gumpy's Outing.* Henry Holt, 1990.

Eric Carle. *Do You Want to Be My Friend?* HarperCollins, 1995.

———. *The Grouchy Ladybug.* Scott Foresman, 1996.

Kevin Henkes. *Chester's Way.* Mulberry Books, 1997 (bullying).

———. *Julius, the Baby of the World.* Mulberry Books, 1995 (sibling rivalry).

———. *A Weekend with Wendell.* William Morrow, 1986 (misbehavior, selfishness).

Russell Hoban. *Bread and Jam for Frances.* HarperCollins, 1993 (pickiness).

———. *Bedtime for Frances.* HarperTrophy, 1995 (fear).

Barbara Joosse. *Mama, Do You Love Me?* Chronicle, 1998 (anger, unconditional acceptance).

Ezra Jack Keats. *Goggles!* Puffin, 1998 (problem solving).

———. *Louie.* William Morrow, 1983 (shyness).

————. *Peter's Chair.* Puffin, 1998 (sharing).

Leo Lionni. *Alexander and the Wind-up Mouse.* Knopf, 1987 (envy, jealousy).

————. *It's Mine!* Econo-Clad Books, 1999 (fighting, arguing).

Betty MacDonald. *Mrs. PiggleWiggle.* Lippincott, 1975 (humorous approach to keeping clean).

Helen Oxenbury. *Tickle, Tickle.* Simon and Schuster, 1999 (little books with great drawings of toddlers).

Beatrix Potter. *The Tale of Peter Rabbit.* Frederick Warne, 1999.

Pete Seeger. *Abiyoyo.* Aladdin, 1994 (playing tricks).

Maurice Sendak. *Where the Wild Things Are.* HarperCollins, 1988.

Dr. Seuss. *Green Eggs and Ham.* Random House, 1960.

William Steig. *Pete's a Pizza.* HarperCollins, 1998 (bad moods).

————. *Spinky Sulks.* Sunburst, 1991.

Judith Viorst. *Alexander and the Terrible, Horrible, No Good, Very Bad Day.* Scott Foresman, 1987.

Rosemary Wells. *Noisy Nora.* Dial, 1999 (misbehavior).

Photo by Denise Willis Turner

C H A P T E R   F O U R

"Touchy" Issues: Physical Closeness and Affection

Fred Rothbaum and Elaine Dyer Tarquinio

Four-year-old Samantha likes to hug, kiss, and cuddle with members of her family, especially her mom and dad. As far as she's concerned, the more the better. She's very verbal about why she enjoys the physical contact. Sometimes she says she's cold, sometimes she says she likes the way the other person feels, and sometimes she says she's lonely.

While Samantha's parents enjoy their affectionate daughter, sometimes her mother guiltily wishes for a little more space. Also, her dad worries that Samantha's too clingy and will have problems going off to school by herself.

All of us have a biologically based need for warmth, touch, and physical closeness. This is especially true for children. For example, we know from studies of neglected children in orphanages that infants and toddlers who don't get the physical affection they need have difficulty form-ing close emotional relationships when they're older.

Some children seem to need more physical affection than others. This is partly a matter of the child's inborn temperament, as is the amount of affection the child feels comfortable showing. Culture, too, plays a major role here. How much physical closeness is encouraged and allowed varies from family to family and across communities.

We deal with closeness and sexuality in the same chapter because, as we will try to show, they are often associated. Although sexuality is some-thing we usually think of as existing after puberty, like everything else in adulthood, it has its roots in childhood. A young child's experiences being held, cuddled, and fed lay a foundation for her healthy adult relationships.

Unfortunately, there is little written for parents about either physical closeness or sexuality among young children. Handbooks for parents almost always address issues of physical growth, intellectual understand-ing, language acquisition, and social development, but they are almost mute about issues of closeness and sexuality. We think that it is critical that parents have an awareness of these more "touchy" issues.

This chapter will help you understand the connections between closeness and sexuality, and how to draw boundaries between them. We'll also look at how closeness and sexuality are intertwined with other important aspects of social development, such as young children's talk, games, and social interactions. (It's common for preschoolers to experi-ment with taboo words, and to explore their own and others' bodies.)

Here are some of the common questions and concerns we'll cover in this chapter:

- How different families express affection, and what's "normal"

- Why children need touch and closeness—especially at night—and what to do with a child who won't sleep in his own bed

- What to do if your child doesn't like to cuddle, and you do (or vice versa)

- What to do when your child likes to run around naked, or has no concept of privacy. How to handle children's curiosity about sexuality, including handling inappropriate comments or behaviors

- What to do when a child touches and rubs himself, or "plays doctor" with a friend

- How to talk to your child about privacy and sexual issues

Your Family's "Script" for Closeness

Jackie, a kindergartner, is dropped off at her friend Kelly's house by her mother. Her mother brings her to the door, pats her on the head, and says good-bye. Jackie is greeted enthusiastically by Kelly and her mother. They are arm in arm at the door.

The girls play for an hour in Kelly's room and then go to the kitchen for a snack. Kelly's mother hugs them both before getting them juice and crackers. She sits with them, stroking Kelly's hair and chatting. Kelly thanks her mother for the snack and gives her a kiss and hug before the girls run off to play again.

There are many ways to express emotional closeness—some physical, some not. In a sense, each family has an unspoken "script" about closeness—when it should occur, in what way, and for what reason. For example, "In our family, we hug when saying hello and good-bye, and only Mom and Dad kiss on the lips." There is enormous variation in these scripts.

Jackie comes from a family that is quite reserved about physical closeness, particularly in front of others. Her parents hug or kiss their children at specific times, such as bedtime, when someone is hurt, or when someone is very excited or happy. They enjoy physical closeness when reading together or working on projects together. They also talk a great deal, which keeps their relationships strong. They tend not to be physically demonstrative in public, relying on their verbal connection at those times.

Kelly's family, on the other hand, is very physical in almost any situation. Her parents are openly affectionate with each other and with her. They hug Kelly frequently, stroke her hair, hold her hand, and give her back rubs. This physical connection is an important part of their relationships with one another. While Jackie enjoys the hugs she receives at Kelly's, she sometimes feels uncomfortable seeing Kelly and her parents kiss each other on the lips.

Some families demonstrate physical affection through elaborate hugging without any kissing; others rely primarily on kissing, perhaps on both cheeks at greetings and partings. Still others show closeness through sitting or standing near one another (proximity) with only incidental physical contact. In some cultures, direct displays of contact such as kissing are rare, but there may be much more proximity between family members, which would leave many Americans cringing at the absence of physical space.

Mainstream American culture puts a high value on independence and exploration. Many of us tend to rely more on eye contact from a distance to maintain a sense of closeness. We often place infants and toddlers away from us: for example, in playpens or walkers. This is not the case in most other cultures. In some parts of the world, mothers carry their young child for most of the day, and may breast-feed at least occasionally until their child is four or five. As another example, many children in Japan are never away from their mothers until the age of three. Not only do these moms not work outside the home, but they don't arrange playdates away from the child, nor do they find a baby-sitter and go out on the town with their spouse. Time alone (for the mother or child) is simply not as valued as much as mother-child closeness.

While very visible and associated with strong feelings, the number of kisses given, or the way you touch or hug your child, are much less important than what that closeness means to the two of you. There is a wide range of what's normal and healthy. It's useful to be aware of and perhaps even talk about your family's script for closeness (especially if you grew up in a family or culture that expressed affection differently than your spouse or partner's did) to see if that script is meeting everyone's needs.

Physical Closeness at Nighttime

> Three-year-old Ahmad has a lengthy bedtime ritual. First comes the obligatory game inducing him to go upstairs—a piggyback ride, a race against time, or bargaining about the number of books to be read. Then comes the book, or books, followed by brushing the teeth, another glass of water, and "leave the door open a little more" segments.

One of parents' most pressing concerns about physical closeness and separateness involves sleeping arrangements. The scene above is probably familiar, to varying degrees, to many of us. (See chapters 2 and 3 for help with getting children to bed.) How did Mom or Dad get hooked into this prolonged ritual, which in many families goes on for well over an hour? We believe that powerful biological and cultural forces are behind this scenario. Young children seek proximity and contact with caregivers to increase their sense of security and to reduce their fear, aloneness, and sadness. These feelings are most likely to come out at night. Remember that young children have more difficulty than adults handling transitions. Going to bed is a major transition, even though it happens every night.

Underlying these feelings is an evolutionary process that has selected for survival those children who most resisted being left alone. Over the course of human history, children who have been the most distressed by aloneness, and who have most actively sought out their parents at night, are the ones who have received the most attention to their basic needs.

> Three-year-old Tom has never liked to go to bed. When finally agreeing to do so, he tries to get his dad to stay with him as long as possible. Later,

when his parents are asleep, he climbs into his parents' bed, even though one of them usually awakens soon after and returns him to his own bed. While he rarely protests the return, he doesn't give up; it is not unusual for him to go back to his parents' bed two or three times in one evening.

If his parents ask him why he comes in, he gives them several answers depending on his mood: I'm scared, I'm lonely, I had a bad dream, I want to snuggle. His parents, sleep-deprived and having exhausted every strategy recommended to them—reasoning, rewards and extra daytime attention—are at their wit's end. Tom does not seem too happy with the arrangement, either.

Despite children's need for closeness, American parents rarely sleep in the same room as their children once they reach three months of age. Why are children left alone at the point in the day that they most need trusted caregivers to protect them? Not surprisingly, the vast majority of the world's children are not left alone at night. Infants typically sleep in close proximity to their mothers; toddlers and older children sleep next to a parent, grandparent, or sibling. (Private sleeping may not even be an option because of lack of space or money, but sleeping close together is often by choice.)

One reason that Tom, in the story above, had trouble staying in his bed is that he slept too far away from his parents. They have a large home, and a bathroom and office separated his room from theirs. When Tom was moved to the room next to theirs, there was much less night-time wandering. (Even being two rooms away versus one room makes a difference to a child.)

Young children regularly sleep alone in only a small number of Western countries, including the United States. When asked in interviews about this practice of having children sleep alone, parents who sleep with their children describe it as cruel, and they express profound sympathy for those children who must endure it. One reason why most American children are left alone at night is that parents want to help their children become separate individuals. Children who are able to be independent at nighttime have taken an important first step toward self-reliance. They realize that when they are distressed, they can count on themselves to make the world right.

Many American advice manuals that cover children's sleep habits emphasize the importance of children's ability to "self-regulate": to soothe and comfort themselves when they cry (for example, with a favorite toy or blanket, or a special sleep position). According to this conventional wisdom, a parent's role is to make sure his child's distress doesn't escalate to the point where she's out of control—but the parent should hang back and wait, to give his child a chance to learn that she can deal with her own emotions.

By contrast, in most other cultures, and in certain communities in the United States, parents believe that they should play a stronger role in comforting their young children. They don't see it as a problem if their child doesn't learn to cope with fear or sadness by herself. These parents may reason that later in life, the child will be a more loyal member of her family if she sees herself as needing others (and others as needing her) to satisfy basic emotional needs. While loyalty is valued in most U.S. families, it's tempered by the high value placed on self-reliance.

> Bob and Anne hear the familiar 3 A.M. sound of their daughter's footsteps entering their room. Four-year-old Haley has joined them in bed virtually every night since she was born, first by their choice but now by hers. She climbs into their bed, cuddling in right between her parents.
>
> In the last few months, both parents have begun to be frustrated by this habit. Bob, in particular, wants his daughter in her own bed so that he can be alone with his wife. Anne is the parent who most often sets the tone and timetable of events for Haley. She is more relaxed about Haley joining them in bed, although she had hoped that she would have outgrown it by now.

In addition to fostering their child's independence, most American parents want time alone, away from the children, to preserve and strengthen their bond. In their bedroom at night, parents have some rare privacy and time for essential intimacy, sexual or otherwise. In cultures where there's less emphasis on keeping the romantic flame alive after children are born, parents are less likely to want kids out of the marital bed.

From an early age, children learn about the value placed on private time for parents. When children are repeatedly told they can't sleep with their parents because "mommies and daddies need their special time together," they come to associate closeness in bed with exclusive relationships and with private behaviors.

For American children and adults, then, time in the bedroom at night—right or wrong—may be associated with sexuality. This is one reason many of us feel uncomfortable sharing a bed with an older child. Sleeping with children can also present practical problems, because of our tightly scheduled lives. For these reasons, we suggest it may be best for an American child aged four or older to sleep in her own bed. If your child is sick or very upset, you can lie down next to her until she falls asleep.

In the case of Haley's family, the first step was for Bob to find a time when he and Anne could talk alone about the issue. He explained his feelings, including his desire for privacy and for Haley to be more independent at night. Once Anne realized how important this was to her husband, she admitted her own growing frustration, and the two came up with a plan to help Haley sleep in her own bed through the night.

They chose the weekend to begin, when they wouldn't have to get up early for work. On Saturday morning, they told Haley that she was a big girl, and it was time for her to sleep in her own bed all night. She could join them in bed when it got light outside.

"If you wake up during the night, you can snuggle with Mr. Bear and he'll help you go back to sleep," Bob explained. "If you can't go to sleep, you may call to us, and we will come and give you a go-to-sleep kiss." Anne told Haley that if she came into their bedroom, they'd walk her back to her room so she could go back to sleep in her own bed.

Bob and Anne spent a lot of time playing in her room on Saturday, putting her stuffed animals and dolls to bed. As expected, Haley tested the new rules. When she came into their bed, Bob quietly walked her back. When she called to them, Anne gave her a brief check and kiss, and left the room. It took several nights of crying and a few setbacks over the next few weeks, but finally Haley was happily sleeping in her own bed.

Physical Closeness During the Daytime

The Morales family includes four boys and one girl. When the father, Conrado, drops off his boys, he shakes their hands and tells them to be good. With his little girl, Clara, it's all hugs and kisses. He spends many minutes each morning with Clara, brushing her thick, long hair and tying it up with bright ribbons as they murmur to each other.

While Conrado is crazy about all of his kids, the boys receive that love differently. He gives physical affection to them in a way that shows he values their independence.

Kids crave touching and physical closeness more during "down" times—bedtime, naptime, waking up—and times of transition and stress, such as when they're sick, hungry, or scared, or in a new situation. Knowing that he can get a hug or cuddle when he wants one, or be carried when he's tired or held when he's stressed gives a child a wonderful sense of security—like the feeling a child has when sleeping near his parent.

Closeness during daytime is expressed in different forms (including those in the story above). Many parents typically show affection not by touching but through eye contact. When he looks up after a fall or an accomplishment, a child used to this form of intimacy feels supported and reassured to see his parent closely watching, with a sympathetic or proud expression on her face.

As children grow older, parents more often show support this way, and rely less on physical closeness. Parents also use language more to show affection, praising the child for her accomplishments ("You did it! All that practice with your jump rope, and you jumped five times in a row!") or using a tone of voice that conveys empathy for the child's feelings ("I know you really wanted to play with Alex, but he is going someplace with his family. You look sad and disappointed."). This maintains closeness while supporting the older child's movement toward independence.

Earlier we mentioned that closeness is often intertwined with other important aspects of development. When a child's busy playing, he might seek a simple touch or hug from his parent. Alternately, play may be of the rough-and-tumble, wrestling or gymnastic sort, as it often is with dads, and children come to associate affection with this sort of play.

In teaching language and reading, physical closeness with parents becomes an important part of how children experience learning. Picture a father sitting close to his child while they talk about their day, punctuating the conversation with well-timed and sensitive forms of contact: a touch on the shoulder, a ruffling of hair. This increases the odds that his child will associate talking and learning with these forms of closeness.

> Jim and his five-year-old son, Justin, are reading a book together when the telephone rings. Jim answers it and becomes engrossed in a conversation with his brother. He keeps an eye on Justin, and sees him take the tissue box off the table and begin to shred a tissue. He recognizes this action as a sign of boredom on Justin's part. He calmly takes the box from Justin and hands him a special pen and pad of paper. Justin turns his attention to drawing and Jim finishes his conversation.

There are many other ways that parents can foster their child's sense of security besides being physically close. Parents who closely monitor their child, and are sensitive to his needs for stimulation or for calming (as with Justin above), also help that child feel cared for. As with physical closeness, the key element is whether the parent is sensitive to the child's needs. Simply focusing on what the parent is doing misses the boat; what is more important is whether the parent's behavior is well matched to the child's behavior.

There is no one right way to provide physical closeness. What works for one child in a family often doesn't work for another; one child might be a cuddler, and another might need space. But these generalizations trivialize the complexities of real life. Few children are cuddly in every mood, location, or time, and fewer still are consistently cuddly throughout their childhood. Cuddliness waxes and wanes.

Parents need to trust their instincts, to trust their children to tell them what they want, and to rely on trial and error. Sometimes, the most sensitive thing a parent can do is *not* offer a hug. For some children, in some situations, the most constructive form of physical closeness is maintaining a respectful distance.

WHEN CUDDLING STYLES DON'T MATCH

> Two-year-old Moira trips on the rug in her living room and falls down. She is crying hard, and her mother, Marianne, runs to pick her up and comfort her. But, as usual, Moira resists her mother's hug and runs to sit alone, crying in the corner. Her mother is heartbroken. Marianne is by nature a very physical person and struggles with her daughter's different style. When Moira is upset or hurt, she prefers to be alone. Even when joining her parents in bed in the morning or reading a book with one of them, she keeps a foot or two between herself and her parents.

Marianne believes that physical contact is important for a child, and craves it herself with Moira. With trial and error, she's found ways to balance her daughter's need for space with her own desire for physical closeness. When Moira is hurt, Marianne gives her a couple of minutes to get past the initial shock and upset, and then goes and sits near her. She talks to Moira in a soft, soothing voice and slowly moves close enough to rub her back. At this point, Moira usually relaxes and often leans on her mother—or even accepts a hug.

Back rubs have proven to be a comfortable way for mother and daughter to connect. Also, Marianne puts a pillow (or stuffed animal) on her lap when they read books together, and Moira will lie on the pillow. When they are close to each other, in bed in the morning for example,

Marianne has found that Moira enjoys lying close to her mother as long as Moira is facing away from her. By respecting her daughter's style, Marianne has found ways for them to be physically close that are comfortable for both of them.

Try to find a style of touch that your noncuddler enjoys, such as back rubs, hair brushing, tickling, or touching foot to foot. Rather than holding hands, he may feel more comfortable linking arms. You might also use a family pet as a way to connect physically with your child, holding and cuddling your cat, dog, rabbit, or guinea pig together.

> Michael is a bright, active five-year-old who has always loved physical affection. From infancy, he was most content when held and cuddled. As a toddler, preschooler, and now as a kindergartner, he constantly runs to his parents to give them hugs, hold their hands, sit on their laps, and basically find any way he can to have physical contact with them.
>
> His mother, on the other hand, is quite reserved physically. Candace grew up in a home where there was virtually no physical display of affection. She sees how important physical contact is for her son, but has had to work hard to be comfortable with it. At times, she stiffens when Michael hugs her or plays with her hair.

To further complicate matters, parents have their own temperaments and preferences regarding touch. In contrast to Marianne, Candace was never big on hugs and kisses, and tends to feel uncomfortable sitting close to a child for long periods. It doesn't help a child for his parent to ignore her own needs. It's much better to become aware of those needs, and to try to give her child what he wants in a way that's comfortable.

Candace has come up with creative ways to be physical with Michael. She loves outdoor activities and finds that holding him in the water of a pool or sledding with him on her lap are fun ways for both of them to be close. They both love music, so she also uses time listening to music or playing the piano as opportunities to be close to him. Since she realizes that as the adult, she has to be the flexible one, she's worked on ways to relax and enjoy Michael's need for physical closeness.

Enjoyment of physical closeness can't be faked; to be effective, it must be heartfelt. Physical closeness, like many other aspects of parenting, is more art than science.

Understanding Childhood Sensuality and Sexuality

Four-year-old Eric is playing in a sandbox at a park with his father when a couple on a nearby bench begin kissing passionately. Eric asks, "Dad, what are they doing?" in a disgusted voice. When his father responds that they are kissing in a way adults sometimes do, Eric says, "Oh, gross. I won't ever do that," and returns to playing in the sandbox.

Whether the issue is deciding whether it's okay for your child to see you naked, answering your child's questions about genitals (from what they're called to what they're for), taking baths with your child, whether to allow children to view television programs or films with sexual scenes, or what to make of the phrase emanating from your five-year-old's mouth—"Did he just say 'penis breath'?"—issues related to sexuality are an everyday part of raising children.

To many parents, physical closeness with a child and sexuality have little to do with each other. Children are innocent, and children's expressions of physical closeness, such as hugging, wanting to be carried, and even kissing, are untainted by sexuality. Closeness is seen as providing care and protection for the child, and sexuality is viewed as serving different functions and as emerging later in development.

Parents and teachers sometimes see preschoolers act in ways that suggest complete innocence about and lack of interest in sexuality. But at other times, children's behavior can look blatantly sexual. Caregivers often wonder how to tell normal and healthy behaviors from those that are not. While there are important differences between the meaning and expression of physical closeness, and the meaning and expression of sexuality, the two topics are intertwined, even in children. We'll try here to clarify areas of overlap and difference, to help you better understand your child's thinking and behavior.

WHAT'S NORMAL?

> Danny, age four, was sitting on the floor watching one of his favorite videos. His dad, reading the newspaper on the sofa, looked down and noticed Danny was lying on top of his stuffed dog, and rubbing it against his crotch.

Children's normal "sexual" behaviors fall within an extraordinarily broad spectrum, leaving parents anxious and uncertain about how to respond. Parents often worry unnecessarily because they interpret their child's behavior the way they would an adult's. But research shows that behavior like Danny's above doesn't mean the same thing to a child, or involve the same thoughts and feelings that an adult would have. To make this clearer, see the following examples of three dimensions where the meaning of children's behavior is quite different from that of adults:

- *Curiosity and play, versus knowing and intentional behavior.* Two four-year-old girls showing each other their genitals in the bathroom at preschool, or two kindergarten children daring each other to show their underwear—versus two adults engaged in essentially the same behavior and expecting it to lead to an intimate encounter.

- *Spontaneity and openness versus self-consciousness and privacy.* Preschoolers at a beach on a hot summer day taking off all their clothes and running naked on the sand—versus two adults who do the same thing on a deserted beach.

- *Sensuality and excitement versus passion and eroticism.* Two four-year-olds cover each other with mud and run giggling all over the yard—versus adults doing the same.

Most parents realize that language, social relationships, and other critical aspects of human functioning develop in stages from childhood through adulthood. Yet many parents don't realize that sexuality follows a similar course, and has its roots in early childhood. In a sense, children's sexuality starts developing from the moment they are born. As parents, we affect that process, knowingly or not. Just as we help our child pick up a ball and learn to throw it, find a word and learn to say it, or hear a song and learn to sing it, we can help our children with this vital part of their lives.

Sexuality appears in many forms and places. It shows up in jokes and flirting and everyday conversations. Sexuality is a feeling that can exist in and of itself, entirely separate from making love. It can arise spontaneously in response to people, places, colors, smells, and memories. The American Medical Association Committee on Human Sexuality (1972) broadly defined human sexuality as "an identification, an activity, a biological and emotional process, an outlook and an expression of the self . . . an important factor in every personal relationship and in every human endeavor."

When you respond to children's sexual curiosity or behaviors, we recommend the following approach:

- Adopt an attitude that is respectful, matter-of-fact, and light-hearted.

- Be conservative in responding to the child's actions, and liberal in responding to questions.

- Take your cue from the child: if neither the child nor his or her playmates are showing concern, then in most cases you shouldn't either.

There is, of course, real concern in today's world about sexual abuse and about children's behaviors that might indicate abuse. We focus here on normal sexual behaviors because they play adaptive and educational roles in children's lives, and because a fuller understanding of normal child sexuality is critical to understanding abnormality. In the final section, we briefly address behaviors that we see as abnormal and problematic.

CURIOSITY AND PLAY

> After his dad had left for work, four-year-old Karl climbed into his parents' bed next to his mom. He took off his pants and said, "I won't be needing these anymore."

The adultlike quality of some of children's comments and behaviors confuses parents into thinking that behavior is truly adult. Yet there are often clues that the child is simply practicing a small part of a much larger adult role. For example, the child who removed his pants seemed to regard this act as the sum total, rather than the start, of "seducing" his mother. There was no sign that Karl was thinking about sexual contact. Here, Karl's mom could just say, "You can put your pants on. Sometimes Daddy is more comfortable sleeping with his pants off."

One mother described a time when her four-year-old son asked her to lie down on the couch and close her eyes. When she asked him why, he simply said, "You'll see." He then climbed on top of her, mimicking the behavior of an adult male during intercourse. When later asked about his behavior, he said, "I just wanted to see what it was like to be on you." As far as his parents knew, he'd never observed any kind of sexual intercourse.

Is this behavior normal? What guidelines should we use to decide? At first glance, this behavior seems adultlike and worrisome. Based on the three dimensions described earlier, though, we believe this incident falls within the normal realm. First, there were definite elements of curiosity and play in this youngster's behavior. He said he wanted to see what it was like to lie on his mommy. His demeanor and actions were playful, as opposed to tense, compulsive, or forceful.

Second, the behavior was unselfconsciously spontaneous and open, probably because the child had little understanding of the psychological or physical implications of his actions. While there was an element of privacy involved in asking Mom to close her eyes, there was more of a gamelike quality to this request than a sense of self-awareness or secrecy. Even if the child sensed this was a forbidden activity, his method of being "private" was more typical of younger than older children (e.g., no demand for secrecy). Finally, there was no indication that his behavior was linked to arousal or eroticism, and there was no evidence of awareness of intercourse.

Just as children are curious about adult roles such as firefighters and teachers, they are also curious and playful about sexuality. Much of children's "work" is to play the roles of adults to learn more about those roles. Children's play involving sexual roles and relationships is found in all societies. Through play, children also develop the larger script they will need to experience adult sexuality.

Another mother told of her four-year-old daughter asking her to play a villain while the girl and her father played a princess and a prince. The daughter included in her play the element of jealousy, making her behavior that much more adultlike. Another child flirtatiously asked his mother to play "cereal girl" while he played "sugar boy."

> Five-year-old David is enjoying a back rub by his mom as part of their usual bedtime ritual. Departing from the usual sequence, David turns around to face his mom and touches her breast. His mom, who is slightly startled, asks, "Why did you do that?" David responds, matter-of-factly, "I wanted to see what it felt like."

Similarly, while children's behaviors can be very purposeful, their purposes often differ from those of adults. Consider, for example, children's attempts to touch a father's penis or a mother's breast: many parents have stories like the one above, involving children's determined curiosity, attempts at humor, and limit testing—but without adultlike erotic feelings.

David's mother could respond in an equally matter-of fact way, "Oh,

I see," and return to the back rub. If she is uncomfortable with this type of curiosity, she might add, "Usually people don't touch a woman's breast. It is a private part of a grown-up woman's body."

> Three-year-old Maya is tired after an afternoon of shopping at the mall. She and her mother are in line at the last stop for the day. Her mother is holding Maya in her arms. Maya's head is resting on her mother's shoulder and she begins to absentmindedly stroke her mother's breast. Her mother gently takes Maya's hand, kisses it, and hands her a favorite blanket from her bag. She strokes her back as they finish their shopping.

Sometimes, such touching of private parts may simply be absent-minded, or be part of seeking comfort. For children, touching their favorite blanket, or stroking a parent's hair or clothing, is a warm and sensual feeling. If needed, you can redirect your child's healthy need for touch and sensuality as in the story above.

> Andrea came upon her four-year-old son with a five-year-old neighbor boy in the bathroom "playing doctor" and inspecting each other's private parts. Spotting her, the boys looked sheepish.
> Andrea said, "It's natural to be curious. But it's time to put your clothes back on."

As with their parents' bodies, it's also very common for children to be curious about one another's parts. Play may involve looking at and touching others' genitals, or games to see who can "pee" the farthest. If you come upon a scene like the one above, try not to make a fuss or look upset about such play. If you do, children are likely to assume that their behavior is indeed serious—without understanding why. Also, let the other child's parent know what went on and how you responded.

The only time this sort of play might be a cause for concern is if there's a clear difference in age or size—which means there's a chance the bigger child could be exploiting or threatening the smaller one (e.g., "I'll hurt you if you tell your mom.").

PRIVACY, MODESTY, AND OPENNESS

> While using the restaurant bathroom, three-and-a-half-year-old Erica insists on leaving the door to her toilet stall open, even though others can see her sitting there. Later, when leaving the restaurant, Erica's mom tries to lift her daughter's dress slightly to help put on her boots, but the little girl protests "because everyone would see my knees."

A second way in which the sexual behavior of young children differs from that of adults is that children are much less self-conscious and insistent on privacy. As Erica's story shows, children are inconsistent (from an adult point of view) in how they show their privacy needs.

For example, children enjoy being naked. One mother, echoing the sentiments of many parents, described how her three-year-old daughter "enjoys running out of the bathroom naked after a bath or after using the potty. I think she feels free."

Most young children are aware that running around naked is taboo at least in certain situations, but they aren't really clear on the reasons behind this rule. They know enough to delight in flirting with the taboo, but not enough to experience adultlike shame. Parents can state their rules, according to what feels comfortable to them and to those involved in the situation, in the same way they would convey any other rule. For example, "When we are visiting, clothes need to stay on your body. At home, you may run around naked for a few minutes after your bath."

> Three-year-old Jennifer and three-and-a-half-year-old Sarah nap next to each other each day at nursery school. Midway through the year, Sarah begins to put her hand down her pants, rubbing vigorously, and making loud panting and moaning noises. At first, the teacher decides to ignore it and see if Sarah will eventually stop this naptime behavior. Instead,

Jennifer, on the next mat, begins to copy Sarah, putting her hand down her pants and stimulating herself, albeit with less vigor.

After a few days of observing this joint "masturbation," the teacher decides to separate the two girls "so they can get some rest." Once napping at a new location across the room from Sarah, Jennifer stops these behaviors. Sarah, however, continues panting and arousing herself on a daily basis.

Parents and teachers also note children's lack of modesty regarding more obvious self-exploring behaviors. One father noted that his three-year-old son rubs himself in the bathtub, when having his diapers changed, and at other "times of opportunity." Parents describe three-year-olds who are unabashed about their self-pleasuring, sometimes calling attention to themselves via such comments as, "Look, Mommy, [my penis] is getting bigger," and "We are the vagina girls."

These comments and behaviors do not always occur in the bathroom or bedroom. For instance, one parent reported that her four-year-old daughter sucked her finger and touched her vagina while she was watching television in the family room. As children get older, they're more likely to be private about self-stimulation. For older children, the behaviors seem more likely to occur while playing in groups in "secretive" places such as bathrooms and small enclosed places. One child-care center designed its bathrooms to accommodate children's increasing self-awareness: the five-year-olds' bathroom, as compared with the three-year-olds', is farther removed from the classroom and protected from easy view.

A small percentage of young children are habitual masturbators: they regularly and energetically manipulate their genitals. Masturbation has a soothing, sedative effect for young children and does not appear to be associated with orgasm. What appears erotic to adults is more likely experienced as simple sensuality or excitement by children.

In the example above with Jennifer and Sarah, in which Sarah continues to rub herself after the girls are separated, the teacher might approach it as an issue of noise disturbing other children. He could tell Sarah that the noise she is making is keeping other children from resting. He could also address it more directly by saying, "Please keep your hand out of your pants. You can rub yourself like that at home. At school you may cuddle with a stuffed animal or blanket." The teacher could then mention the behavior to the parents and tell them what was said.

SEX TALK

> Laurent and his six-year-old son were in a hospital hallway after a routine clinic appointment. As a beautiful nurse walked past them, the boy commented, "She's a major babe!" with all the inflection a teenage boy might use.

When children say, "I hate you," we are prone to read complex adult meanings into that simple statement of anger. The misunderstanding arises because we view the child's behavior through our adult lens. Similarly, when children use sexual language, we tend to assume they know more than they do.

Laurent could ask his son, "What does that mean?" The boy may or may not know what the phrase means, but probably has some sense that it means a woman is attractive. His dad might then add, "Yes, she is a pretty woman. She's a nurse who works with very sick people; that is such an important job." That way, he can shift attention away from the term "major babe" and toward a view of the nurse as a person.

Parents and teachers often hear children experimenting with language related to bodies, particularly the "private parts" and the functions of elimination and sexuality. Poo-poo, pee-pee, wee-wee, fart, penis, vagina, butt, and teat and creative combinations such as butt-face and penis-breath often elicit squeals of delight and hilarity among children. This is eminently normal behavior, deriving in part from children's attraction to the forbidden. Because the body's private parts are imbued with special meaning and are generally inaccessible for exploration, children are all the more fascinated with them.

TALKING TO CHILDREN ABOUT SEXUALITY

Keep it simple. Detailed facts are harder for a child to grasp than a few well-chosen words. Match the information you give to your child's level of development. Remember the well-worn joke about the child who asks, "Where did I come from?" After her parent stumbles through an awkward explanation of pregnancy and the birth process, the confused child says, "Oh, I thought I came from Pittsburgh."

Another example comes from a mother working for Planned Parenthood who frequently talked about condoms while preparing lectures about safe sex. One day her four-year-old daughter asked, "Mommy, what's a condom?" This mother wondered how far she should go in explaining intercourse, and, indeed, where she should begin. But she remembered to keep it simple. She showed her daughter a condom, and the daughter said "oh," and walked away. The child had gotten the answer she wanted and was satisfied with that level of knowledge.

Listen carefully to your child. The less you say, the more energy you can devote to listening to and observing your child—which is how you can be most helpful. Look carefully at the actions of children before reacting. For instance, a preschooler who says, "Suck my dick," has not necessarily been sexually abused; more likely, the child has a teenage sibling. Children's use of sexual words can make it seem they know more than they do. Language play is normal and common, and awareness of that type of play makes setting limits and reacting positively that much easier.

Give your child basic facts before discussing feelings. Children need to know what's going on before they can figure out how they feel about it. Adults often make the mistake of probing feelings, which are hard for young children to understand and express, without giving a simple explanation or correcting a child's misconception.

When the child asked her mother, "What's a condom?" the child didn't need a dissertation about the social and psychological significance of birth control; she just wanted basic information about a physical object. Sometimes parents worry that giving too many facts will take away a child's innocence. Remember, children don't have an adult's ability to understand or reason, and that won't change no matter how much they're told.

Talk over your own feelings first, with another adult. Sex-related issues can be uncomfortable to talk about. The clearer you are about your own feelings (e.g., embarrassment, anxiety, anger) and what's behind them, the better you're able to separate your feelings from your child's. This makes it easier for you to respond calmly to your child and help him understand his own actions and thoughts.

Use "teachable moments." When a child reacts to or comments on nudity, a door closed for privacy, a racy joke, a TV or movie scene, or a pregnant woman, this is a natural time for a parent to comfortably talk about sexuality with her child. Here's an example:

> Five-year-old Sam comes to his parents' bedroom early on a Saturday morning, only to find the normally open door closed tight. He opens the door and his parents pull the covers over themselves. His father gets out of bed, puts on a robe, and takes Sam to the kitchen. Sam asks, "Why was your door closed?"
>
> His father responds, "Mommy and I wanted some privacy, so we closed the door."
>
> "Why?" asks Sam.
>
> "Sometimes we like to be alone. Next time you come to the door and it's closed, please knock and we will let you in."
>
> "Okay. Why were you naked?" asks Sam.
>
> "Married grown-ups sometimes like to cuddle when they are naked," replies his father.
>
> "Yuck! I'll never do that!" exclaims Sam.
>
> "You can decide when you are a grown-up man," answers his father.

It's much easier to use a natural opportunity like this than to awkwardly bring up the "birds and bees" out of the blue. When children's interest is already engaged, they're more likely to share and explore their own ideas.

WARNING SIGNS OF PROBLEMS

We've said a lot about when not to worry—but there are times when children's behavior can be abnormal and require attention. Otherwise normal behaviors, such as masturbation or use of sexual language, are a problem if they happen very often, persist despite efforts to redirect the child's behavior, and become a preoccupation for the child. Sex play between two or more children is a problem if force is involved or if there is several years' age difference between the children or a notable difference in size. Using an object to penetrate any body cavity is abnormal and problematic. In addition to these behavioral signs of disturbance, look at the child's emotions: healthy sex play is typically happy and spontaneous, whereas maladaptive sexuality usually involves secretiveness, anger, and tension. Talk to your pediatrician if you notice behaviors like these, or have any other concern related to your child's sexuality.

WHERE TO SET LIMITS

There are good reasons why certain behaviors are taboo; in any society or family, there are important barriers that must be recognized and respected. How sexuality is handled within the family is one of many factors that affect a child's sense of identity within the family, and how children grow and develop within, and eventually away from, the family.

While parents should set firm limits around problematic behaviors, such as those described above, the limits are fuzzier for other sexual behaviors: a child repeatedly caressing and kissing a teacher's face; a child saying to another, "Suck my dick"; a seven-year-old boy getting on top of a four-year-old girl who is lying on her back and making all the moves suggestive of intercourse (both children are fully clothed); a child taking a bath and asking his parent, "Would you pour water on my penis? It feels good."

In responding to these and other "iffy" sexual behaviors, we believe it's best to err on the side of limits. Children's positive attitudes about, and future enjoyment of, sexuality are not likely to be endangered if restraints are placed on their behaviors. For example, it is helpful for a parent to say to a child: "That's not an appropriate way to play." As long as parents sensitively and thoughtfully redirect the child's activities ("If we pour water on your boat, will it sink?") and adopt a respectful, matter-of-fact, and lighthearted attitude, there is little downside to imposing limits in these cases. In fact, the parent is steering the child away from activities that can be problematic in certain situations and from practicing behaviors that, over time, might get the child into trouble.

Children's sexuality needs a balanced approach. Focusing on open communication alone fails to fully respect the potential physical, emotional, and social dangers we associate with sexuality. And arguing for boundaries without a free flow of information denies the parental guidance a child needs so he or she can develop positive attitudes about adult sexuality based on both facts and values.

Some Final Words

Most parents have two seemingly conflicting agendas for their children: to foster feelings of comfort about physical closeness and sexual matters, *and* to teach appropriate limits about physical contact while preserving children's innocence about sexuality. The dilemma is that too much comfort may stretch boundaries and jeopardize innocence, and too many limits may raise anxiety about closeness and sexuality, and stifle discussion of sexual topics, at least in the parent's presence. Keeping the focus on the developmental differences between children and adults helps resolve this dilemma. *Young children need closeness in order to establish connections with their parents, and young children are innocent in that their sexuality is dominated by curiosity, playfulness, openness, spontaneity, sensuality, and excitement.* Making children comfortable about closeness and sexuality is fully compatible with setting limits regarding physical contact and sexual behaviors.

We live in an overly sexualized society. It's tempting for parents to counterbalance that by denying their children's sexuality. But if we don't guide and give facts to our children they will get it somewhere else—and what they're likely to get is myth and misinformation, without the context of ethics and values that parents want to provide. It's a sad comment on our society, perhaps, but parents who want to provide guidance about sexuality need to start early and beat others—peers, movies, other media—to the punch.

Suggestions for Further Reading

Adults

Sol and Judith Gordon. *Raising a Child Responsibly in a Sexually Permissive World.* Adams Media, 1999.

Debra Haffner and Alyssa Haffner Tartaglione. *From Diapers to Dating: A Parent's Guide to Raising Sexually Healthy Children.* Newmarket Press, 2000.

Lynn Leight. *Raising Sexually Healthy Children.* Avon, 1990.

Children's Books

Robert Brooks. *So That's How I Was Born!* Aladdin, 1993.

Sol and Judith Gordon. *Did the Sun Shine Before You Were Born? A Sex Education Primer.* Prometheus Books, 1992.

Peter Mayle. *Where Did I Come From?* Lyle Stuart, 2000.

Margaret Sheffield. *Where Do Babies Come From?* Knopf, 1987.

CHAPTER FIVE

The Importance of Friendship

Betty Nolden Allen and Deborah LeeKeenan

Robyn had been looking forward to the playdate between her four-year-old daughter, Cara, and her friend Ivy. Having the girls play together would give Robyn a much-needed break during a long and stressful day. But two minutes after she'd left them in the next room happily playing with their dolls, she heard a screech. She rushed in to find her daughter holding two dolls and both girls in tears. Why was friendship so hard for them?

You'd think that making friends would be an easy, natural process: just put them together and let them play. But the skills children need to make friends and maintain friendships seldom come naturally. When Cara and Ivy each wanted the same hat for their dolls, they weren't able to trade or take turns without adult help. In other words, friendships are made, not born.

Toddlers often play alongside their friends, doing things in parallel without much need for tuning in to one another for meaningful interaction. As children mature, friendship requires that each child share and respond to the other's fantasizing: a huge development indeed. This often leads to conflict about the way play should go—and important lessons about sharing control and fair ways to resolve conflict.

The nature of friendship changes significantly during the toddler and preschool years. It sometimes helps if you think of friendship as a laboratory in which children try out new types of social relationships and experiment with their newfound power. You can see this in the phrases they use: "If you give me one of your cookies, I'll be your best friend!" "You won't be invited to my birthday party!"

Children do remember their kindergarten friendships, and some turn into lasting relationships. The old Girl Scout song "Make new friends but keep the old, one is silver and the other gold" speaks of the lasting nature of friends. Most of us recall sharing secrets, special games, or food with a best friend, and difficult times when we fought with a friend or lost one forever. While friendships may seem less significant and more temporary for preschoolers, research suggests that getting along well with peers at this age is linked to doing well in later life—a good reason to help your child with friendship skills now.

Being popular is not the same as having a close friend. Not every child should become a social butterfly. Our goal is to illuminate the process of making and keeping friends so that your child can make choices about how she wants to relate to others. This chapter will help you see how and why children form friendships, and how to help your child develop the social, play, and negotiation skills she needs to make friends. We'll also help you decide when and how to intervene in friendship problems.

We'll cover some of the most often-asked questions about young children's friendships:

- What "my friend" means to preschool children, and how early friendships grow

- How children choose a playmate, including why boys and girls often don't play together

- Helping your child make friends

- How to plan and manage playdates

- Understanding conflict and negotiation in friendships:
  - how to handle fights
  - helping bossy or shy children
  - helping a child with "no friends" or too many.

How Early Friendships Grow and Change

For most preschool children, the bond they share with their parents is their first experience with love and friendship. Peer relationships represent a step into a new social world.

FIRST PLAYMATES (AGES TWO TO THREE)

> TEACHER: What is a friend?
>
> JASON: I don't know.
>
> TEACHER: Do you have any friends in this classroom?
>
> JASON: All.
>
> TEACHER: Everyone is your friend?
>
> JASON: Yeah, everyone is my friend.

At ages two and three, a friend can be someone who's playing alongside you whose name you may not know. To a child at this stage, a friend is "someone I play with." Friendship is more often a matter of convenience than selection: children who live near each other or whose parents often socialize will become "friends."

Friendly relationships among two- and three-year-olds involve basic give-and-take: chasing each other up and down the yard, all the while smiling and laughing to show that it's just play. It's important that the chaser sometimes becomes the chased because then you know the children are taking roles that fit together. The roles are simple and concrete (run toward while chasing, or run away while being chased) and don't call for much imagination.

> TOMMY: Malik is my friend.
> TEACHER: Why?
> TOMMY: Because he likes blocks.

Three-year-olds Tommy and Malik are in the block area, each building a road for cars. They focus intently on their constructions, unaware of each other's work—though they are next to each other and doing similar things. This is called "parallel play."

An adult could help them connect their play by commenting, for example, "I see Malik has a red car on the ramp. And Tommy, you have a blue car under the bridge." Or, "Let's build a block city together, with lots of roads."

Another way to create interaction between young children is to give them a large piece of paper, allowing each to start his drawing on a different part. But don't expect two-year-olds or many three-year-olds to negotiate or share: they often grab what they want, or give in quickly.

Toddlers behave differently with familiar playmates, who can be considered first friends. For example, when a child says, "Me-and-Tim want ice cream," running together his name and his friend's, it shows he views the two of them as a set.

You can also see the evolution of friendship in how children choose what to do at the start of the preschool day. Does Jorge go to the building toy section to work on a tower, or because he wants to be next to Mary Lou? Is it the activity, or the closeness to a friend? (You'll see it both ways at ages three and four.) It's good sometimes to follow a friend, and other times to follow an interest.

PRESCHOOL FRIENDS (AGES FOUR TO SIX)

At this stage, children talk a lot about friendship. But the main purpose of friendship talk is getting play started: "Are you my friend?" means "Will you play?" or "May I join you?"

> MARTA: Are you my friend?
> SIERRA: No, I'm Lila's friend.
> MARTA: Will you be my friend later?
> SIERRA: Okay.

When a child says, "You are not my friend," that usually means "I'm angry or I want to be alone" or "I want to play with someone else right now." A "friend" might be someone whom I like and play with today. Friends share food, toys, adventures, and perhaps the same adults (teachers or extended family friends). While preschool children are likely to develop an intimate relationship with one or two close friends, brief short-term friendships are established easily and often.

> At the city playground, Brendan and Dean, who had never met before, were jumping around the wading pool. The two were showing off and clowning for their mothers. Suddenly Brendan's mom noticed he was shivering.
> MOM: You better get out of the pool. You look cold.
> BRENDAN: But I'm playing with my friend.
> MOM: Well then, invite him to play out of the pool.
> BRENDAN (to Dean): Do you like Pokémon?
> As the two boys sat on the side and looked at a coloring book, Brendan asked Dean: "What's your name?"

Like a younger child, a child of four or five may start off playing next to another, watching him play, or perhaps copying what he's doing. But this is now likely to lead to conversation and interactive play, with no adult encouragement needed.

Like most relationships, the friendships of preschool children often go through a "honeymoon" period. During this time, the friends may seem like each other's shadow: whatever one child suggests, the other follows. Imitative play is an effective way to communicate, "I want to be your friend." It's less complicated than shared-fantasy play.

Friends this age often develop their own rituals and routines.

> Caitlin and Ashley have been companions since infancy. Their frequent reunions begin with a happy exchange of nonsense words:
>
> CAITLIN: Let's go play foo-a-foo.
>
> ASHLEY: Let's play foo-a-foo-goo-poo.
>
> At this point the two girls burst out in laughter and run off and play.

In time, most friendships become more challenging; back-and-forth bickering is common. Although parents may find these squabbles hard to take, they're an essential part of developing a solid relationship. They also help children establish their individual likes and dislikes. At the same time, with some adult help, children can learn to appreciate each other's different points of view and learn to cooperate and share.

At ages four and five, children also use the language of friendship to get what they want:

> BRIAN: I'll be your friend if you let me use the purple crayon.
>
> CARMEN: Okay.
>
> BRIAN: I'll be your best friend if I can use the purple crayon and the silver glitter.
>
> CARMEN: No. I want the glitter first.
>
> BRIAN: Then I won't be your friend anymore.
>
> CARMEN: Okay. I don't care. I don't like your picture anyway.
>
> (The two children finish their drawings separately. Fifteen minutes later . . .)
>
> BRIAN: I'm doing dress-ups now. Do you want to play?
>
> CARMEN: Okay.

This can seem manipulative, but it's also a start at negotiation skills. It is not unusual to see children trading apparent insults with each other, then playing independently for a few moments, then drifting back together again.

With older preschoolers, shared ideas come into play. They organize their friendships around negotiating fantasy play (either through dolls or toys, or by taking on roles themselves) where they have to interpret each other's symbol making.

> Taro and Adam, both four, are playing with a firehouse set. Adam has the fire-chief doll driving a toy truck. Taro walks another doll toward it.
>
> TARO: Pretend the chief gives the fireman a ride in the truck.
>
> ADAM: No.
>
> TARO: Pretend the house blew down. (He tips a toy house onto his fireman.)
>
> ADAM: Pretend somebody trapped the man in the house: "Aaagh! Get me out of here!" Now pretend he pushed the magic button.
>
> TARO: Yeah. (He pushes the "magic button," making the doll fly out of the house.)

Here, the two boys learned to build on each other's ideas, instead of arguing or rejecting them. As young children mature, their fantasy play becomes more detailed, the rules of their games more complex, and their "turns" longer. This shows off their growing ability to negotiate and agree, and to take each other's point of view. They are also more skillful at using language to influence behavior.

By age six, friendship becomes qualitatively different. Friends do nice things for each other, from teaching a new game to sharing popcorn—and later, sharing secrets and promises. Children now start to see friendships as lasting over time, and will talk about friends when they're not present. They are also more able to empathize and take someone else's perspective. For example, when six-year-old Lindsey was sick in the hospital, the kids at kindergarten missed her, asked about her, and wanted to draw her pictures or bring flowers—without adult initiation, as younger children would need.

By this age, children who get together only occasionally (such as cousins who live in different cities and see each other at holiday gatherings) can now pick up where they left off. When Lina's eight-year-old niece and her family come to visit, the niece and Lina's six-year-old head straight for each other. Going off behind the sofa or under the table, they create a private imaginary world with their stuffed animals and dolls.

How Do Children Choose Playmates?

> SOPHIE: Olivia is my best friend. We like to do everything together. We both like to play with the wagons and tire swings outside, and we like to do dress-ups and the dollhouses inside. She is the princess and I am the queen. We are best friends.

Our observations suggest that for two- and three-year-olds, gender, color, or size often don't matter in picking playmates. Gender is more of a factor with older children (see page 130). Sometimes a small child gravitates to a bigger one, or a shy child to a popular one. Sometimes an attraction starts with admiring a T-shirt or action figure, or another child's fast running or other desirable skill. As you'd expect, children who are friendly, happy, and physically attractive are more sought after as friends.

Sophie's words are typical of four-year-olds: Olivia is my friend because she likes what I like. Similar interests and styles are especially important, e.g., a child who likes to climb and swing will seek like-minded friends. Children also prefer playmates who will take turns and not always dominate or follow, as well as those who handle and express their emotions appropriately.

Often a child with good verbal skills is attractive. If a child wanders over and says, "What can I do?" the answer may be "Nothing!" But with verbal skills, she can help organize the play: "Let's play house. You can be the mom. You be the baby. I'll be the kitty."

"I want to be the baby!"

"Well, you can be the dog, then."

This last remark shows some social skills as well. (If children get stuck in this kind of situation, an adult can model for them how to generate options: "Can there be two dogs? Maybe a beagle like Snoopy and a poodle with a bow?")

Finally, access and proximity are key factors in young friendships. Some of the most intense and rewarding relationships evolve within the context of an extended-family–friend relationship. In these situations children naturally become friends because they have frequent contact and the parents are usually present. The result is intimacy without tension.

BOYS AND GIRLS, TOGETHER?

> Teacher to four-year-old girl friends: Karen, I've noticed that each day you and Julie sit in the small loft and watch Michael and Jacques build with blocks. Come down and join them.
>
> KAREN: If I play with blocks, they'll think I'm a boy!

Cross-gender friendships are not so common among older preschoolers. (While we see boys in the dress-up corner at age three playing "mom" in lacy hats, that's no longer true at four and a half.) The problem of boys excluding girls, and vice versa, is often seen at preschools and day care centers as well as family gatherings. Children between the ages of two and six are learning what it means to be a boy or girl, including what they "ought" to want, wear, and do. Preschoolers don't yet understand that gender identity doesn't change when those things do. Often they reach for the extremes of masculine and feminine: a jackhammer operator or a Barbie doll.

One three-year-old refused to take the role of doctor in dramatic play, insisting that as a girl, she had to be the nurse. Her own mother, a physician, was completely perplexed by her daughter's behavior. At this age, it was hard for the girl to grasp that Mom can be both a doctor and her mother. Children need adult help to learn about gender stability without embracing stereotypes about what men and women can be and do (which are still easy to find in everything from cartoons to toy ads).

Helene regularly meets with a group of mothers who've helped and supported one another since their kids were born. Lately, when the group gets together, her five-year-old, Melissa, won't play with her old friend Cory. She just says, "Boys, ugh!"

Patience is key in promoting boy-girl friendships. Melissa and Cory will find ways to interact if they have similar interests and their families continue to plan activities together. To promote play, think of activities that appeal to the skills and interests of both boys and girls (drawing, kicking a ball around, playing "grocery store").

Introduce males and females in nontraditional roles both at home and at school, as well as in books and television shows. Families can invent their own stories rather than playing out stories from popular culture that reinforce stereotypes. Once gender identity is more firmly established (by early elementary school) children may be a bit more flexible in their thinking about gender roles. Still, some children will have many more cross-gender friendships than others.

Helping Your Child with Friendships

PREPARING FOR FRIENDSHIP AT HOME

Children's first relationships at home form the foundation for those that follow. The balance of independence and sociability, as well as the comfort with give-and-take that children need to make friends, start with lots of practice at home.

Give your child small choices to make: "Do you want to bring your elephant or your truck to Grandpa's?" "Today, you can wear the green sweater or the lion sweater." This helps her later to see options during play.

Teach your child that relationships are reciprocal. One way to do this is to practice negotiating, trading, and taking turns: for example, with small stuffed animals, collector cards, or toy vehicles. Sit on the floor across from each other, and set up your items. Then open the negotiations.

"I'll trade you two sheep for the cow and the hay bale."

"No, I want the horse."

"Okay, it's a deal."

Scoot your trades to each other across the floor. Keep this up until most of the toys have gone back and forth at least once.

Take time to play with your child. Remember, the basis of young children's friendships is play, not conversation. Children who don't play as much or as easily have trouble making friends. Play side by side with your child, or work together, making castles, forts, and igloos. Draw a zooful of imaginary animals, cut them out, and build them a home. Share make-believe: "Let's pretend Big Bird and Ernie climb the humongous tree. What do they see way up there? What does Ernie do next?" (See chapter 8 for more on the social value of play.)

Give your children opportunities to meet potential playmates. It helps to have an active friendship circle that includes everyone's kids. During group get-togethers, parents can monitor children's play and offer coaching as needed ("Junie, can Nadia dress your kitty if you dress her teddy?"). Studies have shown that parents' supervising and coaching helps children get along better with peers. Respect your child's style and temperament; for example, some children need time to watch and warm up before starting to play.

Finally, find out what toys, games, or television shows are popular in your child's classroom or neighborhood. If they are acceptable to you, encourage your child to play with or watch them now and then (try to watch with your child—more about this in chapter 11). Shared experiences like these help children start talking and sharing in fantasy play.

For some children who are very attractive to others, making friends is easy. It is keeping them that's difficult. For the shy child or one who has special needs, the initial formation of friendships may be the hard part.

ENCOURAGING FRIENDSHIPS AT GROUP CHILD CARE OR PRESCHOOL

Two children in the sandbox are building castles.

MARYLOU: My sand castle is bigger than yours.

JULIA: But mine is prettier and has more windows.

MARYLOU: I wish I knew how to make those windows.

TEACHER: Maybe Julia can show you how. Would you be willing to do that, Julia?

JULIA: I guess so.

Children's friendships often take root in home neighborhoods. But increasingly—especially for families who must move often—the child care center and the preschool are sources of potential friends. Teachers and child care providers become key figures in the lives of families and children, making a cooperative effort between home and school even more vital. These relationships are not frills; they are essential connections for children and their families.

In many ways, entering a play group or a classroom is like joining another culture. New rules, skills, and routines have to be learned. Children must figure out what behaviors are approved and rewarded, and how best to get their needs met. Temperament, family circumstances, special needs, and cultural background can all influence the ease with which children make these adjustments.

Increasingly, preschools and child care centers are aware of their role in the facilitation of friendships for children, and work to create a sense of community in the classrooms from the earliest years. If parents and teachers emphasize that the neighborhood, child care center, and the preschool are places where children learn how to be social beings, places where children can make mistakes, the work of making friends will be enhanced. Often parents will ask the teacher, "Does Susan like to play with anyone in particular?" or "Which children should I invite to John's birthday party if I can't invite the whole class?"

Encourage your child to invite children home to play, if possible. Or, pack a snack and invite a friend to play in the park. You can also bring young playmates to the local library for story hour. Sometimes a playdate outside of the group is all that is needed to solidify a budding friendship.

Playdates

It's pickup time at preschool. Lucas says to his mom, "I want to go to Richard's house to play! Can I go, Mom?"

"Please please please?" adds Richard.

"We can plan a playdate for next week," says Lucas's mom. "I'll talk to Richard's dad."

Lucas says, "Yeah, that will be real cool . . . I'll bring my subs and we'll play ocean monsters."

PLAYDATE PREP

Parents sometimes see playdates as a break for themselves, hoping the children will keep busy with each other. As we saw with Cara and Ivy at the start of this chapter, this only works to a point. Be prepared to spend time with the children yourself, as they will often have a hard time sharing their space and their things.

Before the playdate, adults need to communicate with each other about:

- Goals for the playdate, or what you hope will happen: "Celie wants to show Geeta her new toy pet shop." "Maybe you can get the kids outside if the weather's okay."

- Expectations and limits: "We're trying to keep Tony away from commercial TV until he's older." "I'll pick him up at five. If he's feeling overwhelmed or wants to come home sooner, I could make it earlier."

- Participation by the adults: "I'll be paying bills in the next room while they work with LEGOs, but I'll keep an ear out for problems." "I'm going to make cookies, and I'll have the kids decorate with me."

- Special concerns or issues unique to the child: "Celie is allergic to nuts, so please keep her away from peanut butter." "If Geeta gets upset, I find it helps to move her a few feet away and distract her with a picture book."

- Special likes and/or dislikes: "Tony loves pasta, but won't eat anything green."

One rule of thumb is that the younger the child, the shorter the visits should be. For instance, invite one friend along for a short period of time (not more than two hours) for a three year old. Parents have to be firm, because children will want to get together more frequently and for longer periods than they can manage gracefully.

At home, head off problems by putting away things that are dear to your child and therefore emotionally difficult to share. Be prepared to stay with them as they play, especially at first. A visiting three-year-old may need an adult by her side until she knows the house and family well.

Most four-year-olds will be a bit more independent, but visits still need to be limited in time—for instance, not a whole afternoon after a morning at preschool. Pay attention to the play. If children are increasingly difficult to manage, it may be that they are too tired to visit for the full scheduled time. Some four-year-olds have many friends and can manage to play with two or three children at the same time; others can barely manage an hour or two with one friend. Most often, groups of three do not work because someone feels left out.

Group playdates in general are hard for preschoolers. That's why at the end of a birthday party, it's not uncommon to see overwhelmed kids crying or even vomiting. With a group, adults need to play a bigger role structuring and orchestrating activities. The rule of thumb for birthday parties: the number of guests should equal (or be less than) the child's age (e.g., three guests for a three-year-old's party). If your child wants to include more children, you might bring cupcakes to school, and have several kids over to your house another time. You might also try a shorter party at a more structured age-appropriate activity, such as a puppet show or indoor play space.

SETTING LIMITS

> Constance always wanted her kindergarten classmate Elizabeth to play at her house. After each visit, Constance's mother, Ellen, would call with an explanation of something Elizabeth had done wrong. It usually had something to do with a typical child-child conflict such as who got what toy. Yvette, Elizabeth's mom, became exhausted by this reporting, and also felt that the visiting should be more reciprocal.
>
> When Yvette suggested to Ellen that their girls take a break from each other, Ellen became furious. She and Constance began avoiding Elizabeth and inviting Elizabeth's good friend whose family lived in the same building to ride to school with them, leaving Elizabeth to walk alone.

Several things stand out in the case of Constance and Elizabeth. The children were tired and cranky by the end of the day and needed more reasonable visiting times (e.g., a couple of hours, a couple of times per week). They were also likely overexposed to each other. A broader circle of friends lets a child experience a variety of personalities and cuts down on the power struggles often seen with an intense pair. Finally, more back-and-forth visiting was needed so that both girls could learn to share their space and their things. Constance, on her home ground, always had more control.

Another factor here: the two mothers had very different needs. Yvette had an infant at her house, and wanted to minimize visits to keep a more balanced household. Constance was an only child, and her family life revolved around her socializing—so Ellen always encouraged Elizabeth's visits. Since the girls clamored to see each other almost daily, Yvette didn't want to play the heavy and always say no. Yvette also began to resent the phone calls, feeling that her child was being painted as lacking something all the time.

Sometimes a story like this ends with bitterness and avoidance. Sometimes, if parents are willing to reach out, it can still work.

> After the playdate, Ellen phoned Yvette as usual, saying, "The girls had a good time with that toy grocery store today . . . but Elizabeth did have a little problem with sharing."
>
> YVETTE: Yes, all kids have trouble sharing at times. You know, you've mentioned problems a few times lately. Maybe the kids need some breathing room so they'll have more fun when they're together. I'm afraid they're overtired.
>
> ELLEN: Oh, but Constance misses Elizabeth. She asks to play with her all the time.
>
> YVETTE: How about we make sure they have time together by agreeing on a schedule? Maybe Tuesdays and Thursdays after school?
>
> ELLEN: I guess that would work for us.
>
> YVETTE: That way, if the girls ask to play together, we can just remind them that their next visit is coming soon. And you know I need quiet sometimes for the baby, but I do enjoy visiting with Constance. I can watch the girls over here, say every other Tuesday. . . .

While there is no magical solution to such problems, Yvette has things moving in the right direction. She tried to focus on the positive—not just say what went wrong—and enlist Ellen to problem-solve with her. This was also a nice way to model negotiation for their kids.

DIFFERENT VIEWS AND CUSTOMS

> Sally keeps asking her mom to invite Ruhiya over to play, but Ruhiya's parents don't seem interested, and have politely declined twice. Sally's mom worries that she has offended them somehow, or that Ruhiya doesn't want Sally as a friend.

Ruhiya does like Sally. But just as children have different understandings of friendship at different ages, different cultures have different
views and expectations of friendship. Cultures, such as some Latin and
Middle Eastern groups, that do not encourage independent socializing
for children outside the family circle before age five can sometimes create
difficulties for children in this country.

In some cultures, friends are part of the extended family: close friends
are like uncles, aunts, and cousins. If the child does not visit alone, try
asking the child and parent over for an after-school snack. Or, perhaps
inviting the whole family to dinner could break the ice.

When children of different backgrounds become friends, cultural
differences in values and expectations may also influence interactions and
play. For example, in some families, individuality—the expression of
self—is highly prized. Children are encouraged to "be who they are" and
stand out from the crowd. In other families, however, interdependence is
the primary value. Contributing to the functioning of the family as a
whole is more important than expressing one's individuality.

One example is a group of children arguing where to sit at meeting
time in the preschool classroom. Three children are trying to fit into two
spots. Finally, Srivats, a child from India, says, "You can sit here. I'll give
you my spot." He is used to thinking of the whole group's needs.

Different styles of communication may lead to misunderstandings
when families of different cultures get together and attempt to develop
friendships. Cultures differ in the amount of information that is explic-
itly transmitted through words versus the amount of information that is
transmitted through the context of the situation, the relationship, and
the physical cues. (For example, see chapter 4 on differences in physical
closeness.)

One factor that complicated the mothers' communication in the
story of Elizabeth and Constance is that Elizabeth was the only African-
American girl in her kindergarten class. Yvette was alert to her daughter's potential self-esteem and racial identity needs as the only child of
color in her class and in her neighborhood. Another factor was their dif-

ferent parenting styles: Ellen's style was more permissive and casual, while Yvette focused on clear rules and more planning—a result of her having a baby at home, as well as of her family-culture belief that that adults should more closely supervise the decisions of five-year-olds.

While people of any age can make friends across cultures, it comes more easily to children, who are more flexible and adaptable. Like language, a culture's rules and preferences are acquired very early in life, and are typically established by age five. Every interaction, sound, touch, odor, and experience has a cultural component that is absorbed even when not openly taught. Lessons learned at such an early age become an integral part of thinking and behavior. But in most instances, when children of varying ethnic groups play together, they find constructive ways to adapt to new rules, to new languages, and to negotiate resolutions. They may ignore behavior they do not understand, or confront the other child about the behavior. Parents and other adults can foster cross-cultural friendships by being open and accepting about differences. The main point is to be aware that differences will exist and not to make assumptions about others—and not to be embarrassed when kids notice the differences and make comments. (Raul: "Teacher, my skin is darker than his." Teacher: "Yes, it is darker. What about Joseph's skin? Is his lighter or darker than yours?")

Nedra's five-year-old son, Ariel, has made friends at school with Jacob, a boy who has cerebral palsy. While Ariel has asked for a playdate, Nedra is nervous that something will go wrong and she won't know what to do—especially since Jacob has trouble getting his words out.

There are many kinds of special needs. Some require parents to have specific kinds of knowledge, and others do not. If you are unsure, it makes sense to consult with the parents of the child and/or the child's teacher before the visit. (It's generally good for parents to talk before *any* young child comes to your home.) Usually, planning such visits requires a bit more thoughtfulness about the physical environment, or the ways in which the child communicates. The parent or caregiver may want to accompany the child on his first playdate, or until everyone feels comfortable. Just being open and honest about concerns is the first step.

Many children with special needs are left out of the usual social circles of birthday parties and playdates. Socializing is harder for some because of delays in language, cooperative play, or other skills. For instance, "What did you have for breakfast?" was Sean's standard conversation opener in his afternoon group of four-year-olds. (Sean was a child with developmental delays.) At that time of the day, children likely could not remember what they had for breakfast. In any event, it was not a topic that got them talking.

> "If you look directly into my eyes, it means you want to fight," Fred would say to his fellow five-year-olds. Fred, a gifted student who also had special needs, was totally consumed by the behavior of wolves. The subject was not so engrossing to his classmates, and they didn't know how to respond to such a comment.

The interests of gifted children are often more rarefied and sophisticated. If they are not in tune with the toys, TV shows, or other preoccupations of their age mates, this makes it harder for gifted children to connect. Children like Sean and Fred need more adult support when playing with peers. For example, parents can help children get started by finding some common ground: "Fred, in what ways are wolves like dogs? Billy, you have a dog at home. Does he look like a wolf to you? Tell us about your dog."

As with special physical needs, it's okay to talk to a child's parents before a playdate about any special emotional or behavioral needs. You already know, for example, what kinds of play your child handles most comfortably, and warning signs that she needs a break or needs redirecting. At the Eliot-Pearson Children's School, parents asked teachers to hold a meeting on encouraging and supporting friendships with special-needs kids. This allowed everyone to ask questions openly, air concerns, and share stories of what works.

Conflict and Negotiation in Friendships

> Francesca and Maya, both two and a half, spent the last hour of their playdate drawing pictures and happily running around. As Maya's uncle herds the girls onto the porch for good-byes, Maya sits down on her shiny tricycle—and Francesca tries to clamber on behind. Francesca's dad pulls up in his truck just as the screaming and hair pulling begins.

Alas, these behaviors are not terribly unusual for two-year-olds. If Francesca were five, we'd have cause for concern. Such behavior is one of the reasons that two-year-olds need to have short visits that allow them to work alongside each other (say in the sandbox or on the swings) with a lot of adult supervision. Francesca's dad and Maya's uncle knew this, and separated the children without laying blame: "I see everyone is tired, it's time to say good-bye now." They also checked to make sure there was no broken skin or other safety issues.

One of the lessons of friendship is how to disagree and work out conflicts in noncoercive ways. With very young children (twos and many threes), don't even try to strike a balance. Faced with conflict, they respond with grabs and shoves, or immediately give in to avoid a fight.

Young children who have not yet developed good language skills—either because of age or developmental delay—and children who've had limited opportunities to socialize are especially prone to disagreements. Youngsters' fights tend to be brief and not very serious. Most of the hitting and kicking among two-to-four-year olds is about objects, although sometimes it's about hurt feelings for the threes and fours: "Will you be my friend?" "No!" Or, "Now you can't come over and see my puppy!" Or, "Your lunch looks gross!"

Guidance, modeling, and support from adults are the most useful responses during these times, so children can learn how to behave. For instance, when you help three-year-olds solve a problem about who had the truck first, use words that you want them to use, and show them either that there is another similar truck nearby (as there often is) or that they can take turns.

> John's mother hears him wailing, "Mine!"
>
> MOM: What's wrong, John?
>
> JOHN: Dennis took my truck. I had it first.
>
> DENNIS: No, mine. I had it first! (Now he is crying as well.)
>
> MOM: Dennis, let's help John fill the dump truck. We will fill it three times, and then it will be your turn to drive the dump truck.

As they gain more skill with language, older preschoolers learn to use it to solve problems in play: they can refer to rules, or give reasons to support their plans. At first, negotiation may mean just exchanging agendas rather than working to coordinate them: "You're making a skyscraper, right?" "No, I'm making a barn." "Well, I'm making a bridge."

> Stefan, five, is playing at Nina's house. Both are constructing airplanes from a shared pool of parts. As Stefan reaches over to grab a wheel, Nina says, "Hey, I was gonna use that!"
>
> "My plane can't take off without wheels!"
>
> "Wait, I think I have more wheels. Let's check the blue bin."

Several things helped keep this playdate from going off track. First, Nina was able to use words (instead of grabs and shoves) to solve the problem. Second, her play space is well organized, with labeled bins on shelves. Third, she's old enough to remember and apply that knowledge: "Let's check the blue bin." If Nina and Stefan were three, they would have needed intervention: an adult to set out piles of each kind of part or to fetch more wheels. Otherwise, they would just fight and cry, not thinking to look for wheels on their own.

Ever hear of "Grandma's Rule" about children's fights? Basically it says stay out of them—or at least keep some distance. This refers to letting children (at least age five or six) try to settle their own conflicts first. You can coach, observe, and ask questions: "What pieces does Katie need to finish her phone booth? Could you make the walls mixed yellow and red so she could have some yellow bricks, too?"

If that doesn't work, try redirecting their attention: "There's your garage—I can get washcloths, and you could play car wash," or "Let's take a juice break and watch your firefighter video."

We also see another meaning in Grandma's Rule: in order to guide your children well, you need to keep some *emotional* distance. Helping kids to learn to distinguish between tragedy and an ordinary occurrence (e.g., a minor disagreement) is a big part of our job during the preschool years. In the land of two-, three-, and four-year-olds, small problems can feel like calamities. But if the adults are as emotionally involved and/or upset as the children, they can't be good role models and the children can't learn from them. Confidence and calm allow us to provide alternatives and the means to problem solve.

All of us have trigger points and "hot buttons" about social behavior. For instance, comments such as "I won't be your friend if you don't . . ." can send us back to emotional childhood quicker than we'd like to admit. Remembering that children live very much in the moment, and that the very same two who are carrying on now will be hugging within the hour, can help us keep perspective.

UNEQUAL FRIENDSHIPS: HELPING THE BOSSY OR WITHDRAWN CHILD

Marvin, age four and a half, is the only child among many adults at home, and has trouble understanding the needs of other children. He always wants to be the star of the show and control every move: "Let's play knights. I'll be the king, and tell you who to fight." Needless to say, Marvin has lots of conflicts with playmates.

Bossy children like Marvin want to keep control and get other kids to follow their lead. Because they aggressively seek out others, such children often find temporary playmates—but can't keep them long enough to become friends. When Marvin kept insisting on being "director," the "actors" sooner or later would object, and abandon the scene.

There are several ways you can help a bossy child make friends. First, give your child feedback to help him see consequences of his domineering behavior. "When you *always* want to be the boss, other kids don't want to play anymore." "Morgan wanted to play firefighters; how do you think she felt when you said that was stupid?"

Coach him on other options: "Maybe you could have added to her idea, and been the hook-and-ladder driver . . ." You can also work with puppets to model the kinds of behavior you want, or read him stories of kids who learn to share control with playmates. Have the family practice taking turns as they play with your child: "Now the bears play tag." "But the bears want to eat their cake." "The bears can have cake after they play."

Build on his skills. Reframe and channel his need to control, and think of it as leadership potential. The trick is to find appropriate ways for him to be the star of the show. This worked for Will, an often overbearing child in our preschool. The teacher gave him the role of master of ceremonies for all the "shows" the children created. Will did a wonderful job.

His teachers found other ways to help Will control his impulse to dominate. He was very fond of Gumby, so his teachers gave him a small Gumby figure to work with. By explaining the rules to Gumby, Will reinforced them for himself : "Remember, Gumby, always raise your hand before talking!"

Will also felt a strong need to express his ideas during group time—to the point where others could hardly get a word in. To balance this, he was given three turns to talk at group time each day. Each time he spoke, the teacher would signal how many turns he had left (two fingers, one finger) and then enforce the rule: "You've used your turns, Will; save that thought for later."

Jayne brought four-year-old Derek to their neighbor's birthday party. When she tried to leave after exchanging hellos with his parents, Derek clung to her sweater, not wanting her to go. Embarrassed, Jayne stood in the hall while Derek silently watched the other children giggle and toss balloons.

Children may behave this way for many different reasons. Here, Derek longed to join the play but felt too shy do so without the supportive assistance of an adult. If your child has a temperament like Derek's, you may need to stay for a while at a few birthday parties, perhaps making an agreement about how long he needs you there. Don't force the issue or demand that he participate right away.

Sometimes children don't seem to know how to join in with their peers. If you watch a preschool classroom over time, you'll notice a few children who tend to wander around the room, watching what others are doing but not joining in. They don't suggest ideas for play, or try to change or control what others are doing, but just wait around to be led. By watching and wandering instead of playing, these children make themselves unavailable for give-and-take play. Most children want an equal as a playmate, not someone who waits to be told what to do.

A parent or teacher can help such a child not by leading him, but by starting to play next to him, and gradually getting him to make suggestions and pitch in: "How can I keep this tower of blocks from falling down? Do you think we should build two smaller towers instead?"

Once an interaction is going, you can allow another child or two to join in; then, you can slowly pull out and move on. Doing this multiple times gives the child the skills and confidence to take part in play.

Shy children often find it easier to interact with one child at a time, both at home and in other environments. It's important to set small goals for such a child so both of you can see progress and won't feel discouraged. For instance, six-year-old Kris-Ann was afraid to speak at group gatherings. After a private chat with her kindergarten teacher, they agreed that the teacher would ask Kris-Ann a specific question each day, and she would answer it.

Later in the year, Kris-Ann made friends with one of the strongest girls in the class. The teacher soon became concerned because of the child's willingness to go along with anything her friend proposed. So, the next goal became to help her to be a decision maker within her friendship. The teacher coached and modeled in real situations (e.g., "Kris-

Ann, is that what you want to do?" and "Kris-Ann, do you have another idea?"). Over time, the friendship became more balanced.

Kris-Ann will likely always have a few rather than many friends, and that is all right. There is no magic number of friends that one needs to have at a certain age in order to be socially competent. If your child is happy with one or two friends and they are happy with her, that's fine.

Sometimes children may be withdrawn or lonely because of family matters that they cannot set aside. Mary was such a child. At age five, she was diagnosed with juvenile diabetes. Her family came to school to tell others about the illness, and they demonstrated how she administered insulin. A few months later, Mary's parents separated, and her behavior changed markedly. She lost interest in school and would suddenly say in the middle of the day, "I need to talk to my mother." She also spent a great deal of time drawing human figures with their insides visible, a sign of her emotional distress.

After thinking and talking together, Mary's teachers and parents felt that it was time to seek professional help (in this case, a psychologist). Sometimes when children appear withdrawn it's due to temporary family stress (a recent move or a new baby), but it can also be more serious. If this kind of worrisome behavior persists for more than a few weeks, talk it over with your pediatrician or a mental health professional.

NO FRIENDS, OR TOO MANY

As usual after preschool, Kirsten sat in her aunt's kitchen having a snack. Looking glum, Kirsten chewed on her bagel as her aunt asked, "What did you do at preschool today?"

"Nothing."

"Who did you play with?"

"No one. I don't have any friends. Nobody likes me."

"What about Fred and Ella? I've seen you play with them."

"They just like to play with each other."

"How does that make you feel?"

"Angry . . . and I guess sad."

No parent wants to hear "Nobody likes me." Yet almost all children feel this way at some point. It's hard not to empathize with those feelings of rejection (in fact, it may hurt you more than your child). When it does happen to your child, listen carefully, make sure she knows you understand her feelings, and offer reassurance. Find out more: "Did someone say or do something that upset you today? What did Fred say?"

Don't forget to do a reality check. In the story above, it may be that Kirsten is getting along well with her classmates—but a minor snub by Fred or Ella at day's end stuck in her mind, overshadowing any fun she had. That's why it's helpful to talk with her teacher.

If the rejection is real and ongoing, look for other issues. Try to be realistic about potential contributing factors. Does your child hit or kick first and negotiate afterward? Does your child always want her ideas to prevail, or is she able to share her ideas and her things? Does your child have the language and the social skills for entering, sustaining, and ending play situations? If you think your child may be behind in language development, talk to your pediatrician (see chapter 9). You can also ask your child's preschool teacher what she or he has observed.

If the problem is aggressive behavior, find ways to help your child be more aware of his feelings and to begin to use words instead of actions. At gatherings, stick around the children and see how your child is getting on. Coaching and modeling in the context of real play situations works best with preschoolers (ages three and up): "Jay, do you like what Justin did?" Or, "You can say, 'Justin, I don't like it; don't do that to me.'" Help the child identify his feelings, and find ways to better manage them: "What can you do when you know you are starting to feel mad?"

Brainstorm solutions together. Sometimes taking a deep breath, walking away, or finding an adult to help will work. Older children can try counting before acting. Try to agree ahead of time on what your child will do when he has a problem.

Three-year-old Marisa is in very high demand; it seems everyone wants to play with her. At her preschool, children fight to sit next to her. Usually they all end up pushing and shoving and dissolving in tears.

We don't usually think of popularity as being a problem, but if that kind of high demand occurs before a child is able to handle it, it can be overwhelming and exhausting. Preschool children typically don't have the cognitive ability to negotiate with more than one friend at a time.

Marisa is friendly and smiling, but not very assertive. She needs help to be able to say what she wants rather than always being guided by the desires of her friends.

Fortunately, her teachers realized that Marisa was not enjoying all the attention. They removed one problem by assigning seats for all the children at group. Together with the parents, teachers concentrated on helping the popular child stand up for herself and become a decision maker.

Some Final Words

Forming and maintaining balanced friendships is *one of* the most important and most difficult aspects of childhood. As a parent, you can help your child take on the task of creating balanced and lasting friendships that help him learn how he fits into the world around him. It is a skill that will last him a lifetime.

Doing this well requires understanding which behaviors are normal at different stages of development so that you can help children solve problems as they relate to each other. Just remember that neither the children nor you have to get everything right the first time. Mistakes can teach as much—sometimes more—than successes. Learning how to make friends is an ongoing process that gets better over time.

Suggestions for Further Reading

Adults

Ruth Charney. *Teaching Children to Care: Management in the Responsive Classroom.* Northeast Foundation for Children, 1992.

Louise Derman-Sparks and the A.B.C. Task Force. *Anti-Bias Curriculum: Tools for Empowering Young Children.* National Association for the Education of Young Children, 1989.

Lilian Katz and Diane McClellan. *Fostering Children's Social Competence: The Teacher's Role*. NAEYC, 1997.

Eleanor Lynch and Marci Hanson (eds.). *Developing Cross Cultural Competence: A Guide for Working with Children and Their Families*. Paul H. Brookes Publishing Co.,1998.

Vivian Gussin Paley. *Boys and Girls: Superheroes in the Doll Corner*. University of Chicago Press, 1986.

———. *You Can't Say You Can't Play*. Harvard University Press, 1993.

Amy Phillips (ed.). *Playing for Keeps: Supporting Children's Play*. Redleaf Press, 1996.

Patricia Ramsey. *Making Friends in School: Promoting Peer Relationships in Early Childhood*. Teachers College Press, 1991.

Videotapes

Creating Caring Communities. Beacon Communications, Inc. Arlington, MA: (617) 643–1141.

Starting Small: Fostering Kindness in the Classroom. National Association for the Education of Young Children, Washington, D.C.: (202) 232-8777 or e-mail: pub-aff@naeyc.org.

Start Seeing Diversity (video and book). Ellen Wolpert for the Committee for Boston Public Housing. St. Paul, MN: Redleaf Press: (800) 423-8309 or *www.redleafpress.org/bookstore*.

Children's Books

Janell Cannon. *Stellaluna*. Voyager, 1997.

Eric Carle. *A House for Hermit Crab*. Aladdin, 2002.

Tim Egan. *Metropolitan Cow*. Houghton Mifflin, 1999.

Kevin Henkes. *Chrysanthemum*. Mulberry, 1996 (teasing).

———. *Jessica*. Mulberry, 1998 (imaginary friend).

Steven Kellogg. *The Mysterious Tadpole*. Dial, 1993.

Leo Lionni. *Alexander and the Wind-up Mouse*. Knopf, 1987.

Arnold Lobel. *Frog and Toad Are Friends*. HarperCollins, 1970.

William Steig. *Amos and Boris*. Sunburst, 1992.

Judith Viorst. *Rosie and Michael*. Aladdin, 1988.

Bernard Waber. *Ira Sleeps Over*. Scott Foresman, 1975.

Transition, Change, and Crisis

Janet Zeller

Four-year-old Rachel's mother was surprised to hear her telling a play-mate that her preschool teacher (who had left school suddenly for a family emergency) had died. When her mother asked, "What makes you think Miss Lu died?," Rachel said, "If she didn't die, then she would've said good-bye and hugged us!" Mom explains that the teacher had no choice, and had to leave too quickly to bid farewell. Her daughter seems to understand.

A few weeks later, Rachel learns she'll be moving to the "big kids" preschool soon. She asks excitedly if her "dead" teacher will be there.

For all of us, change means uncertainty. Adults have many strategies for coping with these moments of flux. They can remember past changes and how they weathered them. For example, the nervous anticipation of a new job is tempered by memories of succeeding at past ones. Relocating to a strange city becomes less stressful when you apply coping tactics from previous moves. Grown-ups can reflect upon the pattern of past changes, a pattern that reveals safe bridges from the unknown to the familiar.

But young children cannot yet see the strong links between the past and the future. Their history is too short, and their minds, while complex and powerful in many marvelous ways, have only begun to develop the capacity to understand and to predict the outcomes of changes in their lives. Rachel knew her teacher would never leave without saying good-bye; therefore, Miss Lu must have died. Rachel doesn't yet understand that death is not reversible.

Young children are firmly embedded in the present. Their boundless energies, their robust responses, and their intense explorations are tied to what is happening in the here and now. They focus on the present, wringing from it every last possible bit of meaning and feeling.

While three-year-olds can happily anticipate events in their near future, such as an outing to the park or a birthday party, they are not yet sophisticated enough to use their past experiences as comforting sign-posts during times of transition. This is particularly true of changes involving separation from a loved one, a sudden alteration of physical environment, or a disruption in a set routine. That is why entering a new child care program, moving into a new house, and switching to a new bedtime schedule are all challenges for the preschooler. Changes that involve real and substantial loss, such as death, divorce, or foster care, are an even greater challenge.

But take heart. The preschool years are a wonderful time to help youngsters master the full array of changes, transitions, and even crises that mark each of our lives from time to time. And attention to these issues during the early years will certainly help your child to approach the uncertain future with an array of flexible coping strategies.

In this chapter, we will present both the principles and the particulars of helping young children negotiate a number of typical transitions and crises.

We'll look at:

- *Transitions:*
  - temporary and permanent separations
  - moving to a new home

- *Changes to the family:*
  - getting ready for a new baby
  - welcoming a foster or adopted child
  - dealing with divorce
  - remaking the family

- *Crises:*
  - serious illness or disability
  - coping with death

The Mind and Soul of the Preschooler

The preschool years herald many exciting new capacities. Thoughts become more organized and much more complex. Language becomes a much stronger means of communication, and social interactions become more sophisticated. Even the physical contours and proportions of the preschooler's body have been altered by the developmental process. No longer does she have the disproportionately large head of an infant. The lines of her face have become more chiseled, melting the curves that we associate with the toddler. Your three-year-old has certainly come a long way from those earlier stages.

It is important to remember, though, that your three-year-old is not simply a small adult. Especially during times of change, families and other loved ones should resist the impulse to support the preschooler in the very same way they would the older child or adult. On the other hand, don't sell the preschooler short. Nothing is lost to this insatiable observer and recorder of the moment: every event is processed, and the quest to make sense of the world never ceases. Your active support during times of transition will be a priceless gift to your child, one that will bear fruit throughout his or her life.

CONSIDER INDIVIDUAL AND FAMILIAL DIFFERENCES

Your preschooler is a jewel like no other! While the stages of early development are useful guideposts for describing all children, every individual offers us a singular variation on these central themes. No two children are exactly alike. That is both the beauty and the challenge of loving them, raising them, and teaching them. Not only has your child already had a host of unique relationships and experiences, but she or he also "arrived" in the world with a one-of-a-kind personality and character. This uniqueness should be an important consideration when guiding your child during times of change. Never forget that you are the very best judge when it comes to your own youngster.

The same rule of variation applies to families. How you help your child deal with the changes presented in this chapter will also depend on your unique family history, values, customs, and beliefs. Where you spent your childhood, your ethnicity, nationality, and sexual orientation also influence your parenting practices.

While the United States is the most diverse nation in the world, it is sometimes more difficult if you're not in the majority culture. This is especially true for families who have recently immigrated to the U.S., or who enjoy lifestyles different from the "typical." They are sometimes made to feel that practices dear to them in their places of origin or in their "worldview" are inappropriate. For example, when a woman from India told a group that her children slept with her and her husband until they were eight years old, the room fell silent; judgment was as thick as smoke. Americans aren't supposed to do that! She, on the other hand, was aghast to hear how Americans put their children alone in dark rooms for the whole night. We all could do a better job of acknowledging and validating the parenting practices of families from other lands and other persuasions. So, add your own ideas to the suggestions in this chapter, and make sure to share them with your friends and neighbors.

Transitions

The way you prepare a child for a transition depends on her age, developmental stage, temperament, and the type of transition. There are two ways to look at transitions: minor versus major (the difference in intensity, for example, between staying overnight at Grandma's and moving to a new house), and benign versus serious (the difference between getting a new puppy—with positive anticipation; and getting ready for surgery—with trepidation). When you decide how much time to give your child to get ready, both axes are important. As parents, we often think only of one or the other, and don't put both together.

SEPARATIONS: TEMPORARY OR PERMANENT

> Six-year-old Lisa is having her first sleep-over at a friend's house, one she's lobbied hard for since last summer. Two hours into the night, she's on the phone in tears, saying that she's afraid and wants to come right home.

What's striking about Lisa's situation is that we all do this: set up big expectations for an important event, and sometimes end up disappointed. Children, though, are especially prone to setting expectations for themselves without understanding the implications.

A child visiting a park may rush away from her parent to play, but every now and then she'll check in with "home base," balancing her needs for independence and security. For Lisa, it's nighttime and she's in someone else's home, so there's no home base to return to. And bedtime is a time with a high need for nurturing—similar to meals and naptime, when kids in school often miss their parents.

A situation like Lisa's puts parents in a bind. They want to rush to her aid, but worry about causing damage with a premature rescue. But there's nothing wrong with admitting this was just too soon for a sleep-over. Children that age are not good judges of what they can handle.

First, talk with the other parents and your child. Say, "If you really need me to come and get you, I will." Then get details on what your child is worried about. It may be something that can be resolved with a little extra comfort or another stuffed animal. If not, bring the child home. Tell your child it's okay, and that it's not her fault.

Look for ways that she can take smaller steps toward her goal, such as having dinner and spending an evening with friends, but sleeping at home. She could also have a guest sleep over. Or just wait until she's older. Your child won't be sleeping at home for the rest of her life.

When your child seems ready to try again, reassure her in advance, "If you decide at any time you don't want to sleep over after all, it's okay. Sometimes kids sleeping at someone else's house don't feel comfortable." Giving her permission to be homesick may actually boost her confidence.

> Jon's parents are going on a weekend trip. They are unsure of when to tell their three-year-old about their plans to leave him with his grandparents. Furthermore, they wonder whether to bring Jon to his grandparents' house or to have Bubbe and Poppy come to Jon's home for the weekend.

In this situation, ready or not, Jon is going to sleep away from his parents. The family must make the best of the situation. If Jon has not slept at his grandparents' home, it would be best for them to stay at Jon's so he's in a familiar space with familiar things. If his grandparents' home is well-known to and comfortable for him, and especially if he's slept there before, then having him sleep at his grandparents' is okay.

Jon's parents are wise to consider when to tell him about the trip. There's an optimal amount of time between when you introduce the idea of a change and when you actually make the change, which depends on the child's age and temperament. If you tell a young child about an event too soon, it puts him in a place of ambiguity. He may build up a web of fears in his mind about the change, instead of anticipating good things.

A child Jon's age could be told a day or two before—or even that morning, if there's lots of time to discuss and process the change with him before the sleep-over. But don't take a three-year-old to his grandparents and say, "By the way, you'll be spending the night here." This leaves the child feeling tricked and fearful that soon someone will pull the rug out from under him again.

If this situation were more serious—e.g., Jon's going to an aunt he hasn't stayed with before, perhaps because his parents must fly to a very ill relative—more discussion time would be needed. Even if you haven't told your child you're visiting a sick relative, he'll still sense that it's a stressful time for you. If your child has never been to the aunt's home, if at all possible let him visit and explore it before the sleep-over day. (This kind of orientation visit is useful with any transition, including starting a new school or preparing for a scheduled hospital stay.)

Whatever the situation, it's your job as an adult to be upbeat about the whole thing. The child needs to know that this transition is nonnegotiable, no matter how much he cries or fusses; it's not his behavior that determines what happens. (In fact, it's very stressful for a child if he *does* feel responsible; he feels that to show loyalty to his parents, he must act as upset as possible. With older preschoolers, you can say, "I know that you're upset. But even so, Mommy and Daddy are still going. What can we do to help you?")

> Romaine has to leave for a weeklong business trip, and feels worried (and guilty) about how her five-year-old daughter will handle it. Corrine has never been apart from her mom this long before.

With a longer separation, it's important to make the time between leaving and returning real for the child. For kids, time is boundless, so adults must bind the transition in time by translating days into objects. This is similar to the traditional Advent calendar, which helps children mark the days until Christmas.

For example, when a teacher from one of our lab schools goes on vacation, we create a paper chain with one link for each day the teacher will be gone. Each morning, the kids take down the link and read the note inside, prepared in advance by the teacher. Monday's note might say,

"I'm still on the plane today, and looking forward to the sunny beach." On Tuesday, it's "Today there will be a sing-along. Enjoy it, and I'll be thinking about you."

One mother prepared a cracker, candy, or tiny toy for each day she would be away. When the crackers were gone, her son knew that Mom would be returning that day. She also recorded bedtime stories for him to listen to each night.

You can also give numbered "countdown" notes: day five, day four, and so on, with a loving message or drawing for each day until the parent comes home. When the child goes to bed, let him know, "Only three more sleeps until Daddy comes back."

E-mail is another tool for staying connected despite physical separation. When the father of a child in our preschool was hospitalized with a long illness, his daughter E-mailed him every day from school. She dictated letters to a teacher, who also helped her scan or fax drawings. She kept all of her dad's responses in class, where they were always accessible.

> Ricky's grandmother has just moved from his neighborhood in New York all the way to Florida. Ricky is very close to his gran, but won't talk to her when the family calls for a telephone visit. He seems to listen to Gran's voice for a second, but then drops the phone and leaves the room while his family continues to converse.

Ricky's parents are puzzled by and angry about his "rude" behavior. But what they don't realize is that Ricky is not rude; he's a five-year-old who is upset that his beloved gran has moved away. Ricky's parents cannot attribute the same motives to him that they would to an adult—as if Ricky were an adult in miniature. But a preschooler like Ricky is unable to put his grandmother's move into a larger perspective. In his mind, it has only to do with him. This leads him to conclude, "She left me, she didn't want to be around me—so I'll show her!"

When faced with a relationship that's "ending" or involves someone who is moving far away, adults also try to cope by diminishing the importance of the relationship: "She did a lot of things that annoyed me." "I have lots of other friends." Some of us, like Ricky, substitute anger for sadness, because it can be easier to handle.

Ricky's parents need to understand that his response is typical and even healthy. Their job is to help Ricky understand that Gran's reason for moving had nothing to do with him: "It's cold here. And when you get old sometimes you don't feel well in cold weather, and walking in snow is harder. Florida is always sunny and warm, and Gran knows people there, so she had to go. But she still loves you just as much, and if she could have you right there with her, she would."

> Portia's teacher is leaving school at year's end. The teacher has been talking about her upcoming departure, but Portia resists hearing any news of this change. She is very angry with the teacher and tells her, "You should go now before the good-bye party."
>
> Portia's mother is very embarrassed at her daughter's seeming rejection of the teacher, and has asked for a conference to apologize.

The teacher understands that this is Portia's way of steeling herself for the coming change. She's distancing herself now so she won't hurt as much when her teacher leaves. Once she has successfully negotiated the transition, she will return to her usual engaging self.

In a similar vein, young children sometimes manage transitions by ignoring those from "past lives." For example, when a spring graduate, Jakie, from one of our classrooms for three-year-olds, saw his old teacher the following fall, the teacher said, "Hi, Jakie!" Instead of saying hi back, Jakie walked right by. He was trying so hard to make it through that transition to his new "big kid" class: he couldn't go back now, and if he tried to go back and get nurturing from his old teacher, it would be that much harder for him. But when December came, Jakie had made the transition and felt comfortable in his new setting, allowing him to hug his old teacher with undiminished love. This transition is hardest for the younger ones, as it's their first time handling that challenge. Older children don't have to distance themselves from previous teachers so much.

Our teachers also spend time at the end of the school year preparing children for what's next. A month before, they discuss who's going to which classrooms, and make pictures and maps of where they are now and where they're going. The new teacher visits children in their current classroom. The "old" teacher and the child's family accompany him to his new classroom for a look-see and snack. The child also chooses a new cubby so he knows there will be a place for him and his things. It's good for the child to see his old and new teachers together, and to see that they have a good relationship (e.g., that one pats the other on the shoulder). Finally, the child can take away a joint photo of his old and new teachers to look at over the break.

> Felix's mother has gone to an inpatient drug rehabilitation center. His
> grandmother doesn't know whether she should tell Felix or anyone else
> about the situation.

It's especially difficult to handle a separation for an emotionally charged reason such as drug rehab or incarceration. In the example above, if rehab is treated as a big, bad secret, Felix will feel unnecessary confusion. His grandmother must let him know that his mother has a problem and is working to fix it. (Neutralizing the issue is not the same as apologizing for or condoning the mother's behavior.) It's important to demystify the situation, and not "try to deny the elephant in the room." Once the issue is not secret, it can be tamed. It may be an elephant, but it need not be a monster.

Kids in these kinds of extreme and painful situations may not want to acknowledge what is happening. But parents and caregivers can still offer emotional support. The silence must be broken first at home, and then, we hope, at school—with teacher and best buddies.

Kids may worry that they'll have no access to the parent in prison or rehab, and need to know when and how they can see their parents. At our lab schools, we have had preschool children go on field trips to visit a parent in prison, sometimes bringing a few friends. Again, the situation needs to be talked about honestly: "Your dad still loves you, but he did something wrong and has to make up for it. When an adult breaks the law, he has to spend a certain amount of time in prison; then he can come home."

MOVING

> Louise and her mom and dad are moving to another state, leaving behind loving relatives and a house her family has occupied for over a century. While Louise is less upset than her mother, she does worry: "How will they find the new house to bring my stuff to?"

Louise's mother was born and raised in this house, and found it hard not to project her sad feelings onto her child. However, the feelings of grown-ups come second. Yes, adults need to understand and cope with their own sense of loss, but this is so they can set it aside when needed to take care of the child's needs. In American culture, it's often more difficult to share quiet negative emotions, such as sadness, than it is to express anger—especially for boys. Let your child know that he can cry and get extra comfort now. If you can, save your own tears until the child is asleep.

Louise's parents can help by modeling for her that it's okay to have and share those feelings: "I'm sad to leave this house. Grandma lived here and Grandma's mommy lived here, so there are so many memories. But we can take memories and pictures and other things with us to the new house." In a happier situation—a family moving within the same town to their dream house—parents are less emotionally distracted from helping their child make the transition.

Children often have misconceptions and fears about moving. They may think they, or their possessions, will be left behind. If you are moving, try to visit the new house or apartment so your child can see that there's room for him and his important stuff. Have your child work with you to pack his things. Help him draw a picture of where people, furniture, and toys can go in the new home.

Louise's parents showed her a map of the route the truck would take to move things from their old home to the new. Just as children have trouble understanding time, they aren't cognitively equipped yet to visualize space and distance. In your preschooler's mind, his new home is dangling out in Nowheresville. Make maps together, using appropriate points of reference: "Here's our house, here's Grandma's, here is Aunt Sheryl's, and here is the new house."

Take lots of photographs of both your current and future homes—if possible, with family and friends present. It's helpful for your child to see these important people showing positive feelings toward the new home. If you can, arrange to bring a symbolic piece of the old home with you (e.g., a fireplace mantel, a patterned tile, a swing from the yard).

A child's school or day care can also help prepare for the transition: for example, making a memory book with photos and drawings of teachers and friends, and activities they did together. He can also bring some class materials to play with at his new school. One child who moved away sent us a picture of himself at his new house. We sent back a photo showing his picture in a place of honor in his old classroom. We also encourage kids to take "inside pictures": using their eyes and brains as a make-believe camera to capture images of friends and places in memory. Things may change, but you carry people with you in your heart and brain.

On moving day, try to have something of your child's already in his new room when he arrives. Let him carry a box of his treasures into the new house. Bring pictures of him in the old house and hang them in related places in the new one. Kids love to tie the past to the present, but need help from us to do so.

It's important for your child to build a connection to his new neighborhood, as well as his new play group, child-care center, or school. Try to introduce him to at least one adult and one peer who live nearby. Help your child create a map of the routes between the new home and important new places: "Here's a photo of your house, and here's the way you'll go to school. This is a photo of your new school, and here's where Mommy is working now." Take him to visit the new school.

If possible, get pictures of the new classroom and children ahead of time. Take the things you brought from his old school and put them in his cubby or post them in the classroom. Try to arrange for the new teacher to visit your child at your home. Gradually introducing new elements to the child helps him ease into the transition.

Changes in Family Structure

New Brother or Sister

> Three-year-old June has a new baby brother with beautiful blond curls. Because of the family's cultural traditions, the grandparents, thrilled that they have a first grandson, shower Labe with gifts and attention.
>
> What's more, when June walks with her mother, next to Labe in the stroller, people come up and coo over the adorable little boy.
>
> One day their mother comes upon June leaning over Labe's crib, singing to him sweetly, "Oh, Labe, I'm gonna cut off your arms, and I'm gonna cut off your legs, and I'm gonna send you to Africa . . ."

Any child competing for attention with a new baby occasionally wishes that baby to the other side of the earth. June's story is classic. June's parents worked hard to show her that they still have room for her in their hearts and lives, but the behavior of extended family and friends was beyond her parents' control. Parents may need to prod friends and family to pay special attention to the older child, e.g., bringing a small gift for her when they bring one for the baby.

While the prospect of a new baby is exciting, preschoolers have fantasies and ideas about babies that aren't based in reality. For example, they may picture an instant, smiling playmate. They also can't predict the many demands the newcomer will place on their parents' time, and may not grasp that he will, in fact, be a permanent part of their household. When that idea is finally rooted, the honeymoon is over; that's when anger such as June's can emerge. Parents need to be very sensitive and recognize an older child's "right" to this anger. Despite their fatigue, it's important for parents to schedule separate, *special* time alone with their older child.

One way to help the big sister (or brother) feel important is to give her some special responsibilities for the baby, such as "official interpreter": "June, what do you think the baby wants now?" (This is also a good way to find out what June is thinking.) She can also introduce the baby to visitors, help out with feeding or bathing, and sing to the baby at night.

At our lab schools, when a parent brings a baby in, we never comment on the baby in front of his preschool sibling. We hold our coos until the big brother or sister is off and occupied elsewhere. This is a subtle way of saying to our students: "This school is for big kids, and babies don't interest us much."

WELCOMING A FOSTER CHILD

Any change in family structure is a challenge for the preschooler. For adults, foster care and adoption are different constructs. We understand that elements of permanence, levels of commitment, and issues of legal rights separate these two arrangements. It is important to remember that young children do not understand these subtle differences. For them, either of these changes represents disruption, confusion, ambivalence, and varying degrees of grief, relief, guilt, anger, sadness, and happiness.

What's more, while we can anticipate future positive outcomes of foster care and adoption, the four-year-old has no such forward view. Our personal history has taught us that the pitches and rolls of the present tend to even out in the future. For the preschooler, the mountain or chasm of today seems like the topography of forever. Children, early in foster or adoptive placement, need lots of calm reassurance and time to slowly reacclimate.

David, four and a half, just moved into a foster home, with a family with two teenage daughters. Because of a drug problem, his mother could no longer care for him. Mabel, his new foster mother, wants to help David feel comfortable in their home.

Tens of thousands of children are placed in foster care in the United States. Some have been removed from their homes because their physical, nutritional, or medical needs were not being met. Some have been emotionally, physically, or sexually abused. While each case is unique, such children share strong emotions about the families they leave behind.

A child who's relieved to be out of an unhealthy or scary home will still have ambivalent feelings. And even a child leaving a loving home (such as one he shared with a disabled parent who can't care for him) will have some feelings of anger toward his family of origin. These conflicting feelings, while hard for the adult to grasp, are even more difficult for the child. Helping the foster child to acknowledge and reconcile these disparate emotions is a task for all who know and love him.

Our lab schools have a long and rich history of schooling and nurturing preschoolers and kindergartners in foster care. This means that we are also working closely with both the foster parents and the family of origin, people often not in contact with one another. We have found that taking the perspective of both families makes us much better able to support the child during foster care.

David was living with his mother, Carole, when he came to school—a mother who certainly loved him, but was periodically unable to parent in a healthy and consistent way. Carole's chronic drug abuse resulted in her incarceration during David's third year at Tufts. David witnessed his mother's violent and tearful arrest. He was immediately placed in foster care.

The foster family accompanied David to school during his first week with them, and the teachers made an immediate visit to David's foster home. For David to see his teachers and foster parents together, both at school and at home, was a critical first step in the work ahead. David now knew that it wasn't his sole responsibility to present himself and his situation to these strangers. He also knew that by our presence in his temporary home, we approved of this arrangement as a safe place for him to be for now.

Having his foster family at school also allowed David to slowly help us to introduce his new living situation to his classmates and their families, all people with whom he shared strong bonds. Teachers helped

David to arrange his new bedroom, making sure that important objects from his past were placed to his liking. This sent a clear message that neither the teachers nor David needed to jettison the past. At the same time, the presence of these objects also signaled that David could, when he was ready and able, "present" his mother to his foster family.

David and his teacher made a map that included the following landmarks: his home of origin, his foster home, his school, the prison housing his mother, and other sites that David chose to add (such as the homes of friends and favorite places he had visited in the past). He also needed to include the home of one of his dearest teachers. The map was fashioned with markers, paper, some photographs, as well as with David's own writing and some teacher transcriptions of his narration. The original map was carefully laminated after several copies of varying sizes were made for use at school, at his foster home, and while David "traveled."

This activity helped David to build a *cognitive* map of where everyone was and where each was in relation to all of the others. As a metaphor for his emotions, the map also allowed David to locate each key party in his heart, which went a long way in helping him to make sense of all of his conflicting feelings. David kept this map close at hand. He also edited the map whenever he wished. The map was used throughout David's foster placement, when he was reunited with his mother, and long after that as well.

David began to communicate with his mother from school, drawing pictures and writing letters. Teachers wrote their own notes to Carole, which were read to David. He attached these to his own work and put it all in the envelope to his mom. When David was ready, he visited his mother in prison. He was initially accompanied by a social worker, but preferred to be taken by his teachers (an arrangement Carole also preferred).

During these visits, David had time with Carole alone, and time with her and his teachers together. Teachers were also able to have private conversations with Carole on the telephone. These arrangements allowed David to maintain his strong relationship with his mother, to see his teachers and mother continuing their relationships, and to express his positive and negative feelings to all concerned parties. It also relieved David of his initial need for secrecy and his feelings of shame surrounding his mother's incarceration.

During this stage, David began to talk a lot about his mother, her imprisonment, his past, and his foster placement. Teachers listened carefully, answering any direct questions, repairing any confusions, and generally supporting this boy's need to make sense of his life. David began to understand that his mother could not presently take care of him, that this was *not* his fault, that she loved him, and that he had every right to be very angry with her. David's great sense of loss ("she can't hug me anymore"), and accompanying feelings of relief ("I was so scared when she was wasted and screaming"), were also much discussed at this point in his foster placement. He was discovering that while Carole would always be his mother, he would not live with her until she was able to keep him safe, comfortable, and happy. We modeled this way of supporting David for his foster family, and they skillfully followed suit throughout David's time with them.

Open communication between David, his mother, his school, and foster home continued throughout the placement. Carole and the foster mother spoke on several occasions, and all parties continued to keep David's needs paramount. When the time came for David and his mother to be reunited, many of the above strategies were used again. The need for gradualness, flexibility, openness, and respect was honored while David negotiated his complicated journey "home."

A YOUNG CHILD'S ADOPTION

Dasheem has just been adopted at age four from a war-torn country. His new family wants to make his new life bright and good, to compensate for what he's been through.

At school, Dasheem steals food from other children's plates. If a child looks him in the eye, he strikes out at him. If spoken to above a whisper, he runs away.

When you adopt a preschooler, that child often comes to you with a long and complex history. Further, he has processed, digested, and stored this history at a fairly sophisticated level. This makes the adoption quite different from that of an infant or even a toddler.

Dasheem needed someplace to take his history—a way to deal with it, and integrate it with his new life. So he began to act out, both at home and at school. With the help of an experienced clinical consultant, his parents realized that behaviors such as stealing food and running away had been very adaptive in his home country, where Dasheem may have lived on the streets for a time.

At school, we told Dasheem, "You know, you don't have to steal food anymore. There's plenty of food." As proof, we took him to the refrigerator many times each day. If he ran away in fear, we told him, "You don't have to run anymore. We will keep you safe." With love and support from parents and teachers, we acknowledged his past without dwelling on it. Dasheem is now doing very well.

Most kids are not adopted from such horrific situations. But the issues of history still need attention. Another child, John, first came to our school at age three. His very young mother struggled with cocaine addiction. Many times she had relinquished him (or had him taken away) to foster care. She would enter treatment, and try again, coming to school sober and caring—but eventually sliding back. Eventually, John was adopted by a loving single man, who wanted to put John's past firmly in the past.

Now that John had outgrown our school, he had no one to talk to about his mother anymore. We worked to convince his new dad that John needed to talk about his mother, as well as his three biological siblings who were under care elsewhere. John well knew that his mother had loved him, despite her limitations, and he did take some good traits and memories from her.

Children who have left their original homes, especially those who've lived in multiple foster homes, may anticipate rejection. There may be a short "honeymoon," then months of testing to see if things will last. It takes time for a child to see that while there are consequences to his behavior, he will not be thrown out.

We have seen many children at our lab school with impulse-control problems whose previous placements had not worked out. We constantly reassure them: "This is your school, and you will be here forever, until you're ready for the school for older kids. We will not let you do things here that aren't safe. We know that other school told your family you couldn't come back. That has never happened here." The same message needs to be given when a child is placed in a new home.

One wonderful thing adoptive families and children can do is make a history book. We do this with all adopted children and families at our school. Elena from Guatemala has such a book. Her mother was very poor, with many other children, and could not care for her. Elena's book has letters from mother, pictures, and a story. "Here is the picture of the village where you were born, and a picture of your mom. Here is the airport where your new family picked you up." Adoption books are very precious to children. It took Elena a year before she was ready to share her book with kids at school.

Divorce

Clive's father has moved out of the family house the day after telling his son that he is getting a divorce. A few days later, Clive hears his mother tearfully telling a friend that she is getting divorced. He runs to her crying, "Now who will take care of me when you move away?"

Makes perfect sense, doesn't it? For young Clive, the concepts of "divorce" and "moving out" are inextricably bound. This is far from the only confusion experienced by a child who doesn't understand what will happen when his parents divorce. In the absence of accurate information, young children's imaginations take hold. They make assumptions based on their own scant knowledge and fears.

Join with your spouse in explaining the divorce to your child. Let him know that both of you still love him very much, and that you will both continue to take good care of him. Share your plans for his physical custody, but don't let him think that he will participate in decisions about how much time he'll spend with one or the other of you. Avoid any comments that encourage a child's fear that something he did contributed to the divorce, such as "Your father didn't like being a parent very much." Kids usually think they are the reason for the split, and that they are responsible for getting their parents back together.

Most published studies on divorce highlight only its negative consequences for the young child. These aspects are inflated, resting on outdated notions our culture used to have about how children experience both bonding with and separation from primary caretakers. While our knowledge in this area of child development has grown, studies of divorce have largely failed to take the more positive aspects into account. Handled well, divorce can actually have positive consequences for your young child—as in the case of Charmaine.

Charmaine told her teacher how happy she was that her parents had gotten a divorce. "Now it's peaceful in my house, and I don't have to put my pillow over my head and press down very hard so I won't hear the screaming." She also reported, "It's fun to be with Daddy now. He never had a good time at home, but now we have fun together at his new house."

While prior to the divorce, Charmaine directly experienced the sadness, anger, and acrimony of her parents' marriage, she has now been freed from that: she's mercifully "out of the loop." Instead of concentrating on the negative aspects of her parents' marriage, she can focus on the good relationship she has with each of them. And, if she played the role of "referee," which even young children may try to do, she can now return to her role as the child.

Lucas, age four, has parents who claim their son knows nothing about their pending divorce because they "never talk about it when he is around. We wait until he is asleep. We close our door." Actually, Lucas has been talking about his parents' imminent "divork" for months, telling teachers and classmates that "it's something you get when you can't yell anymore."

Parents often think that they are successfully protecting their children from the negative aspects of their lives and their marriage. They believe that children do not hear their arguments and their conversations. This wishful thinking, fueled by your genuine desire to shield their youngster, unfortunately doesn't make it so. No amount of resolve or vigilance can completely hide the reality of divorce from a child. Instead of believing that your child *never* hears, operate on the assumption that he *often* hears. Also remember that his ears aren't the only organs through which he is processing the unwinding of your marriage. With his eyes he registers your feelings, and with his brain he evaluates your mood. Don't sell him short; children are extremely accurate in their observations of their parents.

This information is not in any way meant to make you feel like you've been a bad parent. Rather, it should liberate you. Now you can begin to help your child understand the facts of your pending separation and divorce. The "elephant in the room" can now be acknowledged and labeled. Once the child has a name for it, he can begin, with your help, to understand this thing called a "divorce."

> Kelly's parents are in the midst of a divorce and heated custody battle. Kelly, age four, has heard both of them say very negative things about each other, sometimes directly to her. Kelly has told her teacher, among other things, that "My Papa can't feed me," "My Mommy can't make enough money to take care of me," "My Papa is a drunk," and "My Mommy will leave me in the house all by myself."
>
> At school, Kelly has begun to wet her pants and become very tearful, especially at lunch and naptime.

This is an example of what can be called an "out-of-control divorce." It can be very hard to find that balance between concealing information from a child and involving her too much. No matter how true they are, it is wise never to share terrible things about your ex with your child. While your role is to keep your daughter safe, it is not appropriate to burden her with your negative feelings about her other parent (and remember, they are *your* feelings, not hers). This is one of those times when your own impulses and needs should be put aside in favor of your youngster's best interests. If you have expressed negative feelings about your ex-spouse, don't feel too guilty. It's unlikely that you've done permanent damage. Unlike Granny's priceless porcelain vase, your child can definitely mend. It will take some backtracking, though.

Apologize for your temporary lapse in judgment. You will find your child infinitely forgiving. Most important, try very hard to disengage your child from the battle surrounding her custody. Children who are pulled into this arena begin to believe that what they do and say will determine their living situation. They believe that they must choose one parent and therefore abandon the other. The guilt engendered by this is too painful for any child to have to endure.

REMAKING THE FAMILY

Jane's mother, Epatha, has decided to remarry. While Jane has spent some time with Joe, her stepfather-to-be, her mother has wisely not over-involved him in her daughter's life. During the initial phases of dating, both grown-ups were careful to keep the adult facets of their relationship (such as overnights) to themselves. After a recent outing to the zoo, Jane told her mother that she liked Joe quite a bit. Now that marriage is in the near future, Epatha is wondering how to prepare Jane.

We're not making judgments about morality, but if you have a child, her needs come first. As Jane's mother sensed, a date should not spend too much time with your child until he becomes a likely partner. Your own relationships can be sequential, but your child should not be involved in those in more than a very superficial way. Otherwise, you can create a situation where you're asking your child to bond and separate over and over again. Sleep-overs should wait until you are ready to blend the family: if at all possible, after a decision has been made to get married.

Now that marriage is in the near future for Epatha, she can involve Jane slowly but actively with Joe. In a way, it's a three-way marriage. Tradition gives the bride and groom rituals to prepare for what's ahead. Look for appropriate ways to involve your child in those preparations. This is also a good time for Jane and Joe to spend some time by themselves so Jane can help him prepare, too.

While this may be a controversial view, we feel that whatever is planned for the honeymoon, it shouldn't involve a disappearance after the wedding. A wedding, like all important events, is emotional and exhausting. Developmentally, it's very hard for a preschooler not to feel abandoned if her parent and stepparent take off without her. (One child we know was incredibly angry when her parent honeymooned at Disneyland without her!) A small postwedding trip for the three of you—even just a weekend at a lakeside cabin—is a wonderful beginning for, and acknowledgment of, your new family. Later, Mom and Dad can take a private trip to the tropics.

> Five-year-old Amanda lived with her mother and father for the first two years of her life. Since then, she's lived with her mother. Amanda's mother and her female partner have decided to move in together. Amanda's mom wonders how to prepare her daughter, and worries about how this will affect Amanda's life.

Amanda needs to be prepared in the same way that Jane was. But she also needs some extra information. Gay parents need to give a child the words to explain her situation to friends and schoolmates. Tell Amanda, "Sometimes women marry men, sometimes men live together, and sometimes women live together."

Amanda, her mom, and her mom's partner will work things out, as families do. The issue here is to help Amanda be proud of her family.

Amanda also needs to be surrounded by advocates, such as her teacher and Grandma, rather than faced with obstacles to overcome. It's up to Amanda's mom and partner to work to smooth the way for her with these other people. This is not Amanda's job.

Teachers can have books available that show different family situations, and pictures on the wall celebrating all kinds of families (including same-sex-parent families). Young children don't see family differences as bad, unless such prejudices are triggered by adults. Children are curious, however. Since preschoolers tend to be focused more on Mom, they may ask, "Why does Amanda have two mothers and I just have one?" Or, "Where is your dad?" Amanda needs to have comfortable answers ready, such as, "Some families have lots of kids. Some have none. Some families have a mom and a dad. I have two moms."

> Caryn and Beth are five-year-old stepsiblings in a recently blended family. They spend most of their time together in conflict, fighting about practically everything. Their most frequent arguments are about sharing. Each has told her respective parent that she hates her stepsister.

Welcome to the challenging world of blended families. Often when two people with children get married, the parents forget that while they and their new spouse have had time to fall in love, the kids haven't. It's neither fair nor realistic to ask them to have a ready-made positive relationship.

The issues here are territory, things, and time. Caryn and Beth need some private territory where they can control the boundaries, they need control over their own possessions, and they need time to adjust. If at all possible, never put new stepsibs in the same bedroom. After a while, they may be dying to share a room, but at first each needs her own territory. If economics mean they absolutely have to share, put some sort of divider between the sides to mark each one's private space.

Don't push the children to share possessions, and never get just one of something that both are dying to have. Let them control crossing boundaries and sharing objects. It's ideal to have enough resources so sharing only has to happen around activities and objects that require two people, like games or making a mural.

Gradually give them opportunities to mix. For example, start a jointly created poster with a large sheet of paper with a line drawn down the middle, so each draws on her own side; later, you can leave off the line. Or, they can each create links for holiday paper chains, and glue their links together at the end. One goal for each girl is to learn more about her stepsister, and gradually transfer some of the pleasant feelings she has toward her own parent toward each other. Both biological parents also need to model that nice behavior for their kids.

Parents and stepparents can help the children recognize each other's skills, passions, and interests, stressing what they can learn from and share with each other. "Caryn, Beth may be able to help you to build those castle towers . . . and later, Beth, Caryn can show you how to fly a kite." If each child feels valued, recognized, and celebrated by important adults, they are more likely to value each other.

It's also important to schedule private time for each child, both with the biological parent and with the stepparent. Caryn needs to know that she is special to her mom in ways Beth isn't. (One-on-one time is also a nice break from two children's bickering.)

One thing must be crystal clear to all: the blending of the family is nonnegotiable! This issue of nonnegotiability is key for preschoolers' stage of development. On the one hand, they feel helpless and dependent on caregivers, but they also believe they are very powerful. And if a parent says or implies that "I'll only marry Tim if you like him," or "If you cry hard enough I won't leave," that is an overwhelming responsibility.

Here, Caryn may think, "If I really screw up this relationship, maybe Mommy and I will move away." Stepsibs must know that there's nothing either child can do to split the family apart, or create a situation where the stepsib will not be there. Once your child knows that absolutely nothing she can do will split up the new family, you can all move on to finding ways to make it work.

Crisis: Illness and Death

COPING WITH SERIOUS ILLNESS

Five-year-old Chris has been in the hospital following an accident that left his legs paralyzed. After a month of rehabilitation, he is returning home to his parents and younger sister. Everyone wants to make Chris's homecoming as positive as possible. His parents are worried about how the accident is going to affect each of their young children.

What often happens in these cases is that parents try to make believe nothing is wrong. But, of course, something *is* wrong, and Chris now has a tough row to hoe. But he will imagine things are much worse if his parents whisper in corners and cry behind closed doors. Pretending everything is okay, or grieving too much for what's lost (and dragging the child down with you), doesn't help him cope.

What Chris's family needs first is lots of honesty. Look for chances to engage kids in conversation about what happened. Siblings (and friends) need their questions answered: "Will he die? Can he go to the bathroom? How will he get to school? How can he have friends? How will he get dressed or play soccer?" Their concerns will be very concrete. They need to know not to be afraid of or uncomfortable with Chris or his new equipment. They can feel sad for Chris, but should learn to not pity him. "It's true his legs are paralyzed, but he has two good arms."

Chris will have the same kinds of questions as his siblings, and wonder what things he can do: "Will I ever walk again? How will I go to birthday parties? Will I be able to swim?" Chris also wants to know that he's still lovable: "Will people still like me? Does Grandma know; will she be angry?"

Chris may worry about safety: "If there's a fire, how will I get out? What if a dog chases me?" He may also have questions adults wouldn't consider: "Will I still be older than my little sister?" Here, he's thinking of his role as big brother, and worried she will pass him or run faster than he does.

In addition to dealing openly with this setback, Chris's family needs to make an effort to begin gathering new good experiences and memories as a family. They need to see that good things still happen, and that everyone can still have fun together despite the disability.

One of these experiences can be problem solving as a family. For example, before Chris comes home from the hospital, the family can go through the house and talk about changes they can make. "Okay, Chris will have trouble with stairs. What can we do so he doesn't need to use stairs so much?" Perhaps his bedroom can be moved to the ground floor. If that's not possible, what are other options?

A problem-solving focus also helps Chris and his sister see that just because your legs don't work, it doesn't mean you can't go places and do things. "There are things only legs can do. But there are a lot of things that arms can do instead, and there are lots of things we do that don't involve legs anyway. And there are things your legs will still be able to do, Chris. That's what you'll learn in physical therapy. You'll be surprised at how many things you can do." Start a list together of things that Chris can do, from swimming and playing basketball, to going to parties and zoos.

> Morey has muscular dystrophy and is finding it harder and harder to walk. His mother wonders if it would be better for him to learn to use a wheelchair, but his father insists that his son keep working on walking.

Morey's situation is tougher than Chris's since MD is a degenerative condition. He will eventually end up using a wheelchair when his muscles become too weak to carry his weight. But the underlying issue that Morey's parents are worried about is a common one: "How much support do I give my child, and how much do I encourage him to push himself toward independence?" You want to provide a scaffold for your child to lean on, but you don't want to cling too close and rob him of a chance to grow.

For Morey, a wheelchair will give him much more freedom to travel, but at same time rob him of a chance to get there independently. A similar situation is that of a young child who wants to walk alone to school: you want that child to feel the power and confidence of walking on his own, but fear for his safety. Life is full of risks. When do you say, "I've got to let him go?" Should Morey conserve his energy and stamina by switching to a wheelchair, or should he remain more independent by walking?

Here is a place where you, your child's teacher, his pediatrician, and his physical therapist can be a great team. Learn to use these resources wisely so that you can make the best possible decision for your child. Ask all of the questions you have; never be embarrassed about a lack of knowledge. Ask your child's health professionals about the consequences of each of the possible choices you are considering. Then talk with the teacher about how your child might handle each of the choices and how the classroom will be adapted should you decide to introduce a wheelchair. Remember to add your own suggestions during this discussion. With your child's permission and full participation, make a plan to involve the other children in the classroom. Once the decision is made, work hard with your spouse to present a united front. Now you are ready to share your final decision with your child and engage him actively in its implementation.

If Morey starts to use a wheelchair, his teacher and classmates can work together to reconfigure the classroom to help him navigate. In our preschool, we had a child who couldn't fit her wheelchair under the table, which meant she couldn't reach the table to eat her lunch. She didn't want to eat on a wheelchair tray because she and the other kids decided that wasn't like eating together. The solution was to change two lunch tables for higher ones, and raise the chairs assigned to those tables.

If there's a field trip coming up, the class needs to plan how Morey can get there. For example, the teacher can call the public transportation office to make sure the subway-station elevator is working or that the bus is accessible. This teaches children that some problems can be fixed—and for those that can't be, how to adapt and find other ways.

This problem-solving attitude carries over to the home. A child may say, "How is Morey going to get into my house? I want to have a playdate with him, and we don't have ramps." Morey may respond, "I need to be able to get into my school, my home, and stores on my own. But it's okay if someone has to carry me and my wheelchair into your house. I love playing with you."

It is important that parents of children with special needs understand the gift that their child is giving to his peers. By knowing Morey, understanding Morey (both his strengths and his challenges), adapting to Morey's special needs, and advocating with and for Morey, his friends are broadening their own social horizons. Children exposed to variety, whether in their friendships, in food, in music, in physical attributes, or in ideas, will cherish and seek that same variety as adults. And, most important, learning that their classroom is for everyone teaches children that schools, stores, jobs, neighborhoods, and communities are, too.

One general comment about parents and children with disabilities: we find that sometimes parents have more trouble with accommodating to disabilities than kids do. For example, adults often assume that if a child has one disability, such as the difficult speech and uncoordinated movements of cerebral palsy, that he has other mental and physical problems as well. But one of our five-year-old students, who has CP, already reads at a middle-school level.

> Bea is a young mother gravely ill with cancer. As her disease has progressed, through increasingly difficult treatments, she has assured her son, Ray, that she will get better. Ray seems so much happier after each of her reassurances that she hasn't had the heart to tell him that it is likely that she will die quite soon.

This is perhaps the most difficult situation a parent will ever encounter. But even here, a parent can help her child, and in so doing, help ease her own pain.

If you are seriously ill, resist the well-intended impulse to protect your child from the truth. The sad fact is that such protection is not possible. While your child does not fully understand the nature and gravity of your illness, he definitely knows that something is very wrong. And, if you do not talk about the illness, then he will come to believe that this is a secret he's not supposed to talk about. So, he's not only confused, he's also frightened. He wonders what could be so bad that it has to be such a big secret.

Telling your child that you are ill is the first step to guiding him on the journey to come. Your simple but honest explanation of the illness will help him immensely. It will break the taboo that keeps him from sharing his own questions and feelings with you, and it will allow you to support your child during the even more difficult times to come.

Once the lines of communication have been opened, your child will begin to share his deepest fears with you. When he asks if you will die, try to be both reassuring and honest. Tell him the truth—that you are very sick, that no one knows if you will die, but that it's possible that you will. (We'll have more on young children's comprehension of death later in this chapter.) Dealing with an unknown outcome is tough: on the one hand, you are asking your child to wait, and on the other, to grasp a very different kind of situation and prepare to say good-bye.

Children are always looking for reasons; your child may assume he (or someone) did something to cause your illness. In fact, the fear that he's at the root of the problem may be so intense that he feels he can't put his questions and worries into words. It's often a good idea to ask a child if he's worried that he caused your illness. Once you've raised the topic, he can listen to your reassurances that it's not his fault in any way.

Another big fear, from a young child's perspective, is that the death of his parent will leave him without a caregiver. Remind him that if you die, he will be taken care of by people who love him very much and know all about him. Feel free to tell him exactly what arrangements have been made. And tell him that it is okay that he is worrying about these things. Remind him that you have time together now, and that that is the most important thing for both of you. And, most important, help him to understand that your love for each other, even in the face of death, is forever.

Debby's grandmother died two weeks ago, after a short illness. Before, she took care of her granddaughter every afternoon and on many weekends. Right after the funeral, Debby was sent to stay with an aunt for several days and has come home to find her mother still very teary and distracted by her own grief.

While Debby is cooperative and very pleasant at home, she is acting out at school, where she is aggressive, destructive, and unable to sleep at naptime. Usually very cuddly with her teachers, Debby is now very withdrawn and inconsolable when upset or hurt.

Parenting often involves putting your own needs aside in order to attend to those of your child. It is rarely harder to do this than immediately after the death of a loved one. Awash in your own grief, you may miss the signs of your child's suffering. But helping your child to cope with her grandmother's death may actually also help you through your own sadness.

Share your feelings with your child directly. Peeking at you grieving from afar is too painful for a young child to endure. Be open and invite your child to share her sadness with you. Let your child express any confusion she may be experiencing. Until children are five or six, they don't understand that death is permanent. She may believe that death is like a trip to Florida, and that Grandma will come back.

Remember, for the young child, death and abandonment are inextricably tied together. She may feel angry at being left. Be sure your child understands that her loved one did not want to leave her, but had no choice in the matter. And send the clear message that all of your child's feelings are *okay* to have. Spend quiet time together sharing both positive memories and hard feelings.

Finally, help your child feel safe enough to share the death of her loved one with other people who are central in her life. The two of you can tell her teachers together. This will open the door for your child to bring up this issue at school if she so chooses. It will also comfort her to know that her caretakers understand her special needs during this difficult time.

Miranda has become extremely clingy since the death of her grandfather. She is having a lot of trouble sleeping and has begun to crawl into her parents' bed several times each night. Usually happy to see her steady baby-sitter, Miranda now weeps whenever her parents leave her for an evening out. Her speech therapist, who works with Miranda three times a week, reports that this usually motivated three-year-old has become extremely withdrawn.

This is a confusing time for Miranda. Unlike an adult, who can process this experience using sophisticated language and thought, Miranda has trouble organizing all of the emotional content involved in the death of her loved one. It is hard for her to make sense of all the emotions churning within her. And her language disability prevents her from sharing her thoughts and fully benefiting from parental feedback.

This is when extra time and warm contact between child and parent can do a lot of good. If it's to your liking, offering the family bed can be very comforting for the young preschooler. If you choose to gently discourage your child from spending the night in your bed, consider suggesting long cuddles in your bed each morning. This is an opportunity to open the door for helpful conversation. Without pushing, offer gentle invitations to talk about your mutual loss. Without distractions, children with language difficulties are most apt to comprehend what they hear and express what they are thinking and feeling. And wrapped in the comfort of your arms, your child can best integrate the myriad emotions surrounding the loss of a loved one.

The whole class was gathered in a circle around the body of their hamster, which had died that morning. They were sharing fond memories of their beloved pet and preparing for the upcoming funeral and burial.

"How do we know that he's dead?" asked Claire.

"Things can't move when they're dead," Susan tells her friend.

Later, the teacher notices Claire prodding the dead hamster. When asked, Claire tells the teacher that she is "moving him so he will be alive again."

This is a poignant look into the mind of the preschooler. It is a great example of how different the brain of the young child is from the brain of an adult. Adults know that one of many criteria for "living" is the ability to move. We also know the difference between "moving" and "being moved," and that the latter is *not* a sign of life. Furthermore, we have a good grasp of cause and effect, a principle that guides all learning. Claire, on the other hand, is in the early stages of grappling with these complex notions, and her marvelously logical "mistakes" are the hallmarks of preschool intelligence.

Peter insists that his dead dog is coming back home as soon as she "finishes being dead." Is Peter unable to handle his grief? Is he in the throes of denial? Does he need to be in therapy? "No" to all three. Peter is thinking like a typical preschooler; he's missing a few concepts that will not be mastered until a bit later in development. He can't understand the finality of death. After all, Pooch has always returned from her absences.

Peter also can't yet grasp the profound differences between going to sleep and dying. Hasn't Pooch always arisen after bouts of lying still with her eyes closed? Don't we all wake up after sleeping through the night? And Peter, like all young children, lives both in the present and in the concrete. Hasn't everyone, or practically everyone, in his life remained constant so far? Haven't Mommy and Granny always come home from their outings?

The most appropriate strategy right now is to guide Peter through the death of his beloved Pooch without trying to make this into a lesson about the entire abstract subject of death. Remember, knowledge, for the young child, always moves from the specific to the general, never the other way around. Peter's understanding of the finality of death will come as he ages and integrates many experiences involving this ultimate loss. This first experience can be an important foundation for the future. Here are a few guidelines that may help.

A simple but clear acknowledgment that Pooch is dead and will *not* be getting up is a critical first step. This affords an excellent opportunity to let your child know that death and sleep are entirely different. Avoid making any allusions to death as rest or as the ultimate sleep; this would be extremely confusing and even scary. Try something along these lines with your son or daughter:

"Pooch is dead, Peter. That means that she won't ever be getting up. Her body has stopped working, forever. When she was sick last year, she had an operation and she got better. Before you were born, Pooch had cancer, and she got better from that, too. She won't be getting better now. She was very old and very, very sick, and that's why her body stopped working. I know how sad you are. I am very sad, too."

Once you have helped your child accept the finality of his pet's death, you can give him a truly wonderful gift that will last him a lifetime. You can teach him how to harness his grief and keep his dog in his heart forever. Talk about the wonderful times you had with Pooch. Talk about her terrific attributes. Look at photos. Write stories. Put her collar in a special place (perhaps the start of a box of treasures). Have a ceremony to share this time of sadness but also to share a celebration of Pooch.

Finally, if it fits with your traditions, I suggest having a burial. This concrete event does help children integrate and accept the finality of death. It is also the clearest of indicators that death and sleep are unrelated.

> Kris has come home from school and told her mother, "When you die you get to be an angel and fly in the sky." Furthermore, her buddy has also told her, "In heaven, God will be your teacher." These are not beliefs shared by Kris's family, and they wonder how to respond to their child's newfound ideas about death and the afterlife.

This is a thorny situation, but a few guiding principles will help you here. First, while adults other than parents might best steer clear of discussions about religion and politics, children need not. For grown-ups, issues of religion are filled with ethical, moral, and emotional content. For preschoolers, death and religion are much more matters of magic and curiosity. As a matter of fact, these topics, not unlike work, money, and race, are the preschooler's fodder for delightful, original, and thoughtful explorations about how the world operates.

Second, while death and religion are inextricably bound together for the adult, they are often separate and unrelated for the young child. Talking and thinking about death are ways in which the child comes to first realize his or her own mortality—a startling realization indeed. You can help ease any fear or upset by explaining the many years and stages your child has yet to go through.

So, what should you do when your child shares other people's views on death and religion? How about a simple, "Well, some people believe what Janeca thinks and some people have different ideas about what happens after you die. In our family, we believe that God is in your soul, but won't be your teacher in heaven. Some families believe that after you die you become an angel who can fly. We think that after you die you will not become a flying angel. It sounds like you and Janeca have some interesting talks about lots of things. Friends can believe different things and still be good friends."

Some Final Words

Change nudges us, sometimes even propels us, into new worlds, new relationships, and new conundrums. It's impossible to shelter a child from change. But without the stimulation of the unfamiliar, we would surely stagnate. Children are special beneficiaries of change. Each new experience, even those that are painful, is fodder for cognitive growth, emotional expression, physical development, and social expansion. So make the most of transitions and change, however painful they may be. Doing so will make your child stronger and more ready for the real world, which is always filled with transitions and change.

Suggestions for Further Reading

Adoption and Foster Care

Geraldine and Paul Blomquist. *Zachary's New Home: A Story for Foster and Adopted Children.* American Psychological Society, 1991.

Jolene Durrant. *Never Never Never Will She Stop Loving You.* JoBiz! Inc., 1999.

Randall Hicks. *Adoption Stories for Young Children.* Wordslinger Press, 1995.

Trish Maskew. *Our Own: Adopting and Parenting the Older Child.* Snowcap Press, 1999.

Fred Rogers. *Let's Talk About It: Adoption.* 1995.

Moving

Aliki. *We Are Best Friends.* William Morrow, 1987 (a friend moves).

Frank Asch. *Goodbye House.* Scott Foresman, 1989.

Judith Viorst. *Alexander, Who's Not (Do You Hear Me? I Mean It!) Going to Move.* Atheneum, 1995.

New Siblings

Alden Carter. *Big Brother Dustin.* Albert Whitman and Co., 1997.

Joanna Cole. *I'm a Big Brother/I'm a Big Sister.* William Morrow, 1997.

Different Kinds of Families

Bobbie Combs. *ABC: A Family Alphabet Book.* Two Lives Publishing, 2001 (same-sex parents).

Rosamund Elwin and Michele Paulse. *Asha's Mums.* Women's Press, 2000.

Rosmarie Hausherr. *Celebrating Families.* Scholastic, 1997.

Meredith Tax and Marilyn Hafner. *Families.* The Feminist Press at CUNY, 1992.

Divorce

Laurene and Marc Brown. *Dinosaurs Divorce: A Guide for Changing Families.* Little, Brown and Co., 1988.

Stephen Herman. *Parent vs. Parent: How You and Your Child Can Survive the Custody Battle.* 1990.

M. Gary Neuman. *Helping Your Kids Cope with Divorce the Sandcastles Way.* Random House, 1999.

Brigitte Weninger. *Good-bye Daddy!,* 1995.

Blended Families

Leslea Newman. *Saturday Is Pattyday.* New Victoria Publishers, 1993 (blended gay family).

Elaine Fantle Shimberg. *Blending Families: A Guide for Parents, Stepparents, and Everyone Building a Successful New Family.* Berkley Publishing Group, 1999.

Disability
Tricia Brown. *Someone Special, Just Like You.* Owlet, 1995.

Fred Rogers. *Extraordinary Friends.* Puffin Books, 2000.

Illness
Adrienne and Abigal Ackermann. *Our Mom Has Cancer.* American Cancer Society, 2001.

Claudia Mills. *Gus and Grandpa at the Hospital.* Econo-Clad Books, 2000.

Fred Rogers. *Going to the Hospital.* Paper Star, 1997.

Death
Adjoa Burrowes. *Grandma's Purple Flowers.* Lee & Low, 2000.

Earl Grollman. *Talking About Death: A Dialogue Between Parent and Child.* Beacon Press, 1991.

Michaelene Mundy. *Sad Isn't Bad: A Good-Grief Guidebook for Kids Dealing with Loss.* Abbey Press, 1998 (ages four to eight).

Photo by Richard Howard

Children and Parents as Learners

Photo by Sharon Flavellan

Home as the First School

Susan Steinsieck

An Eliot-Pearson teacher recently took her car in for a tune-up. In conversation with the mechanic, she told him a little about her work in the child development department. He excitedly began talking about his two-year-old daughter.

"I'm teaching her the alphabet. Is that all right?"

"Sure, it's all right—but there may be better things you can do with your two-year-old."

This thoughtful father was already concerned about the skills his two year old would need for school. But diving into the alphabet at age two is somewhat like jumping in at the deep end to learn how to swim. His daughter is having early literacy experiences just by connecting words to objects. When she says the word "bottle" as he hands it to her, or when she says "car" when they are in the garage together, her father can encour-

age her understanding of the importance of words—in a much more natural way—simply by acknowledging these events. He can say: "That's
right! It's a car!" Or, if he wants to extend the conversation a bit further,
he can say, "That's right, honey, it *is* a car. It's a big pink Cadillac car!"

Parents want to know that they are doing the "right thing." They
want to prepare their child for school in the best possible way. And it is
true that a child's ability to be enriched by new experiences, to explore
unfamiliar activities, and to interact with new people will be heightened
by what she's learned at home. But in wishing to help, parents may overlook the way their child learns.

Children are learning all the time. They learn through daily interactions with their parents, household, and community, and they learn
through their play. Children are interested in everything—they have a
large appetite for new experiences and activities. As a parent, you'll do
better to support your child in her natural mode of learning than to try to
teach specific academic tasks or offer expert-endorsed "learning experiences" that may not be appropriate for the child's age.

A well-meaning mother whose four-year-old daughter showed an
interest in music hired a singing teacher for her. But instead of teaching
the little girl to sing scales, as the mother had expected, the teacher sat
with the girl under a tree and let her sing whatever she wanted to sing—
which were the improvised songs of a four-year-old. The teacher encouraged the child to tell her *own* story with music. It is developmentally
appropriate to experiment with notes and words. Scales don't matter
when you are four.

In the natural course of listening to, observing, and interacting with
your child, you can support her sense of self—which is grounded in the
ability to express that self and communicate with the world. This means
helping her feel secure enough to detach a bit from you and explore. It
means listening to her and appreciating what she's doing—saying, "Tell
me about your picture," instead of "What's that supposed to be?" It
means observing what she's interested in and finding ways to support it;
if she likes to dance, keep the music playing. All of this builds the foundation for learning.

There's a lot of pressure now to push the kinds of learning appropriate to kindergarten or first grade down to younger and younger ages—perhaps because of parental insecurity and pride, boosted by marketing pressure. Sooner or later, there may be a backlash against this. But regardless of the trend, it's not appropriate to push reading and writing at three. Young children's preparation for formal schooling is anything but formal. In this chapter we will look at the best ways you can support your child's capacity to play and to learn.

- Laying a foundation for learning

- Promoting security and independence

- Meeting the neighborhood

- Building confidence

- Nurturing your child's intelligences and interests

- Outlets for, and building connections with, creative expression

- Creating a child's work/studio space

Laying the Foundation for Learning

Amelia was almost two years old. She was sitting on the basement floor, her legs straddling a piece of green construction paper. Next to the paper were three cups of paint: red, blue, and yellow.

"What color would you like, Amelia?" her aunt asked.

"Booooo (blue)," she said, her voice lilting, excited.

Amelia's aunt handed her a paintbrush. Amelia dipped it into the paint, looked at the color, and squealed, "Oooooh." She was excited to be changing the world, making a mark. She then gently, slowly moved the brush toward the paper. She made a tiny mark and looked at her aunt.

"Oh, Amelia, look, you made a mark!" Her aunt's voice was joyful and approving.

"Me made it," said Amelia.

"Yes, you did it, Amelia."

Amelia asked for "wed." This time she made circular marks on the paper with red paint.

"Circles, Amelia, you're going 'round and 'round," said her aunt.

"Wound and wound," the child said with glee.

Amelia's aunt gave the child the opportunity to enjoy the sensory experience of painting, and then a sense of accomplishment for every mark she made. When Amelia made a circle, her aunt gave her the words for her achievement. Amelia understood that she had made a "shape," and was thrilled. The interest and delight you share with a child make her feel that trying new things—learning—is interesting and delightful.

Recently, Sam, who is three and a half years old, was watching his mother make letter pancakes. When he asked her what letter she was making, she said, "Why don't you guess, Sam?"

Sam frowned and said, "I don't want to guess. I'm not good at guessing, and I might get it wrong."

His mother told him that's why they call it a guess. "Sometimes you're right and sometimes you're wrong, Sam. And you learn something, and it's no big deal."

Sam relaxed his brow and smiled. He seemed relieved.

His mother was making sure not that Sam knew a particular letter, but that it was safe for him to *try* to know which letter it was. She was telling him that it was safe to make a "mistake." Amelia's aunt and Sam's mother may not realize that they are getting these children ready for school, but indeed they are. *A curious child who is interested in learning and is able to take risks is ready for school.* Think of some of the qualities teachers hope to see in their new students:

- Teachers want children to feel safe enough to be free to explore.

- They want children to form meaningful relationships with peers and with teachers.

- They want children to be willing to experiment with new materials.

How can a parent encourage the development of these qualities?

- If you are emotionally available and responsive to your child, it helps him feel secure; that security enables him to be independent at school.

- If you realize that everyday events can be learning experiences, you can be "curious" together and encourage your child's love of learning.

- If you show your child how to behave in the world—on daily outings to the store, library, bank, and such—you encourage his sense of himself as an individual who is also part of a community.

- If you recognize and support your child's interests and respect his learning style, you promote his confidence and self-esteem as a learner.

All of these help prepare a child for a fulfilling and successful experience in preschool or kindergarten. While attending preschool is not a must, it does give a child a chance to socialize (practicing sharing, negotiating, taking turns, having jobs) and it exposes her to new creative materials, as well as offering chances to work on her fine and gross motor coordination—which will serve her well in kindergarten.

Security and Independence

Amelia, now age two, was playing with a mound of sand. At first her mother played with her, filling a plastic mold with sand and upending it carefully on top of the mound. Then she stayed very near as Amelia patted the mound—changing its shape, smoothing it out, changing its texture.

A child who feels secure can be independent. Encouraging your child's independence, that sense of herself as a person who is able to do things alone, is best accomplished in steps. You need to observe your child, to get a sense of when she is ready to play and explore independently, as Amelia's mother did one day when they were at the beach.

Amelia's mother was cooperating with her child, not interfering. First she showed Amelia how to play with the sand, but without expecting Amelia to specifically "mold" it in the plastic container. She allowed Amelia to pat the sand and experience it as she wished to, encouraging Amelia's self-confidence. When she felt the child was ready, she gradually drew back and let Amelia shape the sand "alone." At the same time, she was available in case Amelia needed her. Amelia didn't ask her mother for help. She perceived herself as able to "make her mark" upon the physical world through her own actions.

The child who feels loved and safe at home will have the easiest time exploring the school environment and all it has to offer. She trusts her parents, and that sense of trust extends outward to the rest of the world. This lets her relate to others more easily and encourages her to take social risks.

Of course, the school experience is different from having a loving parent close by and available when the child feels the need for more security and less independence. School, at least initially, is an unfamiliar environment, filled with strangers. The shifting balance between security and independence may well be upset, and the child may be clingy and fearful at school, or bad-tempered at home. Teachers know that separation from parents can be difficult for young children, and they have various strategies to help you and your child make the transition into the school experience. (See chapter 12 for more on the transition to school.)

Learning in the Neighborhood

Sam, three and a half, was in New York City with his father. They loved to walk around the city together. On their way to the pizza parlor they bumped into Officer Sheehan, a policeman Sam's father knows. Sam's father introduced Sam to the officer, saying, "Shake his hand, Sam, and look him in the eye. People like it when you look them in the eye."

The three of them chatted for a while, and then Sam and his father went about their errands, buying stamps and mailing letters. At the pizza parlor, as they devoured their own hot, delicious slices, they watched the chefs twirling the pizza dough in the air.

What a relief for a parent to know that many moments in the course of a day, involving tasks of daily life, can be rich opportunities of joy and learning for a child. All the parent needs to do is be *available* and *responsive*. Our errands are ripe with opportunities to teach social skills.

For example, the chance meeting with Officer Sheehan was a "teachable moment," as Sam's father told him to look in the policeman's eye when he spoke to him—and especially because Officer Sheehan responded warmly. (Note that in some cultures, this lesson would be different, because adult-child eye contact would not be interpreted the same way.)

When Sam's father shows Sam how to behave with others in their community, he is extending his son's experience, and making the neighborhood into a "village": *a place where Sam feels safe because he knows how to interact with others, and because he has a sense of belonging.* The way a parent says good morning to a neighbor, thank you to the person who bags the groceries, and engages in conversation with workers at the hardware store all show young children how to behave in the world.

For a child, everything is new and exciting; even those moments that seem most mundane to an adult can be extraordinary to a child. With the hectic pace of many parents' schedules, maintaining a feeling of collaboration with their child can be a challenge. But even a weary adult needs to remember that for the child, it can be fun to shop for cereal or to mail a letter.

Most two- and three-year-old children have a short attention span, so long shopping trips tend to be challenging. Also, some children don't like not knowing what's going to happen next. Telling your child you are going to the grocery store—preparing him for the experience with specific details—can make him feel more secure than facing the unknown unprepared. Even details like "We are going to buy milk, bread, vegetables, fruit, and chicken" can help.

While you're shopping, you can repeat the items: "Here we are, in aisle one getting the bread." This also helps him start to understand the beginning (making a list and going to the store), middle (shopping in each aisle, checking out), and end (putting groceries away) of a process—which in turn, encourages interest in stories and books.

Of course some children are perfectly content not knowing what comes next; the unknown is just a new adventure. Either way, it is still important for a young child to be a valued participant in these daily experiences and not just be dragged along. The older child, age four to six, can be more involved in your shopping trip. Ask him to think of things he usually eats—cereal, bananas, yogurt, applesauce—and put them on a list. He can make good use of whatever writing and drawing skills he has to make his own list. At the store, he can identify an item, take it off the shelf, and place it in the cart. You can acknowledge these actions and let your child know that he's making a contribution. He can feel helpful and competent.

Building Confidence and a Sense of Importance

Karen fondly remembers making *koofta*—Armenian meatballs—at age five with her Armenian grandmother. The adult meatballs were big, perfectly round, stuffed with a spicy mixture, and very tricky to make. Grandma never spoke much—her English was poor—but Karen remembers the little sound she'd make when she was satisfied with her work: "Heh!"

Karen helped with the children's meatballs, which were smaller and without stuffing. Karen rolled the meat into little balls, then pinched them between her thumb and forefinger. "Heh!" Grandma would say when she saw Karen's meatballs.

Some of our best childhood memories are of times when we felt important to someone. We didn't have to be on an extraordinary outing or special vacation. What we remember are the times that parents or relatives had us very much in mind, or times we were simply "doing stuff together." Most of us can recall moments from our childhood when we were helped to feel extraordinary.

Karen's grandparents were immigrants, survivors of the Armenian holocaust. They had little formal education. They lived on the second floor of a tenement in Providence, Rhode Island, near a small park. Grandma would take Karen to the park and sit on a bench while Karen played by herself; sometimes Karen played hockey with other children in the park.

Back at the apartment, Grandpa and Karen put on magic shows for Grandma. Grandpa held up a blanket and Karen hid behind it. Then Grandpa said, "Ladies and gentlemen, velcome to de show. Vatch me mek Karen deesapeer!" At this point Karen ran into another room while Grandma cried out, "Ver is Karen? Ver is she?" When Grandpa made Karen "reappear," Grandma was so surprised and relieved!

Alfred, a sculptor in his midfifties, still remembers the puppet shows he used to put on for his family. "My relatives would come. It made me feel good that they wanted to watch. And when I was sick once, I made pots of paper flowers. People would buy them. Making something that someone wanted was important.

"Sometimes I rearranged the living-room furniture, making a little cave out of the sofa cushions and crawling inside to get cozy and secure. My parents would let me do it as long as I cleaned up after. That was important, to feel responsible.

"When my parents weren't working, we'd go on outings, pack a picnic or go to the beach. I think they actually worked harder when they were on vacation, doing things with us."

These seemingly ordinary childhood experiences are recalled decades later with feelings of great warmth. They illustrate how everyday acknowledgments can help support the self-esteem and confidence a child needs to make the transition from the home into the larger world.

Grandma's little "heh" of approval for Karen's meatballs, her presence on the park bench while Karen played, the magic shows where she disappeared—and reappeared to cries of joy—were simple interactions between Karen and her grandparents. The delight Alfred's family took in

his puppet shows and paper flowers encouraged his creativity; the freedom they gave him to rearrange the living room, and the responsibility
of putting everything back as it had been, expressed their trust in him, as
well as their acceptance of his desire to make a place for himself. Both
cases were almost routine expressions of adults enjoying a child's company. But to Karen and Alfred, even years later those memories are
tinged with magic.

Nurturing Intelligences and Interests

Most parents watch for and celebrate signs of their child's intelligence;
they hope she will be "smart" enough to do well in the world—or at least
to get along in the verbal, pencil-and-paper way that is valued by our
society. But math and language skills are only two kinds of intelligence:
"intelligence" being the ability to solve problems or create products
(from objects to ideas) that are socially valued. The psychologist and edu-
cator Howard Gardner has identified nine different kinds of intelligence,
and most people have a combination of them. (Some of Gardner's
research on intelligences was done with three- and four-year-olds at one
of our lab schools.)

Although a person's particular kinds of intelligence—their intellectual strengths—become more apparent as they get older, a young child's
strengths show through in what that child is most passionately interested in: that is, how she plays. A child's play is self-initiated learning; it
is the child's own intuitive quest for meaning.

Below is a list of Gardner's nine forms of intelligence, with examples
of how they might look in a young child:

1. *Linguistic—love of language and words:* the child likes to tell and
   listen to stories and loves being read to.

2. *Logical-mathematical—good with facts and numbers:* the child likes to
   count, to organize objects by size, or wants to know how the
   washing machine works.

3. *Musical—love of music and rhythm:* likes to sing and listen to music, remembers melodies with ease, or likes to beat on pots and pans.

4. *Spatial—has a sense of how things are situated in space:* likes to rearrange living-room furniture, may understand early that two triangles can make a square or the difference between a circle and a sphere; good at fitting shapes together to make other shapes.

5. *Bodily-kinesthetic—has an acute physical awareness of how his body moves through space:* he *must* move, whether in dancing, running, jumping, or simply mastering such skills as sitting down in a chair.

6. *Intrapersonal—understands her own moods and feelings:* knows exactly what she wants to do, or how she feels, and can express it.

7. *Interpersonal—understands other people's moods and feelings:* can mediate between other people who are fighting, or empathize with someone feeling sad.

8. *Naturalist—shows delight in caring for living things and an interest in nature:* brings home bugs and frogs as pets; notices that the bird needs birdseed and water; is interested in the seasons, in gardens and making things grow; recognizes different flowers, rocks, birds.

9. *Existential—interested in fundamental questions of existence, like life and death:* to some extent all young children are like this. Gardner himself calls this a "possible intelligence," in that it may be hard to recognize or pin down. (Albert Einstein, at age three, still had not said one word; he spent his time building houses out of playing cards.)

Most children are strong in more than one of these; they have combinations of strengths. Also, these intelligences aren't fixed: your child will have greater raw potential in, and quicker grasp of, certain subjects—but those areas need nurturing and training for that potential to be expressed. Finally, in real life, intelligences are rarely separate; multiple strengths work together to meet life's demands.

Our educational system stresses the first two forms of intellectual ability: language and logic/math. Recognizing a child's abilities in other areas allows parents to nurture their child's strengths, and therefore his problem-solving capabilities and ability to learn—and ultimately, his success in the real world. Also, Gardner's research suggests that we might draw on a child's strength in one area to help her learn more about another. If a child is not as strong in language or math, for example, as she is in music, parents and teachers can use music and rhythm in teaching those topics; similarly, a child with a good spatial sense might build models of math concepts. An imaginative child who needs work on physical coordination could be motivated to get up and move by making pretending or a story part of the activity.

Some of this crossover learning occurs quite naturally in children's play. Jump rope, for instance, where children chant rhymes and act them out while skipping over a spinning rope, strengthens literacy (with the chanting and acting out of the "story"), rhythm, coordination and balance, and cooperation with others (as it takes at least two other people to turn the rope while the third person jumps).

Parents and teachers can also foster this crossover learning. At the beginning of first grade, a six-year-old boy named Jonathan was convinced that he couldn't write. "I can't do it," was his response to making letters. When he made a beautiful clay dog, his teacher asked him about his creation, and Jonathan told her a long story about his dog. He became so interested in the story that he wrote it down himself; he made a book about a day in the life of his dog. He discovered an ability and interest in writing through his first love, which had been to make a big dog out of clay.

Small children need lots and lots of opportunities to express themselves, whether through drawing and painting, clay and modeling materials, collage, building with blocks or recycled materials, dancing and making up songs, or telling stories and acting them out. One reason for this is that they are not yet using formal symbol systems: letters, numbers, reading and writing.

Supporting your child's strengths starts with helping her feel good about the way she expresses herself and tells her stories. Don't tell a kid who's building an amazing bridge that she should focus on learning to write "bridge"—appreciate and encourage her "spatial" accomplishments. A parent who observes his child will know what she likes to do, whether or not he knows the name for her particular kind of intelligence. A parent who is responsive will be able to support his child's interests, and hear what she is saying.

By acting on their interests, children understand themselves and their world better. Try to provide more of what she likes: more water play, more colored paper and beautiful pencils, more types of construction or music-making materials. While reading to your child is critical, it's also passive: she listens as you read. It's just as important that you listen to your child, not just instruct her—and give her chances to construct her own knowledge.

One note of caution: Whatever goals you are working toward with your child, make sure she is enjoying the experience, and that it has some meaning to her. You can teach a young child who is drawing circles and scribbles to draw a face, but the experience will have no value *to the child* until she is developmentally ready to (and wants to) draw a face.

For a special-needs child, of course, the strategy is different; you will want to teach concepts and skills that he cannot understand without help and may never, on his own, be "interested" in. But even with special-needs children, you do best to begin from and follow the child's interests.

Outlets for Creative Expression

At two, Amelia is a very active little girl who needs ample opportunities to move her body in space (aka work with "bodily-kinesthetic" intelligence). Every day Amelia's mother gives her opportunities to "mess about" with a variety of materials that interest her, and to explore her environment through movement or dramatic play.

A recent self-initiated challenge was to hang from a bar at the playground, a mere two inches off the ground. She'd hang for a minute, then drop to the ground, pleased with the physical sensation. Amelia did this over and over again. Repetition was her way to gain mastery of the task. She also likes to hold objects above her head—a straw basket, stuffed animal, or small stool—and then slowly lower the object behind her until it drops.

All children are creative in some way. Very young children, who have not learned formal academic subjects with their right and wrong answers, are most in touch with their creativity. Creative expression is the way a child makes sense of the world outside and the world inside, and reconciles the two. Creativity is the way a child expresses feelings and thoughts, and tries to communicate them. In creative play, children tell their stories and learn to speak in their own voices.

No one knows your child better than you do. Watch what your child gravitates toward, what activities and materials he likes to use, and then make sure those things are available to him.

Basically, children express themselves in one or more of three different ways:

- Two-dimensional, or mark making, which includes painting and drawing with various tools.

- Three-dimensional, or model building, with clay, wood, blocks, etc.

- Storytelling/dramatic play, as in some form of "let's pretend": we're firemen, we're horses, we're a mother and a father. Singing (and thus music) is part of storytelling and dramatic play; children often sing to themselves and one another as they act out their stories. And children sing to themselves all the time, sometimes wordlessly, as a mode of storytelling.

As another way of exploring the world with her body, Amelia is eager for tactile, or "hands-on" experience. She especially likes toys that offer opportunities for filling-emptying, opening-shutting, fitting in, and just plain "messing about": measuring cups and water, pots with lids, or small and large plastic containers. Amelia says "need Pay-Doh" and her mother gives her the container; she likes to try to take the Play-Doh out herself. "Skeez," she says as she squeezes it heartily with her little hand, her face pink with the effort.

Amelia also "tells her stories" by acting them out. By dressing up in different outfits, she becomes fantasy characters: Rapunzel or Cinderella; or she may explore daily role models: being a mommy serving tea to her doll while she sings, "Here we go, my little queen."

> Three-year-old Marco loved to build. One day, Marco's mother asked him and his friend Lee to draw circles. Lee drew many lines curving around the page. Marco drew a circle, put down his marker, and walked away. He had no interest in expressing himself in only two dimensions.

Amelia showed a beginning love for storytelling and dramatic play. In contrast, Marco showed his love and flair for three-dimensional creations. He often came out of preschool empty-handed when other children carried drawings or paintings. He was more interested in building intricate LEGO constructions and block towers.

Marco was encouraged to express his interest with three-dimensional materials at home and at school. If he wanted a lump of clay (or Play-Doh) with his egg in the morning, it was there. On outings, Marco carried a portable case of LEGOs. He also organized his own kits that he kept in plastic briefcases (once containing Transformer parts or a doctor kit). These kits held tools like Popsicle sticks, plastic spoons, toothpicks, sponges, wire, and a (not so sharp) knife. Marco loved organizing and using these tools.

Marco used three-dimensional materials in much the same way that another child might use paper and crayons. He made a clay pancake and added texture and pattern not by drawing on the surface, but by sticking

other objects into his pancake. He organized shapes, marking and stacking them, and finally produced recognizable forms, such as a dinosaur, a
car, or a cave.

Asking a child about his creation is another way to listen to him and
make him feel that his creation is valuable. Instead of saying, "What is
that?," say, "Tell me about that," because it might not "be" anything, in
the usual adult sense. To allow the child to tell you in his own words
leaves him free to do so.

Sometimes children don't want to tell adults what they're doing, but
it's still best to ask and show an interest. One preschool teacher noticed
her five-year-olds playing a game they called "wolf-dogs and kitty-
cats"—wherein all the boys were wolf-dogs and had swords and all the
girls were kitty-cats fleeing from the wolf-dogs. She asked one boy to tell
her about their game. He replied, with a swish of his imaginary sword,
that it was nothing; he was only "cutting up strawberries" with his
sword!

We all have the ability and need for creative expression, but for many
of us it gets lost along the way. Drawing, singing, and dancing get
pushed aside by more formal and "important" pursuits. This motivated
the creation of a graduate course we teach at Tufts University on child art
for grown-ups. It's become quite popular. Some students are from the
museum school, and want a better understanding of child development.
Others are future teachers, who realize that they need to reconnect with
this part of themselves in order to create meaningful activities for children.

To take away any pressure to "do it right," students draw with shoe
polish and coffee, Vaseline and grape juice. They talk about creative
experiences they had when they were younger. One man, a doctor, wrote
and illustrated a book for children that he could take on the ward, about
what it means to be in a hospital.

Exploring your own creativity can open up new dimensions in your
relationship with your child. As well as encouraging children in their
chosen creative expression, you can share your interests with them, and
inspire new ones. For example, in one kindergarten classroom, the teach-

ers showed a video of *Singing in the Rain* to their five- and six-year-olds. Then they taped pennies to the bottom of the children's shoes, and the whole class tap-danced down the long halls throughout the school, singing and pretending to be Gene Kelly or Debbie Reynolds—disrupting every other class in the building, but having a wonderful time.

BUILDING CONNECTIONS THROUGH CREATIVE EXPRESSION

Greg had trouble expressing himself in words and joining other children's play. He dealt with his anger by kicking or knocking over others' work. After sitting apart on a bench to calm down, he would come back and do it again.

Sometimes young children's interests surprise and dismay us, as when themes of war, aggression, and power emerge. Yet interest in these subjects is part of the child's exploration of her place in the world. One first-grade teacher used this interest in combat among some members of her classroom to create math and literacy activities with multiple toy soldiers. Children counted, sorted, and strategized, then recorded their experiences. If a child is learning to manage challenging social situations through compromising and negotiating, or obtaining adult support when needed, then an interest in issues of power is no need for alarm. (See chapter 8 for more on war play.)

In Greg's case, parent-teacher support of his interests—his intellectual strengths and preferred creative expression—led him out of a dead-end cycle of behavior problems at school.

Greg's preschool teacher said that he enjoyed "tinkering with materials like a watchmaker." When Greg reached kindergarten at age five, his intricate work and patience with materials and tools stood in contrast to his penchant for roughness on the playground—which was a concern to his parents and teachers.

At school, Greg loved to use clay. At home, he expressed an interest in coins. His father brought him to school one day with a book about the history of money. This simple act of support of Greg's interests—along with a home/school connection—helped launch Greg on an investigation that lasted the school year. Greg carefully made hundreds of coins out of clay, of all different shapes and sizes, with beautiful markings. He traded his coins with friends, and even taught other children how to make the coins—a much better way to relate to them than pummeling them on the playground. He also arranged his coins by size, supporting his emerging math skills, and proudly took his work home. By seeing that people valued his ideas, and being given materials that suited his needs, Greg was able to connect with the other children over his chosen interest. It helped him.

When his parents invited the teacher for a visit, she found that they had set up a table in their home that beautifully displayed Greg's work with clay coins that year, along with a photo of Greg skateboarding, his other passion. The parents acknowledged their appreciation for Greg's work by displaying it with such attention and respect, and validated their child as a person of importance in the world.

As a four-year-old boy recently arrived in America from Japan with his mother, Yoshi did not speak much English. He was enrolled in a pre-school that encouraged creative expression with diverse materials. Although he was withdrawn because of his inability to speak English, the teacher soon discovered Yoshi loved to draw. Every day he would sit quietly drawing his favorite Japanese cartoon characters, Fujiyama (a volcano in Japan), and other things native to his homeland. The teacher shared his drawings with the rest of the class, and his classmates wanted Yoshi to teach them how to draw those things, too. Through his artwork Yoshi was able to connect with the other children and he quickly made many friends.

Yoshi drew everything: the birds on a poster in the classroom, his own copy of the weather chart used at school, all of the cartoon characters he saw in America, and ones he remembered from Japan. He copied letters, observed nature, remembered experiences, and drew them. Yoshi always carried a little notebook and a pencil in his pocket. When his mother or teachers took him to museums or aquariums, he carried a clipboard and pencil attached with a string. These drawings were not only a means of expression but also a social tool, as the teachers gave him opportunities to share them with the group. Without needing English words, Yoshi could communicate with classmates and adults through his drawings.

Amelia, Marco, Greg, and Yoshi—whether using mark making, model building, or dramatic play—discovered, and were encouraged to use, their chosen outlets for creative expression, for telling their stories and communicating them. Fortunately, people were listening.

Organizing a Work/Studio Space

Amelia lives in a four-room apartment with her parents. In her room there's a bed, a changing table, a chest of drawers, a bookshelf, and a small couch. Under the changing table, her mother has stored Amelia's box of plain wooden blocks.

About twenty beloved board books, which are read again and again, are on the bookshelf. Each night, Amelia "reads" (with one of her parents) several books, which are propped up on the back of the couch.

Amelia works at the kitchen table. Markers, crayons, paper, glue, tape, paint, and Play-Doh are kept on top of the refrigerator; sometimes Amelia asks for them, and sometimes they are offered to her.

At two, access to a wide variety of materials is daunting and can lead to chaos. Amelia's parents are beginning to give her access and limited choice, such as between the blocks and markers. Toys are in plastic boxes in the living room, and her mother might say, "Would you like the tea set or wooden fruit, Amelia?"

Making a studio space for your child at home is another good way to prepare him for school. It lets him explore ways to play with different materials, and teaches organizational skills.

You don't need to live in a mansion to make a workspace for your child. Whether the child has his own room, shares a room, or has a desk or a shoe box, it is important for him to have some special space where his things are kept. (This lets him know where to find things, making the experience less frustrating, and teaches him that part of caring for his materials is putting them away where they belong.) As in school, there should be a special work area, even if it's just the kitchen table. If you have room, it can be fun to build a workspace together.

When introducing materials to your child, start small: for instance, with crayons and markers and one size of good heavy paper. (To help two-year-olds, who may have trouble putting lids back on markers, you can fill a tin can with plaster of paris and put the markers, top down, into it as it dries. Then the child just has to aim the marker at its top, which the hardened plaster of paris will hold steady for her.) When the child has mastered those materials, you can add new ones—such as different sizes of paper, hole punches, scissors, Scotch tape, stickers, paint, clay—a little at a time.

To give a child too many new materials all at once is overwhelming. Children are empowered by being given the chance to choose. The choice between two toys or activities is a good starting point toward being able to make choices from a wider variety of materials. In the course of trying out different materials, the child's natural leaning toward one or the other will become obvious, and you can then make sure that she has what she needs.

When a child is ready to have access to his tools and toys, it is helpful to have an organized way of keeping and storing these materials. Clear containers are pleasing and convenient ways to store smaller materials. A child can label the containers with letters, words, or pictures, and see what's inside. The drawing/writing box can hold different markers, erasers, glue, scissors, stencils, rulers, and papers. A modeling box can hold Play-Doh and clay (a piece of plywood makes a good work surface) plus some Popsicle sticks. A science box might hold found natural objects, a magnifying glass, tweezers, an eyedropper, and a little bug box.

For dramatic play, put together a dress-up box. The box of dress-up clothes in Amelia's bedroom holds some hats, old skirts and blouses, a vest, scarves, shoes, and a dress or two. Check a secondhand store or a fabric store. A large square of satin or velvet, for example, can serve as a royal cape or a magic carpet.

At around age five, a child may keep a "word" box, writing down words she has begun to read: "a," "the," "cat," her name, and the names of family and friends. You can start by putting in words that your child dictates; later, she can write them herself—with the option to ask for help with spelling. Collections kept in boxes become great math experiences: sorting and classifying pebbles, and counting plastic milk lids or bread-bag fasteners.

Acknowledging the child's work and world can be done by displaying artwork and photographs, as Greg's parents did. Often, young children are learning from the process of doing, which does not culminate in a final product. Making patterns with different-colored stones, pouring water through a funnel for the first time, or putting some groceries in the cart are examples. A photograph is a way to record the significance of these tactile experiences and of important people in the child's life, and can be revisited by parent and child and shared with others.

With a child's artwork, a parent can encourage language development and gain a deeper understanding of a child's intentions by asking, "Would you like to tell me about it?" and then writing the child's words under the drawing, painting, or sculpture. Children can sign their own names and sound out words when they are ready to experiment with writing.

The Sissamagona Fact Book

Sissamagonas sometimes have streaky wings. They sometimes even look smudged. Sissamagonas are at the top of the food chain. Sissamagonas live on clouds. To Sissamagonas, surfing is bathing. Sissamagonas don't sleep.

The Sissamagona Book was a gift from a five-year-old kindergartner, Mary, to her teacher at the end of the school year. This extraordinary piece of work could only have been created with support from Mary's home environment.

Mary was a quiet girl at school. She made just one special friend in a classroom of over twenty children and was much more interested in her stuffed dinosaurs than in the classroom curriculum. She was very competent with a variety of art materials. To encourage Mary to express herself socially and with materials, her mother and teacher worked together. Katie, her friend from school, began having playdates with Mary, first at Mary's house, then at Katie's. Both girls had special stuffed animals that traveled with them—Leppy, Katie's stuffed leopard, and Mary's assortment of dinosaurs. The girls engaged in hours of dramatic play with their animals.

Both at home and at school, Mary had access to plenty of art materials; she had a ministudio in her playroom with pencils, markers, scissors, glue, and paper. At school and at home, Mary painted, sculpted, and drew her dinosaurs. She eventually invented the Sissamagona, a tiny dragonlike creature. In the above example, you can see some "facts" that Mary wrote about her invented character.

Mary's book richly expresses her skills in writing, organization, and thoughtful detailed drawings. It shows her ability to focus and to remain on task, and a respect for her own imaginative power.

Some Final Words

The foundation of support at home for the young child is a warm, loving environment and respect for the child's intuitive methods of learning and being in the world. Her belief in herself is developed through absorbing experiences: building, playing, exploring, and just being with her family; and by her ability to communicate: through her interests, the stories she sings and tells, the things she makes, and the questions she asks.

Creative play is how a child "makes something" of the world. The parent can foster the child's work by responding with interest and by providing materials and experiences that allow him to tell his story. In this way the parent builds a bridge from the curious learner at home to the absorbed student in the school setting. A child who can express himself, and who knows that he is heard, has confidence in himself as a special individual, and as someone who can learn.

The play of a young child is not separate from learning. Creativity is an expression of intelligence and a method of learning.

Suggestions for Further Reading

Thomas Armstrong. *In Their Own Way: Discovering and Encouraging Your Child's Multiple Intelligences.* Tarcher, 2000.

Marie Clay. *Writing Begins at Home: Preparing Children for Writing Before They Go to School.* Heinemann, 1988.

Marian Diamond and Janet Hopson. *Magic Trees of the Mind : How to Nurture Your Child's Intelligence, Creativity, and Healthy Emotions from Birth Through Adolescence.* E. P. Dutton, 1998.

Trish Kuffner. *The Preschooler's Busy Book.* Meadowbrook Press, 1998.

Vivian Gussin Paley. *The Boy Who Would Be a Helicopter: The Uses of Storytelling in the Classroom.* Harvard University Press, 1991.

———. *The Girl with the Brown Crayon: How Children Use Stories to Shape Their Lives.* Harvard University Press, 1998.

———. *Wally's Stories: Conversations in the Kindergarten.* Harvard University Press, 1987.

Fretta Reitzes and Beth Teitelman. *Wonderplay : Interactive and Developmental Games, Crafts, and Creative Activities for Infants, Toddlers, and Preschoolers from the 92nd Street Y Parenting Center.* Running Press, 1995.

CHAPTER EIGHT

Not Just Fooling Around:
Supporting Your Child's Play

W. George Scarlett

Evan, age two and a half, wanted nothing to do with car washes. Over the weekend he had been obviously upset and scared as he sat in the backseat while his mother's car made its way through a car wash. All the swishing and confined space had brought him almost to tears.

But several days later, Evan began building a car wash with his set of blocks. He carefully reconstructed the tunnel, then placed blocks to represent brushes. After finishing constructing, he slowly had his Matchbox cars make their way through the tunnel and out the other side—all the while keeping a very serious expression on his face.

Given the opportunity, young children play: with sticks and sand or expensive model sets. This fact alone should indicate something important happens in play. As Evan's story suggests, children can use play to make sense of the world, and to deal with their emotions.

Denny and Will, energetic four-year-old best friends, play on the floor with blocks—each doing his own thing, but keeping track of what the other is doing. Denny announces, "I'm building a humongous cave!"

Will responds, "I'm making a building for dinosaurs."

"Dinosaurs don't live in buildings," objects Denny. "They live in humongous caves."

"Well, my dinosaurs live in a building."

This friendly disagreement goes back and forth until Denny suggests that dinosaurs live in both caves and buildings. The two start work to connect their structures.

At first glance, this scene may not suggest much about the value of play. But these two boys are exercising newfound abilities to make and use symbols. Also, their disagreements seem to bind them together, not drive them apart, as they pool their imagination to create a fantasy world together. Perhaps there is more to play's role in cognitive and social development than meets the eye.

Our experiences with children in the Eliot-Pearson community, along with careful observations by educators, clinicians, and researchers, reveal a rich intellectual, social, and emotional life in play. What's more, playing well as a young child—building with blocks like Will and Denny, drawing elaborate pictures, or creating detailed fantasy worlds— is associated with better social and academic development later on. But play also has clear benefits in the here and now. In play, you see your child's mind at work. You see her express, make sense of and control her emotions, and make healthy connections to others. Play helps your child thrive.

In this chapter, we'll explore the value of play for children, and address common questions about how best to support healthy play. We'll cover:

- *The value of play:*
  - using play to make sense of the world
  - using dolls, blocks, and art materials to construct, be creative, and develop the ability to symbolize
  - using play to manage emotions and wishes

- **Supporting your child's constructive play** *(including how to play with your preschooler)*

- *Play and your child's social life*

- *Common concerns about play:*
  - war toys and violent themes
  - "girl" and "boy" toys
  - imaginary playmates
  - computers and electronic play

- **Sports and outdoor play** *(including concerns about coached sports for young children)*

What Children Get Out of Play

> Michael, almost three, is fascinated with vacuum cleaners. His idea of a great day is going to the shopping mall to visit a display of vacuums and pushing each one in turn across the carpet.
>
> One day, he turned to a little girl nearby, saying, "I like vacuums. Do you like vacuums?"
>
> "Yes!" she replied.

As a small child, you're surrounded by newness and bombarded by interesting stuff that is barely intelligible. How do you begin to understand all of this? Among other things, you study and explore those fascinating objects, the way an adult might swirl a new wine around the glass, admire its color, and let its taste linger on her tongue. One use of play is to make sense of the world, to slow it down and savor it at an understandable pace. When you're two feet high and have little experience and nothing approaching adult competence—Can you drive a car? Cook a meal? Open a can?—play lets you take a little control. Instead of feeling helpless, bewildered, and frustrated, you can manipulate big vacuum cleaners or become a gigantic dinosaur.

One way to become a true believer in the value of play is to watch how play develops over time. But observing this is tricky because play develops differently in different media: doll play, block play, drawing, and so on have their own special line of development.

Also, children start playing with these kinds of toys at different times. For example, play with dolls usually begins very early, shortly after the first year. Play with blocks usually begins several months later, and play with markers and paper starts later still. The point here is not to dictate an ideal sequence; when children play, and with what, depends as much on individual interests as on age and stage. Rather, the point is that getting started is easy in some media and more difficult in others.

SYMBOLIC PLAY: A DEVELOPMENTAL MILESTONE

Once children begin playing with different media, they usually spend time exploring how these work. For example, when children start drawing, they figure out how to make different kinds of marks: dots, spirals, scrawls, curvy lines, and such. This experimentation prepares the way for an exciting milestone in your child's development: the use of play to *symbolize* or represent. In symbolic play, children take images or fantasies in their heads and represent them in concrete visual form. Dolls, blocks, markers and paper, and a host of other materials now become a means to enact or depict family life, hospital emergencies, and space combat with alien life-forms.

Symbolic play provides children with a powerful tool for thinking, for relating to others, and for mastering feelings. Think of how limited your understanding of the world would be without the aid of symbols: signs, words, gestures, pictures. Think, too, how central symbols are to forming relationships and expressing feelings. Without symbols, you would be confined to grunts and pointing, and your emotional life would resemble an infant's.

With symbolic play also comes the ability to *consolidate* knowledge obtained outside of play. For example, we knew one little boy who became fascinated with American wars before the twentieth century through books, museum visits, movies, and holiday pageants. Without play, Garth would have been lost in a sea of information. But with play, he could take the information fed to him and use it with toy soldiers, bridges made from blocks, and a host of other play props. In the process of playing, Garth consolidated what he'd learned and became remarkably knowledgeable about early American history, even before the age of four!

Of course, not every child needs to become a minihistorian. The point here is about play's role in helping children make sense of and integrate information that would otherwise be forgotten. The information may be about wars, how pies get cooked, or Tyrannosaurus rex; it really doesn't matter. What does matter is that in their rich, symbolic play, young children orient themselves in the world, make their world less strange and more predictable, and develop that crucial capacity to symbolize.

Symbolizing in play begins simply and concretely. Sometime during the second year, toddlers usually play by representing familiar events: going to sleep, ironing clothes, eating ice cream, and so forth. In fact, for the next year, children's play remains fairly realistic. But from two and a half on, play becomes more and more fanciful: doll play depicts imaginary worlds; block play creates scenes not found in the neighborhood; and drawings show both everyday life and life that is hardly everyday. Play develops, then, to the extent that it increasingly represents not just the real world, but unreal, imagined worlds as well.

You can watch for these developments in your own child's play. (We focus on dolls, blocks, and drawing not because they are essential toys, but to show how different media offer different opportunities and challenges.)

> Three-year-old Rose says to her buddy Jenn, who has climbed laboriously into the doll crib along with her Raggedy Ann, "Silly Jenn, this is a pretend baby room, not a real baby room. Get out of that crib—you're squashing her!"

Doll play provides a wonderful means for children to develop a *dramatic frame,* to help them make sense of the many real-life dramas around them. This dramatic frame develops slowly. At first, a child's dolls are passive: they may be fed, put to bed, or held tightly, but they never appear to act on their own. As the child grows, dolls become actors in small dramas; they face problems and resolve them, seemingly through the doll's own initiative and skill—at least, that's the illusion created through imagination. And in time, dolls take their place alongside other characters in full-blown make-believe story worlds.

One of the great paradoxes here (expressed so well by Rose) is that learning to separate fantasy from reality allows children to create believable fantasy worlds—not unlike a good writer of fiction. And just as the more talented writers often have greater insight into the workings of the real world, the child with a flair for creating fantastic worlds in doll play generally has a better grasp of reality.

> When tucking in four-year-old Flavia one night, Mom noticed six wooden blocks stashed under the covers. When asked about them, Flavia replied, "I'm going to build a house for my dreams."

Block play goes through a similar evolution: from something to stack to a tool for symbolizing. While dolls offer opportunities to represent stories, blocks let children represent structures—structures with specific, recognizable contours and space, that we give names to, such as "house," "fort," and "bridge." When we say blocks, we mean the plain wooden blocks sometimes referred to as "unit blocks" that come in standard sizes and shapes; just about every early childhood program has them, and ideally, so does your home.

Just as stories come late in early childhood, so, too, do complex block structures. Early on, around the age of two, children show more interest in stacking blocks up to knock them down than they do in building structures. And when they do start building, the final structures don't look like anything that has a name.

Between three and four, children who are into blocks often produce structures with recognizable contours and space, but building usually occurs along two dimensions only (e.g., a block wall). After four, children can create block structures that have height, width, and depth. From then on, blocks become a wonderful medium to represent the world.

Perhaps more important, blocks are now a means to create props and scenes that ground children's fantasies: a block mountain and block bridge form the setting for a battle, or a block ship provides the center-piece for a maritime disaster. After four, actions become a focus in block building, but unlike the earlier, real action of knocking over stacks of blocks, the actions now are just pretend—such as calling out battle instructions from a built fort, and manipulating dolls inside a built house.

> When her dad says, "Can you tell me about your painting?" four-year-old Shani responds, "It's colorful, colorful, colorful—more than where we live, or even in your brain!"

Markers and paper offer opportunities to represent objects and scenes with precise shapes and colors: the family dog chasing a stick, a *Star Wars* battle, a girl on a swing. As we noted earlier, drawing starts out as mark-ings, not symbols, but these markings soon become organized into designs: perhaps an interesting curvy line marking the right border of the paper, a scrawl on the lower left, and a circular shape or two in the middle.

Between three and four, many children use what they have learned in creating lines and shapes to create *schematic drawings*. These are more like cartoons of people, animals, and objects than they are pictures faithful to reality. One or two features of an object can stand for the whole. This is the time of the "tadpole" figure: a single oval counts for both body and head, with lines serving as limbs and hair. Stick figures and solid figures come later. Increasingly, drawing becomes realistic, and persons, animals, and objects appear not only alone but also in scenes. (See chapter 7 for more on children's art.)

These examples make clearer the important role of play in children's development. We've emphasized symbol making because in early child-hood, that's what's most valuable about play. However, *action-based,* rough-and-tumble play is valuable as well. It's not only important for physical development—research suggests that action-based play in early childhood can help with friendships later on, especially for boys. Symbolic play and action-based play are important, too, in the development of gender identity (more on these later).

EXPRESSING FEELINGS AND WISHES THROUGH PLAY

The waiting room is full of toys: doctor, nurse, and patient dolls, plastic syringes and other medical apparatus, a small plastic hospital, a toy ambulance—along with young children anxiously anticipating (or remembering) getting shots.

While the youngest children cling to their parents, a few older preschoolers laugh and play: "I'm Dr. Brown. It's time for your shot. Hold still!"

"Here is your medicine. You have to take it every day until you're better."

"He's going in the ambulance. He needs an operation fast!"

The children seem to like taking the doctor's role best.

These older preschoolers have found in their play a way to control or master difficult emotions related to the hospital scene. Where reality places them in a vulnerable, passive position (getting shots, taking bad-tasting medicine), play places them in control. Play, then, becomes a way for children to take care of their emotions—a step up from relying on others to do this for them. The clingy toddlers in the waiting room have yet to develop their symbolic play into a tool for mastering emotions.

Play also offers ways to manage frustrations and realize wishes. Think how frustrated you would be if you lived in a world of giants able to do lots of interesting things you could not. This is how it is for young children. But in play, children can do anything. They can fly planes, scold their "kids," drive trucks, and cook fancy meals. Reality may frustrate, but play satisfies. Play, then, offers ways both to cope and to heal.

One last comment about play's ability to help children express and manage feelings. There is research to show that play's role in helping children manage difficult feelings is more selective than you might think. If feelings are too strong and scary, young children may not bring them into their play. If the feelings are too weak or peripheral, again young children may not bring them into their play. It is, then, the moderate levels of anxiety that children play with to gain control. Think again of the opening example of Evan and his feelings about the car wash. His play about car washes did not begin right after being traumatized by a real car wash. Rather, it began after a short "cooling down" period—when his emotions were not running so high.

The important point for you to remember is that play can be a tool for expressing and managing feelings. Supporting your child's play, then, means helping your child develop this invaluable tool. The question is how?

Supporting Your Child's Play

Being father to two-and-a-half-year-old Ryan brought back to Gary memories of his own childhood, including the fabulous block constructions he used to make. One day, Gary proudly brought home a huge set of wooden blocks of all shapes and sizes. As he unpacked the carton, Ryan became excited, too—but not about the blocks. He climbed into the big carton and began playing "train."

SHARED IMAGINATION

The good news is that there are lots of ways to support young children's play. The bad news, at least for many tired parents, is that providing support is not always easy: especially when it means playing with your child. At the end of a long day, your first-choice activity may not be getting down on the floor to build with LEGOs, and it's probably been some time since you got out crayons and paper to draw on a Saturday afternoon. So, playing with your child can be work. However, the benefits are many.

Parents tend to play with babies and toddlers spontaneously and naturally, playing peekaboo and other games that help prepare children for social interaction. Around age two and a half, kids start to invent their own games. This requires a little more thought from parents. If your child says, "You're a doo-doo! You're a foo-foo!," is it a challenge or a game? If it's play, what are the rules, and how do you respond? This one could be a game of naughty-sounding words, or it could just be sound-alike words. Your child is probably waiting for you to say, "And you're a koo-koo!" It's the natural next step from the back-and-forth imitation games you played together earlier.

As Gary found, it's possible to enjoy preschooler play in ways reminiscent of your own childhood. Not only that, but you'll enjoy the special bond that grows when you and your child play together—and we mean together, not with you as the teacher.

This is a great opportunity for you and your child to take on different roles and to try new media. Try to follow your child's lead. Kids who boss their parents around in play tend to be more cooperative later; by three or four, you're likely to hear "Let's pretend this . . ." and other signs she's moving on to sharing control through joint make-believe. When you pool your ideas, the imagination is no longer located just in your child, but in your relationship with her. This can also be tremendous fun. (If your child remains unusually bossy, see chapter 5 for ideas.)

You can also help your child deal with feelings through play. Your child may insist that you play a monster and do "scary" things while he skips away as the "victim." When a protective parent takes on a "monster" role, it can help a child master his fears—by allowing a child feel those fears in a safe environment. That is the issue with difficult feelings—they need a safe environment to get expressed and dealt with.

As we noted earlier, the more children can become involved in a detailed imaginary world, the more grounded they are in reality. Ironically, kids with problems often play in ways that most resemble ordinary life. Children don't get lost in fantasy worlds; they find themselves—and they better understand the real world, which helps them solve problems.

TRYING OUT NEW TOOLS FOR PLAY

Sometimes a child's problems with play come from problems with the medium: he doesn't know how to get started. Another plus of playing with your young child is that you can start playing yourself with a new medium (cardboard bricks, paints, macaroni and glue) and entice your child into playing along. You don't teach by saying, "Look! This is how you build a tower," but by just sitting down and building the block tower yourself.

In our story of Gary and Ryan, Gary was at first very disappointed in his son's lack of interest. Each time he got out the blocks, nothing much happened. Gary decided to give Ryan some time; after all, he was not yet three. For the next month, at the end of each day, Gary took out the blocks and built with them. He told Ryan, "I'm playing with the blocks. You can do whatever you want to do." If Ryan played with farm animals, Gary would build them a barn; sometimes Ryan put his animals inside.

Then one weekend, Gary's wife said, "Go look in the living room!" Ryan had gotten out all the blocks and built a city featuring walls, towers, and spaces: a marvel of construction more like a four-year-old's. Obviously, Ryan was soaking up everything Gary did, and getting ready to tackle the blocks on his own.

The point, then, is to encourage an exploration phase with a new medium—not just by providing opportunities to play with a new medium, but also by paying attention reflecting what your child is doing, even playing with the new medium yourself—as exemplified in the previous example. Adults usually underestimate how much there is to learn and practice before a child can use a medium well. Kids have to discover many things we take for granted. In your second year of life, you don't realize that a marker has a tip that needs to be dragged along the paper, or that blocks won't stay together if joined in midair, but only on the floor or table. There's a lot to learn about how to create spaces and contours.

One implication of this point about encouraging exploration is that we need to avoid unintentionally undermining exploration. One common example of undermining occurs when parents ask certain kinds of questions about a child's drawing-in-progress, questions that presume the child has a definite goal, questions such as "What is it?" and "Is that a horse?" Even simple praise can cut into the motive to explore, since comments such as "That's beautiful" aren't pertinent to exploring. Better for parents to stay descriptive and give words to how a child is exploring—"I see you made a curvy line," and the like.

Soon, kids can use that knowledge to represent or symbolize, and that process drives increased technical expertise—for example, starting with ovals for hands, and later adding fingers. It's exciting to see your child achieve these everyday milestones, which parents often miss "because it's just play." Great advances can happen over just a few days.

> Six-year-old Zach was impulsive and rambunctious, practically flying around the classroom as a fantasy Power Ranger. His teacher discovered one day that Zach was uncomfortable with drawing; he didn't seem to know how to start. Picking up on Zach's fantasy interest, the teacher sat next to him and drew leaping, kicking Power Rangers. Zach began to get involved, and gradually learned to transfer his interest to a new medium that helped him develop other skills.

One way to redirect a child's energy is to get him into a different play medium. The key here was not teaching Zach to draw, but picking up on his interest (martial-arts moves and all), letting him watch, and opening his mind to new possibilities.

"EDUCATIONAL" TOYS

We also encourage you to support your child's play by buying good play materials. Toy retailers are increasingly clever about labeling and promoting "educational toys." In reality, there really is no such thing as an educational toy. Toys and play materials are educational only with respect to what children *do* with them. So, you'll do much better to stick with old-fashioned materials for your child, such as dolls and human figures to act out stories, blocks and plastic bricks to construct buildings, and various art materials and paper to create pictures. Pass by the expensive, complicated toys and go for the stuff that children really use. And don't bother with toys meant to teach preschoolers to read, write, and calculate; that's not a good use of their time. There is more on this in a later chapter. For now, it's enough to say that there are all kinds of foundation skills that play develops and that are needed before a child can take on the demands of developing academic skills.

Admittedly, some of these old-fashioned play materials can be expensive. For example, a good set of plain wooden blocks is apt to cost well over a hundred dollars. But if you price play materials not by the initial cost but by the hours your child plays with them—sometimes daily, for several years or more—then these old-fashioned materials can turn out to be cheap. There are also good affordable materials, such as printed cardboard "bricks," and of course, big empty boxes.

Another way to get good use from your child's toys is to store and organize them well. Materials need to be stored where your child can easily find them and get at them. This means keeping on top of the clutter, buying plenty of clear plastic containers, and providing special shelving and places to store toys and play materials. Gradually you can enlist your child's help in keeping things tidy, including making labels for shelves and bins. At first, though, concentrate on keeping playthings accessible, both to eyes and little hands.

FOLLOW YOUR CHILD'S INTERESTS

> Castles and knights were six-year-old Tenley's passion. She loved books that showed the insides of medieval castles, and liked to dress and undress knights and ladies in "armor" and clothes she made from felt, paper, and glue. One of her favorite videos showed the history of British castles. Tenley's dad encouraged her interest by helping her find books and Web sites and bringing home scrap bags of fabric. He actually found himself looking forward to her latest fact or construction.

Parents and kids develop closeness not only through shared fantasies, but shared interests. If your child is immersed in names and details of airplanes, birds, or soccer players, try to follow his lead and feed that interest. Try linking your child's play to videos, books, and weekend adventures. If his play centers on dinosaurs, hang out at the science museum. Suggest he write and illustrate a book for you of key dinosaur facts. If you can find something in his topic to get even a little excited about, your child will be thrilled; you're validating his feelings and sharing more of his world. Kids can take ordinary facts you take for granted, and bring out passions you'd forgotten or never experienced before.

Remember, by exploring these passions in different media and different settings, your child is learning to make sense of his world. Be prepared, though: if you rent or buy videos about your child's passion, he'll want to watch them over and over. When a young child has a strong interest, it seems there's no such thing as too much repetition.

The Social Value of Play

Andrew (age five) watched his friends Tom and Cathy pretending to be fish swimming near a beach. Wanting to join their play, Andrew moved closer, making loud roaring noises, which, he explained, was his way of being a shark. Tom and Cathy accepted this suggested story line and pretended to swim away. The three played at chasing and being chased for a while, until Tom and Cathy became bored and proposed a change to the "story."

"You don't have to be an angry shark all the time," said Tom. "You could sometimes be angry and sometimes not." Andrew rejected this suggestion and stuck to his role as an "angry" shark. So, to keep the play moving but change direction, Tom and Cathy created a "rock" where fish could be safe from sharks. This puzzled Andrew. Not knowing what to do, he walked away.

Andrew's play with other children was often cut short because he couldn't seem to play off their suggested lines of fantasy. This often left him on the sidelines. To overcome his isolation, he'd turn disruptive and destructive—anything to make contact and get attention.

Adults often don't consider that preschoolers who don't play well don't make friends. Adults, even teens, develop friendships by chatting with one another. Kids make those contacts by playing together. Play is the springboard to friendship, the soil in which it grows.

Our own observations and research show that children like Andrew often have problems making up stories with dolls, building with blocks, drawing pictures, or otherwise engaging in constructive play. They also may have problems inventing informal games (as in the story above) and understanding the games invented by others. You can put two kids together, but if one doesn't know how to make a roadway, or send little characters to fight fires or rescue kittens, she may find herself struggling to connect.

This problem becomes more obvious as make-believe play grows more imaginative, and fantasies acted out with toys are the products of more than one mind—of the coordinated thinking of children playing with one another (or with adults). This is where practicing play with your child can make a huge difference.

In playing with your child, you can play in ways that bring out what is needed. If imagination and fantasy are needed, you model being imaginative and fanciful. If your child is not leading enough or suggesting enough about how play can become cooperative, you can follow your child's lead by imitating, then playing dumb and asking for direction. If your child is a bit too bossy in play, you can insist on sometimes leading, sometimes following—all the while making sharing ideas very satisfying.

Concerns About Play

Larissa was having a very hard time connecting to her kindergarten peers. Shy, she spent much of her time on the playground just watching and wandering. One teacher took her under her wing and tried to draw her out and help her make friends. The effort was starting to pay dividends; Larissa seemed more secure and happy on the playground, but was still too shy to approach other children.

One day, Larissa bent down and, with a gleam in her eyes, picked up a few pinecones. She turned to her newfound teacher friend and said, "Let's pretend these are food, and we poison it and feed it to the kids."

The teacher was appalled and answered, "Oh, no; the kids are our friends!" Larissa dropped the pinecones and walked away.

Sometime parents worry about play because they assume a connection between what their child plays and what she'll grow up to be. There is not a shred of evidence to support this. Unfortunately, this concern can lead adults to discourage perfectly healthy play—and that concerns us. To avoid this problem, pay attention to what your child's play means to her, rather than assigning an adult meaning to it.

Despite the best intentions, Larissa's teacher spoiled a wonderful chance for this child to connect to her peers. It may be hard for you to believe, but if the teacher had gone along with Larissa's fantasy, perhaps saying, "Great idea! I'll get the cooking pot and poison," not only would the child and teacher have had fun playing together—but other children would have likely joined in, gleefully acting out roles as "victims."

Our experience tells us that children often understand better than do adults that this kind of play is "just pretend." Over and over, we find that the *content and themes* of play matter much less than whether the play is *developed and shared*. Don't sanitize play. Support its development! Think of extended fantasy play with destructive or distasteful themes as the work of a novelist writing a mystery, or a story of war and crime.

One day a boy at the Eliot-Pearson preschool built the outline of a "coffin" with blocks. As his friend joined in, they built two grave sites with headstones made of block arches, then lay down together. They even wrote things on the headstones, such as "rest in peace." An adult looking at this might think these boys had a death wish!

For them, it had nothing to do with death; they just liked to construct things, and they were experimenting with symmetry and arches.

They also liked to see what kinds of things they could (or couldn't) fit inside. The two boys lay face-to-face, talking and playing. It was just another buddy activity. Soon other children asked, "Hey, Jonah, can I go into your grave?" This is just another reminder not to overinterpret and sanitize.

War Play

> Jerome, age six, used his play to act out themes of destruction—nothing out of the ordinary. However, what was out of the ordinary was how often his play got "out of hand": overly excited and unsafe. For example, when building a fort out of blocks along with his friends, Jerome might suddenly yell out, "Let's bomb the bad guys!" and proceed to hurl blocks around the room.

TV news reports and magazine headlines have triggered a great deal of fear about children's war play. Publicity about shootings by children have led adults to connect real violence to pretend violence. As a result, more and more parents are banning play involving toy guns and themes of death and destruction. This is too bad, because war play should not be judged on the basis of its content: its themes about death and destruction. Rather, like the "worrisome" play of Larissa or Jonah above, war play should be judged on the basis of how well it is developed.

Jerome's problem didn't lie in his fantasies of destruction, but in his inability to keep those fantasies embedded in safe play. Part of the reason he couldn't do this was that for him, certain types of play were undeveloped. For example, he had not been able to develop his story lines in less physically active play media, such as drawing. But when he was later encouraged to draw by an adult drawing with him, he did just fine. Their drawings were of bombings, shootings, and all the other kinds of destructive events that interested Jerome. But the fact that they were safely on paper prevented his becoming impulsive and destructive in reality.

To better understand the importance of this distinction between content and development in war play, consider two children: Travis runs around saying, "I'm going to shoot you!" Yochi behaves the same way, but says, "I, Darth Vader, am going to shoot you!"

This is not a trivial difference. Studies show that Travis (the child who uses the "direct I" when engaged in war play) is much more likely to be too aggressive than Yochi. Why? Because Travis is probably less able to engage in constructive, developed play.

Think about this example in terms of what makes for more developed fantasy play. In this example, Yochi's play is more developed because he has taken on a simple fantasy role (Darth Vader). With time and growth, we hope both children will develop much more than fantasy roles; we hope they'll develop entire fantasy worlds.

This example brings out the essential paradox in war play and play with violent themes: the more fantastic and developed a child's war play becomes, the less violent or aggressive a child is apt to be. Consider the previous example of the little boy whose play centered on pre-twentieth-century American wars. Garth was constantly involved in elaborate, developed war play. Armies of toy soldiers were meticulously arranged on the living-room floor; pictures were drawn to depict various flanking maneuvers. Forts and bridges were constructed out of blocks. Entire battle scenes were reenacted in play. Friends were recruited to manipulate the toy soldiers on the enemy side or to command armies on the allied side.

For those who assume a direct connection between war play and real violence, this little boy should have been headed for an aggressive, violent, or even criminal way of life. However, the very opposite was the case. Garth was one of the most gentle in his group of friends, a true pacifist with not a mean bone in his body. One night, while lying in bed, he told his father, "I wish there were no wars." He loved war play, but he hated wars! He was wonderful at symbolizing violence, but more wonderful still at being kind and gentle. That is the way it is likely to be with developed war play.

The point is, don't lump all war play together. A child running around out of control going "bang, bang!" with toy guns is not the same as a child creating elaborate battles using toy soldiers and drawings (of historic or entirely imaginary conflicts). The first kind of play can indeed lead to kids getting hurt and becoming aggressive or even mean. The second kind of play can lead to kids playing constructively together. But neither kind of play predicts long-term future behavior.

So, don't worry that if your child's play contains themes of violence, he will be more likely to become violent or insensitive to violence. Worry only if your child's play remains unimaginative and undeveloped. Help your child move from the out-of-control, less fantastic, and repetitive kind of war play (like Jerome's) to more in-control, imaginative war play (like Garth's).

To support constructive war play, feed your child information about wars: through books, films, and trips to museums. Encourage symbolizing war in more static media such as drawing (where a child can't run around). Encourage war play with small replicas (toy soldiers) that will help your child construct miniature worlds. In sum, don't discourage your child's war play; develop it.

"GIRL" TOYS AND "BOY" TOYS

> Leaf was a girl with a big, outgoing personality. From age three, she wanted a Barbie doll. Her parents, teachers of drama and dance, were concerned. They explained to Leaf that Barbie was not a good model for girls; they didn't want Leaf to think she could only do things Barbie does—and no real woman looks like a Barbie.
>
> Leaf was relentless in her request. When her parents talked to her day-care teacher, she said, to their surprise, "Get Leaf the doll. She is such a together little girl. Giving a child a Barbie doesn't make her into a bimbo."
>
> Leaf's parents continued to resist, until one day she said, "Daddy, I just want to *play* with Barbie. I'm not going to *learn* from Barbie!"

Leaf's parents were concerned that her play with fashion dolls would foster unhealthy stereotypes of what it means to be a woman (e.g., encouraging pursuit of an impossible ideal shape, or emphasizing looks over brains). This is another case where parents assume a direct connection between the content of a child's play and what kind of adolescent or adult she'll become. Life is more complicated than that. What parents do and say matter much more than individual toys their children use. Leaf will not learn to be a sex object from Barbie.

Leaf's parents found that she used her Barbie as a prop for her own original stories, not for fifties-style dates with Ken. And eventually, Barbie spent most of her time in the toy box, along with assorted ponies, trucks, and puzzles.

One young woman vividly recalled her childhood interpretation of Barbie: that impossibly curvy figure didn't mean girls were supposed to look like Barbie; it just meant that Barbie was a *girl*! We adults take for granted that it's easy to distinguish the sexes, to know what it means to be a girl and not a boy. We forget that even the simplest distinctions have to be constructed by young children, through observing and interacting with reality. It helps when those differences are exaggerated—and Barbie, with her amazing statistics, certainly does just that!

With both war play and ultrafeminine play, our focus should be on the development of the play and not on its content. When Barbie becomes part of a miniature world complete with decisions about dressing, friendships, and even dating, we should be delighted—because this means the players are taking control through fantasy, and showing a capacity to share fantasies with peers that will develop and sustain friendships. It's only if Barbie is simply dragged around, and other signs of creative play are absent, that we may have cause for concern.

Sean, age three, was so shy that he had no playmates or friends. His child-care teachers worked hard to help him connect with other kids. Everyone was delighted to find Sean one day playing with a little girl, the two of them pushing around toy baby carriages and pretending to care for their babies.

To reinforce their connection, a teacher took a picture of Sean and Suki and taped it to the wall. But when Sean's father saw the picture, he got very upset and demanded an end to such play.

Little boys playing in girlish ways troubles some parents, especially fathers. Obviously, Sean's father overreacted and missed the point about his child's play being a way to overcome isolation and connect to others. We don't assume that you would react as he did. But you might share some of the father's concerns about play's role in developing gender and sexual identity. As with war play, focus less on the themes or content of your child's play than on whether his play is developed, whether he's using constructive play to make friends, and whether he seems reasonably comfortable and happy. Further, we again urge you to see play more as a way to thrive in the present than as a path to an adult role.

This said, gender-opposite play may be a cause for concern if a child is uncomfortable playing in any other way. If a little boy will only play with girls and in the ways girls normally play, that's a problem for him— because he needs to be able to make friends with boys. If he can't do that, he may become isolated—and be mercilessly teased—as time goes on.

Between three and four, girls and boys usually (but not always!) begin to play differently from one another. This may occur even when parents encourage the opposite, doing their best to engage girls with trucks and other so-called boy toys, and provide boys with dolls and other "girl toys." Influences outside the home (such as television toy advertising) play some part in this, but frequently children take the initiative and separate themselves in "traditional" ways. Boys play more at themes about death and destruction; girls' play is more likely to center on nurturing and family. Boys go for more rough-and-tumble play, and in play on the floor with blocks and action figures. Girls engage more in quieter play, and in play at tables with markers, paper, puzzles, and crafts.

The concern, then, is not about what nontraditional play means for some distant future, but about helping a child feel happy and secure now and in the immediate future. Throughout childhood and into preadolescence, boys will need boys to support their own development. In American culture, a "tomboy" (a girl who likes trucks and frogs) may be accepted and even admired, but not the boy who wants to play only with girls. We hope, then, that boys will become comfortable and motivated to play in boylike ways. Whether they *also* play in girllike ways is not the issue.

To reinforce this last point, we recall a humorous confession by a secure young man. During a discussion of Barbie play, he confessed (to him, it felt like a confession) that throughout his childhood he and his older sister played with Barbies because his sister insisted. But the two of them developed an agreement that this was their secret—that when his male friends visited, Barbies were not to be mentioned. By everyone's account, this boy who played with Barbies grew up to be a very fine man.

IMAGINARY PLAYMATES

> One day on the playground, Nina perched herself on the tire swing with two other children. She suddenly tossed her hand in the air and said, "Here you go, Dumbo!" The other children looked puzzled until Nina continued, "Here are some more peanuts, Dumbo!" The others then laughed and joined her in tossing "peanuts" to "Dumbo."

Nina was shy, especially at school. But she found a way to deal with and, to a point, overcome her shyness. Her method was to employ a variety of imaginary playmates who both made her feel more secure, and offered ways for her to communicate and connect to others. There was timid Minnie and the more adventuresome Alice, and there was Dumbo the elephant. The preceding story is one example of how Nina used these "friends."

By now, you've gotten the point that we feel almost anything goes in play, provided play is developed, shared, and helps a child thrive in the present. This applies also to imaginary playmates. Some parents worry that imaginary playmates indicate a break with reality, much as delusions and hallucinations indicate breaks with reality later in life. But once again, this is imputing adult meaning where only a child's meaning should prevail.

Happily, there is a good deal of research showing only positives for those children who have imaginary playmates. Imaginary playmates seem to be inventive ways for a child to adapt to being alone or to feeling shy. For example, firstborns who are above-average in intelligence are more apt to develop imaginary playmates.

In one study, young children were left "alone" in a place new to them, with toys available for play. The children who had imaginary playmates were more likely to play constructively—even in this stressful situation. The children who lacked imaginary playmates were more likely to get upset and search for their parent.

Finally, researchers of cognitive development underscore the importance of a child's being able to "go beyond the information given"—to invent and not simply react to what is seen. In playing with imaginary playmates, a child does just that—as when one little girl insisted the family set a separate place at the table for her imaginary playmate and make room in the car for her playmate to sit. So, if your child has an imaginary playmate, we suggest you simply sit back and enjoy.

It's easier to enjoy your child's imaginary playmate if you stop worrying that she might be confused about what's pretend and what is real. Your child knows that her imaginary playmate is not real; you don't need to remind her. When she's playing, she will not keep the boundaries between real and pretend sharp and clear, but neither do you when you read a good book or go to a good movie. Imagine if in the middle of a thrilling or passionate scene at the movies, someone tapped you on the shoulder and said, "Don't worry; it's just a movie." Momentarily getting lost in make-believe is healthy. All of us, young and old, get refreshed from these momentary retreats from reality. Fantasy and reality are partners, not foes. We see this partnership especially in the development of young children's play, including play with imaginary friends.

ELECTRONIC PLAY

There is a technology-driven revolution going on in children's play. Parents are faced not only with choices about computer play and play at television-based consoles (GameCube, PlayStation II, or Xbox); there are also an expanding number of "electronic educational toys," from talking books to "kids' laptops." This means you need to be prepared with a good approach to electronic play.

Like most things new, electronic play causes parents to worry. For example, there's concern about the content and educational value of computer or video games, and the bad health effects of too much sitting. There's also worry about possible isolating effects because children often play video games alone.

As we mentioned earlier, preschool children don't need fancy toys that push letters, numbers, or phonics—as many electronic toys do. But there may be social value in electronic play. Research suggests that as children get older, computer play becomes a social activity. Even though children use the keyboard one at a time, it's not an isolating medium. You can observe kindergartners hovering around a computer to watch and teach one another. In fact, for many children, not having access to electronic play can be isolating—since children's friendships today can be built around a shared interest in electronic games. Also, console games allow joint play.

Interactive games are a step up from the more passive use of television, since children's minds are at work. (See chapter 11 for more on children and electronic media.) But they're still a step below developing one's own imaginative worlds through make-believe play. You needn't limit electronic play if you are providing opportunity, materials, and support for playing in other ways, such as block building. If your child seems to be playing too much with computers, take it as a sign that you need to provide more encouragement and opportunity for other types of play. In sum, there's no rational reason for pushing the panic button over electronic play—or for preferring this play over other kinds.

Sports: Backyard and Coached

On a cool fall Saturday morning, parents and youngsters gather on the local school's athletic fields, a modern equivalent of the town square. Parents cluster on the sidelines to watch their children, but also to

engage in friendly chat. Occasionally, the children do something exciting enough for parents to cheer. But at this age, the children are just getting used to the game.

The game is called soccer—but its unofficial titles are beehive or
swarm ball, since the children swarm around the ball wherever it goes,
with no defined roles of striker, forward, or defense and no real understanding of what it takes to be a team. But no one cares, and everyone
seems to be having fun.

This is one typical scene of young children being introduced to
coached sports. Now consider the following, very different scene:

On a seasonably warm spring afternoon, children stand at their respec-
tive positions on the ball field as the batter swats at the ball on a tee. The
second baseman is squatting, rolling dirt into balls. The first baseman is
fixed on a couple of ants making their way across the foul line. The left
fielder has his back to the batter and gazes off into the sky.

Only the parents and coaches, it seems, are interested. They yell
encouragement to the batter and direct the players in the field to "pay
attention and get into the ball game!"

Few areas of our culture elicit more passion than sports. No wonder,
then, that so many families are interested in having their children play
sports, even at a very young age. The increase in the number of children
involved in organized sports constitutes a second revolution in the way
today's children play. By some estimates, there are over 20 million children in this country participating in youth sports programs.

But coached sports don't always serve young children well. In the
first story above, children are focused, active, and having fun, without a
lot of adult interference. In the second, children are unfocused, inactive,
and seemingly bored as adults tell them what to do. This is the nature of
coached sports.

We see these contrasts in coached sports because there are balances to
be kept that are often not kept very well. Between stressing skill devel-

opment and keeping the game lively and fun. Between stressing competition and winning, and getting everyone to participate—even those who aren't very good. And finally, between drafting teams to create well-matched sides, and keeping friends together on the same teams. The world of coached sports, then, requires parents and coaches to strike the right balances for children's development.

Youth programs and coached sports aside, there have and always will be "backyard" sports: even when there are no backyards. Backyard sports are the kid-run variety, the ones that take a handful of kids (too few for a regulation game) and use made-up rules to play games that are highly irregular but incredibly fun. With informal outdoor play, young children participate for sheer enjoyment. They get all the good things that come from play: being in control, being with friends, and having fun. As with make-believe play indoors, every child is active all the time.

In coached sports, kids aren't in charge. Some sit and wait on benches. Often they're doing things that aren't natural, like being placed in the outfield, or are assumed to have eye-hand coordination beyond their age level. Coached sports risk being developmentally inappropriate, which never happens with backyard sports because there, kids choose their own level. Unfortunately, both complicated schedules and safety concerns make it nearly impossible for many parents to just send their children outside into the neighborhood to play. So, like it or not, we are stuck with coached sports, and must to do what we can to keep everything balanced.

As you enter this new role of parent to a child who plays sports, you'll want to support both informal and formal play. Backyard sports without coached sports will leave your child without requisite skills. Coached sports without backyard sports may slow or undermine your child's falling in love with sports. The two should play off of each other.

What do children want when they play a team sport? First, they want to be active. They want to run around, throw, kick, hit, and do all the fun things that they do in backyard play. That is why the second example, of T-ball, is an example of bad play. Second, they want to be with their friends—those they hang around with off the field, and not just on the field. That's why older children's elite teams and even town teams don't measure up, because the drafting system often separates friends. Third, kids want some control of how they play the game. They don't want to be drilling all the time, or have to fit into a highly structured and rule-governed game directed only by adults and not them. This last point deserves discussion.

Coached sports for children have today become a problem not because of the dramatic situations reported in newspapers but because of how much adults have taken over. There are elaborate bylaws governing youth sports organizations and their games. There are complex tournaments and leagues. In short, there are institutions for children's sports that mirror what has developed for high-school and college students. But children are not adolescents or young adults, and the fact that they're treated as such by youth sports leagues is probably why a good many drop out of sports by the time they're thirteen. It's too much pressure and not enough fun.

Another issue is boredom. Some parents squeeze all the competition out of a game, under the misguided notion that any form of competition is harmful to young children. For example, we have witnessed parents awarding children first base, even after an infielder had thrown the runner out. The result usually is kids becoming bored because making good plays becomes pointless.

Parents also foster boredom by not teaching children real skills—skills that allow children to feel in control of their bodies and the game. We have seen many a team show up for games ill-prepared and fall so far behind that they lose interest. Most important, parents foster boredom when they put children in games that are boring—that leave children in the outfield or on the bench without a chance to play.

Here, then, is what we advise if you want your child to play a sport. Spend time playing backyard games that prepare for organized, coached sports later on. Cultivate (don't demand) interest in professional teams in which, later on, sports heroes will provide motives and meaning for your child's sports participation. Infuse games with playful competition that gives your child advantages to level the playing field, and that occasionally allows your child to win. Take advantage of the wonderful new sports equipment for young children: equipment that gives a feel for the real game, but is modified to fit little bodies. Most of all, give encouragement and approval!

Then there's the important factor of the coach—whether he or she can instruct and mentor. By mentor, we mean helping support a child's overall development. Truly good coaches know the game, and know how to communicate with children in ways that help them acquire skills, but they know much more. They also know how to encourage and support a love for the game. Seek these coaches out and, at the same time, protect your child from coaches who do the opposite: who use children to promote their own agendas.

Sports can be a joyous, healthy affair that binds together children, parents, and community. This connecting power of sports happens only with a great deal of individual and collective effort on the part of parents and communities, and only with a close monitoring of coaches and parents who have let their passions run amok. It occurs only if we keep in mind that it's not what the child does to the ball that matters, but what the ball does to the child.

Some Final Words

Play, then, is not "just play." In this chapter, we have tried to convey that play is at the very heart and soul of childhood. Play is food for your child's cognitive, social, and emotional development, and your active support is very much needed.

Early childhood is what author Selma Fraiberg called "the Magic Years," because they are the years when fantasy rules, when children's imaginations hold sway, and when anything can turn into anything else. As we have seen, this fantasy, this imagining, this transforming is no enemy of reality. Rather than escape from reality, children, through play, take on reality—the reality that really matters.

In play, they know that life is a drama and that friends are there to share the drama. In play, they manage feelings and begin to develop skills both mental and physical. So, admire your child's play, take pleasure in it, and support its development. Play's the thing wherein you'll catch the wonder and sense of childhood.

Suggestions for Further Reading

Martha Bronson. *The Right Stuff for Children Birth to Eight: Selecting Play Materials to Support Development.* National Association for the Education of Young Children, 1995.

Nancy Carlsson-Paige and Diane Levin. *Who's Calling the Shots? How to Respond Effectively to Children's Fascination with War Play and War Toys.* New Society Publishers, 1990.

Selma Fraiberg. *The Magic Years: Understanding and Handling the Problems of Early Childhood.* Fireside, 1996.

Barbara Goodson and Martha Bronson. *Which Toy for Which Child: A Consumer's Guide for Selecting Suitable Toys: Ages Birth Through Five.* U.S. Consumer Product Safety Commission Document #285.

CHAPTER NINE

The Child as Communicator

Calvin Gidney

Three-year-old Maria Luisa, describing her day at preschool, says, "Oh! And then we goed to the zoo." Adriana gently corrects her daughter: "You went to the zoo? Great!"

Maria Luisa seems not to notice, adding "And then we goed out for ice cream!" Adriana is puzzled because just a few months earlier Maria Luisa would always say "went."

Parents and caregivers of young children often marvel at how quickly those children learn to talk. In the space of three years, children go from babbling unintelligible sounds to producing complete sentences. Given the important role that language plays in children's education (after all, elementary school is sometimes called *grammar* school), you might worry that you're not doing enough to help your child's early language development.

The good news is that you can relax. All of us are born with the capacity to develop language, and under a variety of circumstances, *all* of us develop language. In fact, it's hard to keep a child from acquiring language. This is because our capacity for language is deeply engrained in our genetic makeup. It is one of the things that most distinguishes humans from other animals.

This does *not* mean that parents can do nothing to enhance their children's language development. On the contrary, there are specific things parents can do to build their children's ability to use and play with language. Surprisingly, the more obvious strategies, like correcting children's errors, or drilling children on grammar, seldom have the desired effect. But when parents and caregivers offer children frequent and regular opportunities for face-to-face interaction, and provide rich and varied experiences like trips to the zoo, the library, or the park, their children's language will, in turn, be richer and more varied. Also, if parents regularly read to their children and encourage them to tell stories, jokes, and riddles, their language will be the better for it.

In this chapter, we will briefly look at how language develops in children and then discuss some ways that parents and caregivers can enrich their child's language. We'll also address common concerns and questions about young children and language:

- Should I correct my child's mistakes?

- Should I talk baby talk to my child?

- My child has begun to curse and use other offensive language; what can I do about it?

- How does being exposed to more than one language affect my child's language development?

- When should I worry about a speech delay or speech impediment? What can I do if I suspect that my child has a language delay or hearing problem?

- What can I do to enhance my child's language development?

Language "Mistakes"

Four-year-old Evan has some unusual pronunciations. He calls a hippopotamus a "hipomanus," elephants are "elfulunts," and an octopus is an "ottopus." "Spaghetti" usually comes out as "pasketti." His family enjoys Evan's "creative" pronunciations, but sometimes his dad worries that Evan has a hearing problem.

• • •

"Doggie!" young Tamika cries, obviously thrilled. Tamika's mom looks puzzled—Tamika is pointing to a cat! Mom says, "That's not a doggie, sweetie, that's a kitty cat. Say, 'kitty cat.' " Tamika, unfazed, repeats, "Doggie! Doggie!"

From a grown-up's point of view, young children make a lot of "mistakes" when they speak. It seems they just don't understand how to say things correctly. Like Evan, children may have cute but incorrect pronunciations of words. Like Maria Luisa at the start of this chapter, they may say "goed" or "putted" instead of "went" or "put." They create sentences like "No want milk!" instead of "I don't want milk!" Or, like Tamika, they have strange notions of what words mean.

While technically these may be errors, linguists and other experts in child development call them *developmental errors,* seeing them not as mistakes but as wonderful windows into the workings of a child's mind. You might think that children learn their first language effortlessly. After all, even with minimal help from parents, children are producing long complex sentences by the time they're four. (Anyone who's taken four years of high-school Spanish knows that four years certainly isn't enough for an adult to speak fluent, accentless Spanish.) But looks are deceiving: the process of children's first language acquisition is in some ways a trial-and-error effort.

On their path to linguistic competence, children formulate, throw out, and reformulate many ideas about how language works—about what words mean, what verb forms make sense, and how words are pronounced. This is part of their ongoing process of trying to make sense of their world; it's also part of their developmental process. That explains why the "corrections" of caregivers and parents may not have much *immediate* effect on children's speech.

Sometimes, as in Evan's funny mispronunciations of animal names, children's language reflects their stage of *motor development*. Remember that speech is, among other things, a physical skill that requires the careful coordination of the muscles of the tongue, jaw, and mouth. Some words require fairly sophisticated movement of these muscles that children, even children as old as six, are not able to carry out. Instead, they simplify the pronunciations: They may reverse the order of sounds ("spaghetti" becomes "pasketti"), just repeat a prominent syllable (*Sesame Street* is "see-see-tee-tee"), or leave out a difficult sound ("first" comes out "fuss").

Children might also have difficulty with *specific sounds* of their first language. Many English-speaking children, for example, have difficulty correctly enunciating the "r" sound, making it into a "w" instead. (You *pwobabwy awen't surpwised* by this.) Other children have difficulty pronouncing *blends,* more than one consonant next to each other. For example, it's not uncommon for children to pronounce the word "truck" as "tuck."

> Take a look at some of young English-speaking children's most common approximations:
>
> "Water" may become "wawa."
>
> "Baby" may become "beebee."
>
> "Candy" may become "kacky."
>
> "Horse" may become "hawsie."
>
> "Duck" may become "guck" or "duckie."
>
> "Stop" may become "tahp" or "tah."
>
> "Scary" may become "kerry" or "gaggie."

Spanish-speaking children sometimes have trouble rolling their "r"s or saying the word *quiere* ("want")—it comes out something like *quele.*

What's interesting about these mispronunciations (we prefer the term "approximations") is that each child has his or her unique combination of them. One woman, who took care of two toddlers, described how the children wobbled into the kitchen one day with outstretched arms, each wanting a cookie. But one was saying, "Cocky! Cocky!" while the other yelled, "Googie! Googie!"

In most cases, parents and caregivers shouldn't worry about these mispronunciations. They represent children's attempts to pronounce difficult sound sequences. Most children grow out of them by the time they reach first grade, though sometimes they may persist beyond age six. If you notice consistent unusual pronunciations lasting much beyond age five, consider seeking professional advice; we'll discuss this issue later in the chapter.

Children also make what sound like *grammatical mistakes* (as when Maria Luisa "goed" to the zoo). A few months earlier, she commonly used "went." What's going on? While such "mistakes" may look like a move backward, they're actually a sign of progress. These developmental errors show that Maria Luisa has come to understand something important about English: that the past tense is *usually* formed by adding "-ed" to the end of a verb.

Before, when Maria Luisa said "went," she probably saw "went" as its own little word, unrelated to the broader concepts of past tense or to the word "go." But at some point, she had an "aha!" moment—she realized that people around her say "walk/walked," "play/played," and "jump/jumped." She grasped that there's a pattern here—not just some assortment of individual words. So, she formed a hypothesis (not consciously, of course): "To put a verb in the past, add '-ed' to it." Giddy with her newly conceived idea, she applies the rule across the board: The past tense of "go" becomes "goed," the past of "put" is "putted," and the past of "eat," "eated."

It makes a lot of sense, doesn't it? Probably everybody who's ever studied English as a second language wishes it worked that way. Of course we all-knowing English-speaking grown-ups know that it *doesn't* work that way—but we should cut Maria Luisa some slack and simply marvel at the genius of her newly created hypothesis. She will get it right soon—*but on her own.*

Finally, what about little Tamika, who doesn't seem to be able to tell a dog from a cat? By now you can guess the answer—that's also a developmental error. Of course, these *word-meaning errors* last well into child-hood—and even beyond. For example, until fourth grade, one of the authors of this book used to think that the Lord's Prayer went: "Our Father, who art in heaven, *Harold* be thy name . . ." And why not? It's not as if most fourth graders (or adults, for that matter) usually use the word "hallowed."

To Tamika, "doggie" might refer to *any* four-legged animal with fur—cats, dogs, even gerbils. Later, perhaps on a trip to a zoo with her parents, she might see an elephant and realize, "Hmm, this doesn't quite fit my concept of 'doggie.'" This viewing of the elephant might cause Tamika to reformulate her ideas about what fits under the category of "doggie." Little by little, her ideas about what words mean will come to match those of the people around her. However, it's a process that for the most part, Tamika will accomplish by herself, without being "corrected."

Baby Talk

Before the birth of their first child, Nathan swore to his wife that he would not speak "baby talk." "I'll speak to the child just as I would to anybody else."

Ever notice what happens when an English speaker is talking to someone who does not speak the language that well? His voice gets louder, as if the foreigner has a hearing problem; his speech slows down, his gestures become more pronounced, and the pitch of his voice becomes more varied. You may be surprised to learn that depending on how much English the other person knows, these strategies are actually helpful, if a bit insulting. The same can be said about baby talk or, as researchers call it, *child-directed speech*.

All of us, usually unconsciously, modify the way we speak to young children. This is because we recognize that young children's vocabulary and general understanding are not as well developed as adults'. Typically, baby talk is characterized by (1) exaggerated vocal pitch or intonation,

(2) a slower rate of speaking, (3) exaggerated facial expressions and gestures, and (4) simplified vocabulary and sentence structures.

Child language experts believe that baby talk helps children acquire their first language. First of all, it holds their attention better than speech directed to adults. Second, choosing simpler vocabulary over more complex words helps children make semantic connections between objects in the world. For example, when reading to your two-year-old, you might come across a picture of a jaguar. Of course, you'd like your child to know the word "jaguar" eventually, but instead, you point to the animal and say "kitty cat." This helps your child understand that a jaguar is a type of cat and is related to other types of kitty cats like lions, tigers, lynxes, and Max, your household cat. In simplifying the word, you are helping her create what linguists call *semantic networks*—complex webs of relations among words and concepts.

Now, we don't mean to imply that Nathan is entirely misguided in his desire to speak to his child in adult language. Children also benefit from exposure to adultlike language. It's just that they can neither pay attention to it, nor understand it, as easily as they can speech that's tailored to them. Exposing young children to adult language shows them new vocabulary, more complex sentence structures, grown-up expectations about how to behave in conversation, and adult ways of thinking and reasoning.

Your child gains these benefits simply by hearing you interact with another adult. For some families, mealtime is where this exposure takes place; for other families, commuting back and forth from school does it. Whatever the situation, *find regular times to talk to other adults in front of your child*—but with the understanding that the child might not be able to completely follow the conversation and probably will not be able to follow adult rules of speaking.

Teaching your child the rules of conversation is part of your role as a caregiver, so it's perfectly acceptable to say to your child, "Surina, Daddy's speaking to Mommy right now. Please don't interrupt me." You're teaching your child an important lesson: "One rule of talking is: Don't interrupt when someone else is talking!"

Also, take time out of your adult conversation to teach the child a word or two: "Surina, do you know what a 'loan' is? It's when you give someone some money for a little while, but they have to give it back to you."

Every community and every family has its own unwritten rules of conversation, and families generally want their children to learn and follow those rules. Some communities value a person's ability to tell a good story. Some value the one-speaker-at-a-time principle. Others expect children to show respect to adults by saying "yes, ma'am" or "yes, sir." Whatever your family's conversational rules, make sure that your children have a chance to practice them—and don't expect them to catch on right away.

Cursing and Offensive Language

> Patrice went to pick up her four-year-old son, Larry, from his child-care center. Before leaving, he said to one of his best friends, "Good-bye you f___a___!" and both of them broke into uproarious giggles. Patrice was mortified; she was worried that the staff would think she used language like that at home. She glanced sheepishly at one teacher, who smiled and said, "Just ignore it! It's going around the class this week!"

Many young children go through a stage that some child care professionals call "potty mouth." They seem to take a wicked delight in saying words that are taboo. For young children, though, "potty mouth" marks an important discovery about language—that words have *power,* that you can *do* things with words: make people laugh, hurt people's feelings, or just make others take notice of you. Add to this discovery a natural glee in crossing the line between acceptable and out-of-bounds. (What student of a foreign language doesn't want to know the curse words?) The motivation is the same for kids and grown-ups—being bad just for the fun of it, for the sheer shock value, for the fun of watching other people's faces.

Given this, the child care teacher's suggestion was a good one, at least initially. If you do not react to "bad" words, you rob them of their power. If the child learns he can't get a rise out of you by using such words, eventually he will stop using them. However, if your child continues to curse, it's time to establish ground rules for speaking, as is done in many classrooms. This might include rules such as, "Only call other people by their name" or "No potty words." Sit down with your child and work these rules out together. Make sure the child clearly understands what kinds of language are not tolerated in your home.

In addition, make sure your child knows that words can hurt people's feelings. By age three, children are sufficiently emotionally developed to understand that it's wrong to hurt other people's feelings. By age six, this knowledge is firmly rooted, so you may be even more explicit with your six-year-old. And remember that children learn by example—if cursing is not allowed at home, the rules also apply to adults.

It's Monday at Dunbar Elementary School. Miss Broome, a first-grade teacher, begins her morning as usual, with time for students to share something they did over the weekend. A little blond girl eagerly raises her hand and, when called on, cheerfully announces, "On Saturday, I saw a nigger! I went to the store with my mama and she pointed to a lady and said, 'That's a nigger.'"

Shocked, Miss Broome keeps her composure and calmly asks the child, "Do you know what that is?"

"No," replies the child, "but it's bad."

Miss Broome is sure that the child doesn't know the meaning of the word; if she did, she'd never have told the story. Miss Broome is African-American.

What happened to Miss Broome in this story is trickier. Children are not born with racial prejudice; it's something they learn from their communities, their peers, or their families. When parents first hear their child use an offensive term, they often wonder where she learned it, especially if they don't use such terms themselves. Once children enter group child care or school, their peers become a major influence on their language development. Kids will use the words that they hear other kids using, especially the words that older children use.

Racist and antigay language perpetuates racist and antigay beliefs. Such language should never be tolerated in any situation—classroom, home, or playground. If your child uses a racist or homophobic term, understand that it does not mean that she is herself a bigot. As the example shows, children often use such words unwittingly. However, the terms themselves are racist or homophobic, so in using them your child is being schooled in these beliefs. If you hear your child use one of these terms, add it to your list of language that is not allowed. Make sure the child understands that these words, too, can hurt people's feelings.

Introducing a Second Language

Charlene, a native of Haiti, wants her son, Dieudonné, to speak Kreyol (Creole). Even though she is married to an American, Charlene speaks to Dieudonné in Kreyol when they are alone. However, it seems no matter how hard she tries, he replies to her in English.

Things have gotten worse since the boy started attending a kindergarten where none of the other children are of Haitian descent. Now Dieudonné begs his mother not to speak Kreyol in front of his school friends. Charlene fears that her efforts to raise her son bilingually will fail.

• • •

Erisson and Fernanda, both immigrants from Brazil, want their daughter, Sabrina, to speak both Portuguese and English. They emigrated from Brazil when Sabrina was three years old. At home, both parents speak only Portuguese to their child, and Sabrina always spoke in Portuguese to them. But now that she's in a new English-speaking school, her teacher says that she almost never speaks in class. The teacher suggests that Erisson and Fernanda should stop speaking to the child in Portuguese. They are torn. Their own English is not so good—isn't it better to speak good Portuguese to the child rather than bad English?

• • •

Recognizing the benefits of bilingualism, Janet and Betty want their son, Tyler, to speak Spanish. However, though both Janet and Betty have studied Spanish, neither of them speaks it as their first language, and Spanish conversation doesn't come naturally. They buy children's books in Spanish and sometimes read them to Tyler before he goes to bed. They've also hired a Spanish-speaking nanny who takes care of him while Janet and Betty are at work. This seems to be working in a limited way; Tyler has begun to say some words in Spanish, but he still overwhelmingly prefers English. What else can Janet and Betty do to promote bilingualism in their son?

Bilingualism, the ability to speak two languages, is a wonderful gift that parents can give their children. Bilingualism has been shown to have both cognitive and social benefits. Bilingual children develop an awareness of language, sometimes called *metalinguistic awareness*, earlier than those who speak only one language. And, because bilingualism usually goes hand in hand with biculturalism (feeling like one belongs to two cultures), bilingual children also have invaluable insights into more than one society.

Bilingualism, however, can be hard to foster in a child, especially if there is not much support for it in the home or community. Even in homes like Charlene and Dieudonné's, where another language is spoken, it can be difficult to maintain a child's bilingual ability. This is in part because children strongly desire to fit in with their peers. Speaking a different language with their parents can set them apart from their friends, especially if the community itself is not bilingual.

Another obstacle is that bilingualism is more cognitively challenging for children than monolingualism (speaking just one language). Children are no different from the rest of us: when faced with two paths—one easier than the other—they will choose the easier path. That's why, despite Charlene's efforts to speak Kreyol to Dieudonné, he still replies in English. He knows that his mother speaks English and that it's easier for him to express himself in that language, so why make the extra effort to speak Kreyol? Add to this the fact that his school friends don't speak Kreyol, and you've got a recipe for English monolingualism.

Janet and Betty's situation is little different. Neither of them speaks Spanish to Tyler. Though having a Spanish-speaking caregiver seems to help, as soon as Tyler goes to nursery school, he'll lose the consistent exposure to Spanish and will also end up monolingual in English.

This is not to say that bilingualism is impossible to attain; after all, much of the world's population is bilingual (at least). The good news is that despite these psychological and social obstacles, children who are systematically and consistently exposed to another language will become bilingual. The key words here, though, are *systematic* and *consistent*.

As the three stories illustrate, bilingualism can come about under a variety of circumstances. Erisson and Fernanda are both native speakers of Portuguese, so little Sabrina *must* use it if she is to communicate with them. However, they worry that her English will suffer because of their home language. Charlene, married to a monolingual American, probably speaks more English at home than Kreyol. Janet and Betty only speak English at home to Tyler. Each of these situations presents different dilemmas, and calls for correspondingly different strategies.

Let's look at Erisson and Fernanda first, because their situation is probably common to more Americans than the others. Until Sabrina entered nursery school, her language development probably more or less mirrored that of other Brazilian kids. Her first real exposure to English was when she went to school at age four, after she'd already acquired the basics of Portuguese (linguists call this situation *consecutive acquisition of bilingualism*). Once she reached school, though, she was suddenly immersed in another language—one that she could not communicate in. Children in Sabrina's situation, especially children younger than six, often initially try to speak their *home* language to other children. So, for a week or two, Sabrina might have tried to speak to the other (English-speaking) children in the nursery school in Portuguese, and to her bewilderment (though not to ours), these efforts failed. Confused and possibly embarrassed, she retreats into silence.

Teachers and researchers have noticed that a young bilingual child often goes through a *silent period* in the classroom. During this phase, she does not interact with her peers and often withdraws into fantasy play by talking to herself in her native language. The other children, not knowing how to interpret the withdrawn child's behavior, begin to avoid or ignore her, which only increases her sense of isolation.

Fortunately, this silent period is short-lived. Children typically emerge from it after one or two months, after they are able to communicate on a rudimentary level with their peers. It is heartbreaking to watch a child in this lonely and uncomfortable situation; the teacher's suggestion that Erisson and Fernanda begin speaking to Sabrina in English was motivated by genuine concern. However, it is not a decision that we would endorse if Sabrina is to become truly bilingual.

As painful as it is to witness, Sabrina is learning some important things during her period of self-imposed silence. She is watching the other children in her class and listening to them. She desperately wants to fit in and so becomes a keen observer of their interactions and the words that they use. When the teacher asks, "Who wants popcorn for snack?" and all the other kids raise their hands excitedly, Sabrina watches and then raises her hand, even though she's not quite sure what the teacher said. When a little cup of popcorn is placed in front of her, she (gradually) begins to see that "popcorn" must refer to what she knows as *pipoca*. She forms hypotheses about this strange language: maybe she'll hear the phrase "Pick it up!" as one word, and so she'll say something like "*Piggydup* the book!"

Eventually, and with some effort, Sabrina's English will improve. By the next year, she'll be able to follow everything. She might even speak her second language without a trace of an accent, unlike her parents. Sabrina's passage from monolingual Portuguese speaker to bilingual Portuguese-and-English speaker will be a tough one, but it won't last long from an adult point of view.

We suggest that Erisson and Fernanda continue to speak to Sabrina in Portuguese, even reading bedtime stories to her in that language. They might read some stories to her in English as well, or find someone who is comfortable in English to fill in now and then. With time, they'll find that Sabrina will prefer to speak English, especially if she attends English-speaking schools. However, if they insist on speaking Portuguese at home, Sabrina will continue to need that language and will grow up to be bilingual and bicultural.

The case of Dieudonné and his mom, Charlene, is a little bit different. Here, Charlene has married an American and speaks to him in English. Dieudonné is only receiving Kreyol from his mother, and he knows that she also speaks English. Taking the path of least resistance, Dieudonné speaks to his mother in English. What can Charlene do to foster and encourage her son's bilingualism? She needs to put Dieudonné in situations where he must use his Kreyol.

This can be accomplished in many ways: joining a Haitian soccer team, going to a Kreyol-speaking community center, finding books or movies in Kreyol, going to a Kreyol-speaking church service, or other types of interaction with the Haitian community. Charlene might have a Kreyol-speaking relative, such as a grandparent or cousin, regularly spend time with the child. If Charlene makes sure that this systematic exposure is an ongoing feature of her son's life, she can rest assured that he will maintain his bilingual ability.

Janet and Betty are in the hardest situation with regard to raising a bilingual child. They recognize that bilingualism is an asset in several ways: culturally (it gives you insight into another culture), cognitively (some studies indicate that bilingual children think more flexibly than monolingual children), and practically (think of what a boost Spanish will give when little Tyler hits the job market in twenty years!).

However, neither of them is a native speaker of Spanish, so Tyler does not acquire any Spanish from *them*. Although his nanny speaks Spanish, once she is no longer a regular part of Tyler's life, his rudimentary Spanish-language ability will wither. Remember that children will become bilingual if, and only if, they *need* to be bilingual. In this case, there's no situation where Tyler needs to speak Spanish, so he probably won't. Occasional trips to Spanish-speaking countries won't help much either. Children need *regular* exposure to the second language.

Janet and Betty, however, need to recognize that Tyler's struggles with Spanish will not be easy. Despite the common belief that learning a second language as a child is effortless, the opposite is true. In fact, research indicates that it's actually easier for an adult to learn a second language than it is for a child.

"Delayed" Language Development

Nathan and Yi-Hsing are worried that their daughter, Lilly, has a language delay of some sort. It seems that most of the other two-year-olds that they meet are talking; some are even speaking in whole sentences. By contrast, Lilly only produces single words, and sometimes simply gestures and makes grunting-type cries when she wants something. Nathan and Yi-Hsing wonder if they should consult a speech pathologist.

We want to stress that the process of language development is a variable one. Each child goes through the stages of language development at slightly different times and in a slightly different order. As far as language disorders are concerned, this means it's important to recognize that *difference does not necessarily mean delay*. In fact, according to the American Speech-Language-Hearing Association, only 2 to 3 percent of preschool children have a language disorder. By the time children enter school, this goes down to about 1 percent.

There are many factors that influence the rate at which a child acquires language. The child's *gender* may play a role: On average, girls begin developing language earlier than boys, and progress more quickly. The child's *birth order* may matter: the more siblings a child has, the slower his language development. Conversely, firstborns and only children develop language more quickly because, in many cases, they receive their caregivers' full attention. Finally, consider the *amount of talk* directed to a child: the more conversation he hears, the faster his progress.

Also, as we have discussed, *bilingualism* also plays a role in how quickly a child's language develops: children exposed to two languages from birth often show signs of language delay—*but only in the initial stages of language development.* Sometimes a child's *language variety*, or dialect, may be mistaken for a language delay. For example, a child might say something like, "My *muvvuh love* me." To someone unfamiliar with this child's home language, it simply looks like he can't pronounce the "th" sound in "mother," or see the need for the "s" on the word "loves." Instead, these linguistic variations reflect the child's native dialect, not an underlying language disorder.

Some children, however, are at greater risk of language and communication delays. Sometimes the risk is due to prenatal drug exposure. Children born to mothers who used methamphetamines (like "crystal" or "ice"), crack cocaine, marijuana, cigarettes, or alcohol during pregnancy are at higher risk for language and communication disorders. For example, children with fetal alcohol syndrome often have problems with speech articulation and fluency as well as with swallowing. Prenatal nicotine exposure, usually through the mother's cigarette smoking, can lead to reduced cognitive abilities. Illness can also increase risk; children who have suffered from inflammation of the middle ear (known as otitis media) are more likely to develop hearing problems, which later show up as language disorders. *If any of these apply to your child, it's a good idea to have his language and communicative skills assessed early by a professional.* Talk to your pediatrician.

Early assessment and intervention is important. Research shows that those children with language delays in the preschool years are the ones who later develop other language-related problems, such as reading disabilities. Even though some children outgrow early language difficulties, most do not unless intervention starts early.

So, how can you tell if your child might have a language delay? A simple rule of thumb in language development is the one-two-three test: by the end of age one, a child should be able to utter some single words. By age two, the child should, at least, be producing two-word phrases. By the end of age three, you should hear sentences of at least three words.

Before you worry too much, remember that young children are still sorting out the complexities of their first language, including how to pronounce its more difficult sounds. Anyone who's ever tried to roll their "r"s, as in the Spanish word *ferrocarril,* can appreciate what a difficult task pronunciation can be. So, when children are young, it's easy to mistake a simple developmental error for one that suggests a more serious problem.

Of course, it's natural for parents to compare their child's development with that of other children their age. This can often lead to unnecessary worries. Let's say your child didn't develop in one area as quickly as her peers, and despite your best efforts to help her "catch up," she's still "behind" the others. In the case of Nathan and Yi-Hsing, it might be too early to tell if Lilly's slower development of language indicates a more serious problem. Her parents need to consider her language development in context, as only one aspect of her overall development. For example, Lilly's motor development might actually be ahead of other children her age.

Remember that in the early stages of development, children are working on many areas—cognitive, social, emotional, motor, and linguistic—and one may proceed more quickly than another. Ask yourself if your child is developing in sync with her peers in these areas, too. If you are concerned, talk to your pediatrician. She will be able to offer a professional judgment and, if necessary, refer you to an appropriate specialist. Also, get a second opinion; language delay is tough to diagnose definitively in young children, so it's best to have the views of more than one professional.

Simple Ways to Boost Language Skills

Talk to your children. This suggestion might seem obvious. Of course you talk to your children, every day! Yet you might be surprised at how much "conversation" involves just giving directions: "Get your socks." "Don't touch kitty that way!" One study found that on average, parents spend less than ten minutes a day interacting with their children on topics unrelated to directions. Other research shows that regular conversation with adults provides children with important linguistic skills.

Deafness: A Special Case

Including deafness in a section on childhood language or communication disorders is a controversial move. Many believe that deafness is more a subculture than a disorder. Indeed, in the United States, the deaf form their own subculture. They have their own language—American Sign Language (ASL)—their own schools and universities, and in cities such as Washington, D.C., their own neighborhoods. And make no mistake: ASL is a language in its own right. And yet, for the 90 percent of deaf children born into hearing communities, their deafness can separate them from their families and peers. Moreover, deaf children are at heightened risk for language delay and for later reading problems.

In many ways, the language development of deaf children follows that of hearing children. For example, prelinguistic deaf infants have been observed to "babble" with their hands. Deaf children's acquisition of signs mirrors that of hearing children's acquisition of words. Interestingly, young ASL signers make the same types of "developmental errors" that young speakers make. If the child is born to hearing parents, he may not receive enough early linguistic interaction, especially if his deafness is not detected early.

Parents and caregivers should make sure that their children's hearing is regularly tested, especially if the children have suffered severe earaches or ear infections. An audiologist can determine the degree and type of hearing impairment. For example, if hearing loss is in the range of sixteen to seventy-five decibels, a child is said to be "hard of hearing" rather than deaf. Children whose hearing loss exceeds seventy-five decibels are defined as deaf. These distinctions are important in suggesting what strategies to follow.

Hearing parents of deaf children are faced with difficult choices: Should the child be taught ASL, signed English, cued speech, lipreading, or some combination of these? Should the whole family begin studying ASL? Should a cochlear implant be considered for a deaf or hard-of-hearing child? Also, what special services and community networks exist for deaf children of hearing families?

An excellent resource for parents of deaf children is the National Deaf Education Network and Clearinghouse (*http://clerccenter.gallaudet.edu/clearinghouse/index.html*) located at Gallaudet University in Washington, D.C. This features a catalog of publications and on-line documents as well as a state-by-state guide of services for people who are deaf and hard of hearing. Their Web site also lists information about how to locate local parent groups.

You might also try the National Institute on Deafness and Other Communication Disorders (*http://www.nidcd.nih.gov*).

First, through conversations with adults, children come to understand how *discourse,* or everyday speech, works. Most of us don't consciously think about the rules we follow when we speak; our conversations with friends and family seem just to flow naturally. But young children need to learn those rules. Parents can model how talk works for children—when it's your turn to speak, how long you should speak, and what makes up a complete thought. For example, when you ask your five-year-old what she did in kindergarten that day, she might say something like, "We saw a movie, and Sheila laughed at the boy."

Of course, there is missing information here: Who is Sheila? Which boy was she laughing at? What movie did the class watch? What was it about? As an adult, you can ask her questions ("Is Sheila your friend?" "How did that make the boy feel?") that model what a complete story should contain. By asking these questions, you are providing necessary *scaffolding* for your child's language development.

Whenever you can, encourage your child to tell stories: made-up tales, retellings of movie plots, or just stories about what happened that day. Storytelling experiences are the foundation of *narrative development—* a key component of literacy. When you ask your child questions that help him fill the gaps of his story, you're modeling how a well-formed narrative is structured. In a typical story, there's always a "when" ("Today in class . . ."), a "who" ("Miss Johnson and my friend Amy . . ."), a "what" and a "why" (". . . had to go to the nurse because Amy threw up."). Often when we tell a story, we also provide some sort of *evaluation* of the action—details about how we felt or about what lessons we take from the story ("It was really gross! You should never eat and then go on the swing.")

Another advantage of regular interaction with adults is that children are exposed to new vocabulary. By the time most children enter first grade, they have a vocabulary of about ten thousand words. This doesn't mean they can actively *produce* each of those words, but they can understand them. Between the ages of two and six, children build their vocabularies at an astonishing rate: a two-year-old may learn as many as ten words a day.

Researchers have noticed significant differences in the vocabulary size (in academic jargon, the *lexical inventory*) of children as young as three. These differences seemed due, in large part, to the patterns of interactions between the parents and their children. Those children whose parents and caregivers exposed them to a variety of words, in a variety of environments, had noticeably bigger vocabularies than their less-experienced peers.

As we discussed earlier, even being around adult speech can foster children's language development. This lets a child overhear all kinds of words and ideas—some of which you should take the time to explain. While your child might not seem to understand, she'll surprise you later with a word you didn't think she knew.

Choose a regular time to chat with your kids. For some families, socializing takes place around the dinner table (without the television on, please). For other families, it might be during breakfast, or in the car at day's end. It doesn't matter when, only that you make time to really talk together.

Read to your children. There's a lot more on reading in the next chapter. For now, it suffices to say that reading is the next best thing to talking for developing children's language skills. Even children as young as three can derive enormous benefits from being read to.

What About Television?

Television is an inescapable part of modern life. Almost all American families have at least one television set, and American children typically watch four hours of television every day. By the time the average child reaches age eighteen, he's spent more time watching TV than on any other activity except sleeping.

TV watching need not be a passive activity, though. As a parent, you can make television into a useful ally in your child's language acquisition. When you get the chance, watch television with your children and discuss the program with them. Be sure to include open-ended questions—questions without yes-or-no answers—such as:

Why do you think Ernie did that?

How do you think Dora felt when she heard that?

Would you want to live on Sesame Street?

Also, give some thought to what your kids are watching. Some shows, such as *Sesame Street, Between the Lions, Barney & Friends,* and *Dora the Explorer* are specially designed to enhance young children's language skills.

Do a variety of activities with your child. As we noted earlier, going to the zoo, to museums, or to the local firehouse helps develop your child's language skills. Let's think about an outing to the circus from a linguistic standpoint: new words to be learned like *trapeze, lion tamer, clown,* and *juggle.* Actually experiencing these objects and activities firsthand may help a child pick up those terms more quickly. At the circus, the child also finds a chance to practice her interactive skills with other children or adults. She might practice routines like "Excuse me!" when getting up out of her seat or, depending on her age, practice making requests at the concession stand. Afterward, there are opportunities to develop her story-telling skills by asking her what happened, or what she liked best and why.

Joke with your children. Child rearing need not be such serious business all the time. Children enjoy laughing. Of course, what young children find funny usually is less amusing to adults. You can use jokes and riddles as a way to develop children's language skills. That's because many jokes and riddles are based on puns and other plays on words. Consider the following knock-knock joke:

> CAREGIVER: Knock-knock.
>
> CHILD: Who's there?
>
> CAREGIVER: Boo-hoo.
>
> CHILD: Boo-hoo who?
>
> CAREGIVER: Why are you crying?

Okay, Chris Rock it ain't—but to a child, it's pretty funny (go ahead, try it with your four- or five-year-old). And the crux of the joke, as if you couldn't tell, is *homophony:* two words that sound alike but are spelled differently. Understanding this type of joke helps in the development of children's awareness of language and helps prepare that child to learn how to read.

Here's another one that works on the same principle:

> CAREGIVER: What did the daddy tomato say to the baby tomato when they were walking down the street?
>
> CHILD: What?
>
> CAREGIVER: Ketchup. Ketchup!

Another example of homophony—this one a bit more complicated since the child must resegment the words (meaning "ketchup" must become "catch up") while at the same time changing a noun to a verb. Tough, isn't it?

Even tongue twisters are potential tools for language development. Most tongue twisters rely on alternating initial sounds: "How much wood would a woodchuck chuck if a woodchuck could chuck wood?"

This tongue twister plays off of several complicated semantic strategies: homophony ("would" and "wood"), *homonymy* (the same word with different meanings: "chuck" meaning throw and the "chuck" in woodchuck), and *alliteration* (all the words beginning with "w").

The older the child, the more complicated the wordplay can become: "How come we *park* in a driveway and *drive* on a parkway?"

When joking with your child, don't hog the stage; let your child practice telling jokes as well. She probably won't get the hang of it at first—jokes require a complicated combination of timing and precision—but eventually, she'll become more proficient, and be able to share jokes with her peers. Jokes and riddles are examples of "painless learning," because the child practices some pretty complex features of language while getting some laughs.

Some individuals and families engage in playful teasing with their children. Of course, teasing is not for everybody—some children are more sensitive than others, and teasing is less natural for some adults to engage in as well. Studies have shown that dads are more likely to tease their children than moms, and that playful teasing of children is more common in some cultures than in others. At first blush, it might seem as though teasing is unnecessarily cruel. But if it is done in a playful, loving manner, children can learn some valuable social and linguistic lessons from it. Look at the interaction between Maricarmen and her four-year-old child (in Spanish and in English):

MARICARMEN: *¡Te voy a comer enterita!* I'm going to eat you whole!

LAURITA: *¡No! No me vas a comer. No te dejo.* No, you're not going to eat me. I won't let you.

MARICARMEN: *Sí, te voy a comer encebollada con frijoles y tortillas. "Laurita encebollada." ¡Que rico!* Yes, I'm going to eat you with onions, beans, and tortillas. "Laurita with onions!" How delicious!

LAURITA *(laughing)*: *¿Y con salsa también?* And with salsa, too?

MARICARMEN: *Pues si, con una salsita bien picante.* Why yes, with a really hot salsa.

Even at age four, Laurita clearly understands that her mother is joking with her, and she starts playing along. Engaging children in playful teasing develops their sense of irony, a very sophisticated adult skill. It also gives children practice in defending themselves from the teasing of other children—something that, unfortunately, most children will experience at some point during their childhood. But forewarned is forearmed; if your child has developed the social and language skills to shrug off teasing, he's less likely to be a victim of it.

Playact with your children. Children's fantasy plays a critical role in their emotional, social, and linguistic development. When children role-play, they are able to experiment with different kinds of language—what linguists call *registers of language.* Studies of children's fantasy play reveal that even children as young as four have some idea that different types of people speak in different ways. For example, if a child plays the part of an adult, he might shift his tone of voice downward. Or, children might use titles such as "Mister" or "Miss."

Children also get to act out different social roles: a daddy, a mommy, a doctor, an evil sorcerer. Each of these social roles requires a slightly different set of linguistic, vocal, and gestural tools. A "pirate" may use phrases like "Shiver me timbers!" and laugh in a demonic way; a "mommy" might scold her children; a "dinosaur" might roar and speak in a loud, gravelly voice.

Although it can be fun to participate, you needn't be present when your children engage in fantasy play. In fact, your child may try different things when you're not around. The next time she gives a tea party for an elite guest list that includes all her stuffed animals, listen at the door. You'll hear how she's trying on new social and linguistic roles for herself.

Some Final Words

Witnessing the flowering of children's language is one of the many rewards that parenting offers. Like a child's first steps, her first words are an occasion for both joy and wonder. As a child's language develops, so does the quality and complexity of her thinking. When a child learns new words, she's also learning new concepts and fresh ideas. While the language emerges naturally, and at its own pace, parents can play a significant role in their child's language development by doing simple things: by *really* talking to their children, by involving them in a rich variety of experiences, by reading to their children, and by always realizing that any experience, no matter how mundane or trivial it may seem, holds the possibility for learning and offers the opportunity for growth.

Suggestions for Further Reading

American Speech-Language-Hearing Association, 10801 Rockville Pike, Rockville, MD 20852. Toll-free, voice or TTY: 800-638-8255. Web site: *www.asha.org/*

Colin Baker. *A Parent's and Teacher's Guide to Bilingualism.* Multilingual Matters, 2000.

Patricia McAleer Hamaguchi. *Childhood Speech, Language and Listening Problems.* Wiley, 2001.

Edith Harding and Philip Riley. *The Bilingual Family: A Handbook for Parents.* Cambridge University Press, 1987.

Katherine L. Martin. *Does My Child Have a Speech Problem?* Chicago Review Press, 1997.

CHAPTER TEN

Learning to Write and Read

Calvin Gidney and Maryanne Wolf

With great effort and concentration, Tara, age four, has filled an entire sheet of lined paper for the first time—with totally illegible squiggles. Crinkling her brow, she thinks to herself, "Hey, how come if I just wrote this, I can't read it?"

She calls to her teacher, "Beth! Hurry and read this to me!"

Why have we chosen to devote an entire chapter to writing and reading rather than covering it under language development? After all, literacy—the ability to write and read—is, in large part, a language skill. However, unlike learning to speak, which children do naturally, learning to write and read requires explicit and sustained instruction by parents, teachers, or other caregivers.

Literacy is a fairly recent development of human civilization, and the idea that *everyone* should read is only about a century old. Humans existed for thousands of centuries without literacy—and even today, most of the world's languages do not have a writing system. Yet in highly literate societies such as ours, mastery of writing and reading is vital to professional advancement and personal enrichment. For this reason, we think it's important to take a detailed look at writing and reading: how they develop in children, and what caregivers and parents can do to foster children's literacy development.

You may have noticed that we use the phrase "write and read" even though most people use the opposite order: "read and write." We do this on purpose because, as you'll see, children typically begin with writing first and from there move to reading. This makes sense if you think about it; from a child's perspective, writing is a fairly transparent activity, akin to drawing. A person sits down with a pen or crayon and makes some marks on paper. A young child might think, "Well, *I* can do that!"

Reading, on the other hand, is more opaque. Imagine what reading must look like to a young child: Mommy sits at the kitchen table with a magazine in hand, looking silently at a bunch of indecipherable characters on a page. When the child tries to speak to her, she says, "Shh! I'm trying to read, dear." Well, what exactly is she doing? Why must there be quiet? It's all so confusing.

In this chapter we will present some of the facts about the early development of literacy. We will address some of the following questions:

- How do children make sense of writing?

- What are children's first steps toward writing?

- How do children make sense of reading?

- How does reading start in young children? Why is letter-sound awareness important? What books are best for developing letter-sound awareness?

- Why do some children have difficulty learning to read? Does speaking a second language delay reading?

- How can parents help their children get more out of books, and develop a love of reading?

Before we enter into this discussion, however, we'd like to clarify one thing. Throughout this chapter we will use the term "literacy" to refer to more than just the mechanics of writing and reading. Of course, in the early years, the mechanics of literacy (for example, how children figure out the connection between letters and sounds) is a principal focus of education— but literacy is more than just that. Literacy, in its broadest sense, includes *ways of thinking and behaving.* In this broad sense, the term "literacy" can be discussed in relation to other activities, such as watching television or having a face-to-face conversation. It implies being able to answer certain types of questions, and to use skills such as analysis, interpretation, and integration.

How Do Children Make Sense of Writing?

Tiffany is playing with a toy phone in her kindergarten classroom. She makes the phone ring, answers it, and then scribbles down several inde-cipherable lines. She takes her message over to her teacher and says, "You've got a message."

The teacher asks her what the message says and Tiffany replies, "I don't know, but it's very important!"

Tiffany has realized something very significant about writing—that it is a visual representation of speech. While this is certainly a profound realization, writing is also different from speech in several important ways. What's more, writing is a complex activity that requires the successful integration of diverse cognitive skills.

How is writing complicated? First of all, writing requires us to break up the speech stream into discrete sounds, called "phonemes." Linguists and other scientists are still trying to figure out how children are capable of breaking up speech into individual sounds—because when we speak, all the sounds blend together so quickly that there are hardly any measurable gaps between them. Think about this the next time you hear an unfamiliar foreign language: it seems like an endless stream of sound, and you can't tell where one word ends and another begins. Recent research suggests that children may be "preprogrammed" to segment speech; infants have the ability to distinguish speech from other noises such as dogs' barks or car alarms.

Another difficulty with writing is that each phoneme must be paired with some visual representation: a letter of the alphabet (what is technically called a "grapheme"). For each phoneme, there may be several graphemes. For example, take a look at the following:

A A A ɑ a *a*

Each of these symbols is, from a drawing standpoint, quite distinct. But as writers and readers of English, we recognize that they all stand for the same letter.

A third difficulty with writing is that each of the words of our language has, usually, only one spelling—and these spellings are far from consistent. Sometimes we use two letters to represent a single sound (like "sh" or "ch"); sometimes we use one letter to represent several sounds (the letter "x" can sound like "ks" or "gz"—compare "box" and "exam"); sometimes two different sounds use the same letters (we use "th" to represent the different sounds in bath and bathe). And these are just the *two-letter* combinations! Consider the many sounds that the letters "ough" can stand for:

"uff"   As in "rough"

"oh"   As in "though"

"oo"   As in "through"

"aw"   As in "thought"

Consider also that some concepts are represented in writing that have no counterpart in speech. Commas, for example, sometimes correspond to brief pauses in speech—but then again, so do periods, dashes, semicolons, colons, and exclamation points!

As writers of English, we know that words run from left to right, and that we should put spaces between them. While this is obvious to us adults, young children only gradually learn this about writing.

A final complexity of writing lies in the fact that writing requires us to change our language in order to make it easily understandable. Speech is, essentially, a face-to-face activity—one in which the person speaking and the person listening often share the same space. This means that when one person says, "Could you hand me that?" and points to, say, a pencil, the listener know what "that" refers to. Even if the listener doesn't know, she can simply ask the speaker ("Do you mean the *stapler*?").

When we write, we must assume that the person who will read what we've written won't be able to ask us questions to clarify what we mean. This requires that written language be more explicit than spoken language; that is, we need to supply more information when writing than when speaking. Speaking relies a great deal on the context, the "here and now" of the speech, while writing does so to a much lesser extent.

In learning how to write, children must understand and master all of these complexities. It's a daunting task—one that requires instruction from parents, caregivers, and teachers, and one that emerges gradually.

What Are Children's First Steps Toward Writing?

Take a look at this child's drawing. One of the things you'll notice is that there are several symbols in it that correspond to letters of the alphabet and to numbers. There's a clear N, P, zero or O and some numbers along with a face and other shapes. You'll remember that we said that to young children, writing is linked to drawing. Well, because of this, the drawings of many young children contain *alphanumeric characters*, or letters and numbers. Even the next picture, which looks to an adult eye like scribble, is a child's impression of cursive writing. *Linear scribble* shows that this child understands that in some way. The writings that grown-ups do on paper represent language.

Nicole Gabrielle, age 3½

In these first stages, children use whatever alphanumeric symbols they know, along with other letterlike symbols. If you ask your child to "read" what he's written, he might not be able to, but you can rest assured that your child will come to understand the complex relationship of speech to writing.

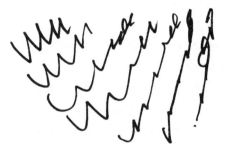

Nicole Gabrielle, age 3½

Young prewriters can hold some interesting notions about writing. For example, many young children think that the bigger an object is, the bigger the letters should be, or the longer the word is. So, to a young child, the word "bear" should be bigger than the word "bird" because a bear is bigger than a bird.

Later, children hypothesize that words should have at least three characters, and that each word should use a different combination of the same characters. Many children assume that each letter represents a word. So, for example, a child might think that "SN2NL" could stand for

"My dog is very pretty." Actually, this is a critical moment because it marks the understanding that letters represent some element of language.

One of the first words that a child can accurately recognize is her own name. Children are probably exposed to their names more than to any other word. After all, it's written on their lunch boxes, on their clothes, in their books, and other places. Learning how to write her name at an early age actually helps a child understand the alphabetic principle: that one letter, or grapheme, corresponds to one sound, or phoneme (that is, unless her name is something like Phoebe!). This is important, because many young children believe that letters correspond to *syllables* rather than to individual sounds (and in some writing systems, this is true—but not in ours). A child's name can help her understand that, generally, each letter in her name corresponds to a *sound* in her name.

Once a child has understood the alphabetic principle, his writing becomes more and more like adult models. Even this, though, develops only gradually. Initially, young writers frequently use a letter's *name* for its *sound*. So, for example, a child might write "RUCINME?" for "Are you seeing me?" (Interestingly, this resembles the E-mail or pager shorthand of today's teenagers.)

By discussing writing before we address reading, we do not mean to imply that one is more important than the other. Rather, writing and reading are interconnected and reciprocal: the more a child practices writing, the more she improves her reading skills. Likewise, the more a child practices reading, the more she practices writing skills as well. Ever wonder why the best writers are usually avid readers? Well, here's why: When we read, we learn new words, new ways of using language, and new ways of expressing ourselves in the written mode. Subconsciously we internalize what we've read so that when we write, we draw on what we've read before.

How Do Children Start to Understand Reading?

Young Craig sits beside his father one Sunday morning, watching him read the newspaper. Craig picks up the paper, opens it up, and looks silently at the pages, "reading." Dad begins to chuckle when he notices that Craig is holding the paper upside down!

The very fact that you're reading this now means that, most likely, you're a fluent reader. This means that you're able to read these sentences automatically, without ever consciously thinking about what you're doing. But if you take a closer look at what we do when we read, you'd see that reading is a very complex process—perhaps the most complicated task we ever master in our lives.

As the story above illustrates, reading is, at first, a mysterious activity to young children. Craig knows that his dad is engaged in some type of activity that involves conscious attention to pages of symbols. He sees his dad sitting there, occasionally turning pages and making comments to Mom about what he's reading. Beyond this, though, it's unclear what's going on in Dad's head. Children only gradually come to understand things about reading that we fluent readers take for granted: that text (in English, anyway) moves from left to right and from top to bottom; that the symbols on the page (letters or graphemes) correspond to individual sounds of our language (phonemes); and finally, that these are combined into words, each of which has a standard spelling, or orthography.

Reading is, in the words of specialists, a *multimodal activity;* it requires our brains to coordinate and integrate many different skills— language skills, meaning skills, visual skills—all at the same time. A closer look at these skills will help us better understand the challenges young children face when learning to read.

For most people, reading begins with the eyes. When we see some printed text, our eyes send this visual information to a part of our brain that is responsible for identifying and categorizing visual information. Over time, our brains come to recognize familiar visual information more and more quickly; the more familiar a pattern, such as a letter, the faster we can process it. The process becomes so quick it is said to be automatic, and this is one of the most important aspects of learning to recognize letters and words.

Of course, reading is much more than just recognizing letters and words; it also requires us to match those visual symbols with individual sounds of our language, what specialists call phonemes. This matching involves another area of the brain: the area involved in hearing. But the type of hearing we use here is important. It's not the same part of our brain we use when we hear a fire alarm or a clap of thunder; it's the part of the brain we use to break words down into their smallest components: sounds. What children must learn to do is automatically match the visual symbol (or grapheme) to a sound (a phoneme). This grapheme-phoneme connection is the cornerstone of reading.

It doesn't just end here: other parts of our brain, especially those that control our attention, also come into play. Attention helps us focus on the reading task and is important in helping us remember and understand what we're reading. Pretty complicated stuff, right? And to think that we ask children to master reading in elementary school. It's a miracle each time a child learns to read.

How Does Reading Begin in Young Children?

Marcia sits in rapt attention, tucked beneath the arm of her mother, listening to words that move like water—words that tell of faraway places never visited and never before imagined. Her mother points from time to time to pictures of giants, and beautiful women with beautiful dresses, and boys brave enough to climb bean stalks that climb as high as the sky itself.

This scene is repeated all over the world in many different cultures and through many different languages—and it holds all the important elements of early reading development. It is under the crook of a loved one's arm that reading best begins. A child learns to associate reading with the sense of being loved and led into a new world of imagination.

This can begin as soon as an infant can sit in his caretaker's lap. And the best part is, at that early age, it doesn't much matter what you read to the child: the newspaper, that magazine article you've been meaning to read—even the weather report! What does matter is that you read: that you begin the habit of reading to your child so that she can start on the road to literacy. And read to her often. Research has consistently found that the amount of time you spend reading to your child is a superb indicator of that child's future reading achievement.

Children's love of reading starts with the delight of hearing their caregiver's voice. Next comes falling in love with pictures. Children become fascinated with the many varied visual images in books. That's why, if you look at quality books written for young prereaders, there are plenty of beautiful illustrations, photos, and in some cases, pop-up dioramas.

At a later stage, the child's emerging language development guides her likes and dislikes. The meaning of the text becomes more and more important (at this point, you should probably stop reading the op-eds and weather to her). After the child begins to understand that specific pictures go with particular stories, and that stories convey wonderful words and feelings, more critical and subtle details of reading are absorbed. Children gradually discover that the book's lines are full of large and small words that stay the same every time the book is read. Next, they discover that these words go in a specific direction: in English, from left to right. Sometimes, a young child will mimic adults and move her fingers from left to right so that she looks like she's "reading"—even when there's not a line of print on the page.

Over time, the squiggling shapes on a page of text become more familiar and, for some children, individual letters can be identified. It is at this point that children begin to make the connection between the printed letter (the grapheme) and a sound (the phoneme). If they are read to often, children as young as four are able to reflect on the sounds of language: an ability that is essential for learning how to read.

It will take time for children to learn the letter names and sounds (many English-speaking children think there's a letter named "elemeno," as in "elemeno—P"). However, be sure to *encourage children to name letters* from the time that they appear to be ready to do so. The awareness that words are made up of a sequence of individual sounds is called "phonemic awareness," or *letter-sound awareness*, and is *one of the most critical predictors of later reading achievement.*

WHAT KINDS OF BOOKS CAN HELP MY CHILD DEVELOP LETTER-SOUND AWARENESS?

As we have seen, children's ideas about what sounds make up words can be quite different from adult notions. Children's phoneme awareness develops over time and depends, to a large extent, on their exposure to reading. There are types of books that foster this awareness. Books that are rich in rhymes, such as *Mother Goose*, or some of Dr. Seuss's books, have been shown to be especially useful in developing children's phoneme awareness. Why? Well, take a look at the beginning of this well-known nursery rhyme:

> *Hickory dickory dock!*
> *The mouse ran up the clock!*

The first thing you notice about this is that the words rhyme—hickory and dickory, dock and clock. When words rhyme, it means that one part of the words, the endings, are the same, and one part, the beginnings, are different. This simple variation helps young children understand that words are made up of sounds by focusing their attention on small variations. Texts that use nonsense words, such as "dickory" (whatever that means), are also helpful because children cannot focus on the meaning of the word but must concentrate only on its sound.

Remember, the development of phoneme awareness takes time and practice, but there's no reason it needs to be a chore: it can be great fun! You don't always have to be reading something to work on phonemic awareness skills: remember the children's name chant, "Janet, Janet bo-Banet, banana-fana fo-Fanet, fee-fie-mo Manet, JA-net"? Well, even though this is not an example of reading per se, it is a game that focuses on sound substitutions. Singing a song like this in the car with a four- or five-year-old is fun and has the added benefit of working on literacy skills (though don't tell your kid that).

Why Do Some Children Have Difficulty Learning to Read?

Clifton and Tanya are worried that their son, Jamal, is having trouble grasping the rudiments of reading. Some of his friends already know their alphabet, and can even recognize simple words such as "cat" and complex words such as their names. They worry that Jamal is "not as smart" as other kids his age.

Even when children are read to early and often, some will still have problems learning to read. Although the majority of children will eventually learn to read using almost any method of instruction, many need patient, systematic, and explicit teaching of letter-sound rules. As we have seen, learning to read is an extremely complex process that requires the integration of many types of cognitive skills: language skills, visual skills, and attention skills. In such a process, even a slight breakdown in these microprocesses can serve as the basis of reading difficulties. A child who has problems with word retrieval—the quick recall of the word for an object or color—may develop reading difficulties. A child who has trouble breaking words into sounds may also have reading difficulties.

What's important to remember is that if a child struggles with learning to read, it does not mean the child's not as intelligent as his peers. Children with *dyslexia*, a learning disability that affects reading, writing, and/or spelling, are no less smart than other children—often they are smarter. Their brains just process some kinds of information differently. (Other learning disabilities can affect how children write letters or grasp math concepts.) Dyslexia runs in families; sometimes more than one child in a family will have problems "decoding" words.

If you suspect that your child needs something different from what is being taught, be open and honest with his teacher. You and the teacher are both advocates for your child, and only want what's best for him. Together, you can develop a plan that may include a change in methods or outside tutoring using another, more appropriate method of instruction. If reading and/or learning disabilities are suspected, work with the teacher to get your child a proper assessment across a range of language, reading, and learning skills; this will show whether he needs special services unavailable in the classroom. Don't just "wait and see"; if a child who is thought to be at risk for having dyslexia can get instruction tailored to her needs early, in kindergarten or first grade, she is much more likely to keep up with her peers in reading.

There are two very simple tasks a kindergarten teacher can give to children that are superb at predicting who's at risk for reading problems. These include a "phoneme-awareness" test, and a "naming-speed" test. The first task gives us a window into how well a child can hear and segment the individual sounds in words. (This ability is critically important in learning the letter-sound correspondence rules that underlie language decoding.) For example, the teacher tells the child: "Say the word 'birthday.' Now say 'birthday' without the 'day.' Now say 'birth' without the 'b.'" At each point, the teacher is getting more and more information about whether a child can segment speech and discriminate between the individual sound parts in a word.

The naming-speed task provides a different kind of window; it gives an idea of how accurately and how fast the child's brain can integrate, or put together, visual processes with language processes. A child is asked to give the name of five letters or numbers or colors. The speed with which he can find a name for a visually presented symbol is related to the speed the brain takes to integrate these same processes used later in learning to read. Together with a child's vocabulary knowledge, these two tasks can tell the teacher a great deal about whether the child needs extra help in learning to read. Preventive action is terribly important for children with reading difficulties, and the phoneme-awareness activities—such as the teacher having the children identify words that rhyme and words that start with the same letter—can help everyone in class.

You can get more information about learning disabilities from organizations such as the International Dyslexia Association (visit their Web site: *http://www.interdys.org,* or call 410-296-0232).

DOES SPEAKING ANOTHER LANGUAGE AT HOME
HINDER LITERACY DEVELOPMENT?

Tesfay and Maryam Dagachew are both recent immigrants from Ethiopia. At home, they both speak Amharic to their son, Hailu, but Hailu attends an English-speaking kindergarten. Tesfay and Maryam worry that Hailu's literacy skills will lag behind the other students unless they read to him in English. They also wonder if teaching Hailu Amharic, which has a different writing system than English, will harm his development of English-language literacy.

The good news about phonemic awareness is that it is transferable: *if a child develops phoneme awareness in one language, he can use that same knowledge in another language.* This is one of the many important insights that have emerged from research on the development of literacy in bilingual children.

It so happens that Amharic, the Dagachews' native language, does not even use the same written alphabet as English (in fact, it's not really an "alphabet" at all: the symbols represent syllables instead of letters). Luckily, though, even this apparent obstacle is not critical. If Tesfay and Maryam read to Hailu in their native language, he will come to understand what English-speaking children learn: that words are made up of smaller units, and that these smaller units are represented by written symbols. When Hailu is read to by his English-speaking kindergarten teacher, he will bring these same insights to his second-language experience.

What's important here is that research suggests Hailu will have an easier time learning to read in English if he has started the process in his native language first. It's easy to see why: Can you imagine learning to read first in a language you don't really speak that well? There would probably be so many unfamiliar sounds—like the strange English "th" sounds, or the subtle distinction between the vowel sounds of the words "chip" and "cheap"—that would make learning to read more difficult than it already is. Therefore, we recommend that, *whenever possible, children who speak a language other than English in their homes should become literate in their native languages before becoming literate in English.* This is why early bilingual education programs are beneficial. However, when bilingual programs are not available, it is very beneficial for non-English-speaking parents to read to their children in their native language.

Helping Children Get More Out of Books

Hanan is reading to her three-year-old son, Ali, in their Boston apartment. As she reads, she points to words like "ball" and isolates some of the individual sounds like "b," but he seems much more interested in the pictures. Hanan and her husband, Mohammed, really want Ali to attend a highly regarded preschool in Boston—but they worry that unless he already knows his letters and the sounds they make, he won't get in.

Today's parents receive messages from the media and other sources that their children should know how to read by the time they enter kindergarten. While it is important to start developing children's literacy skills early, we do not wish to advocate pushing children too quickly. Remember that literacy is a complicated set of skills that develops gradually.

In the story above, Hanan may be asking her son to accomplish more than he's ready for. The major areas in the brain responsible for the integration of sensory information—for example, linking visual and verbal processes—do not develop fully in many children until the years between five and seven. Forcing children to learn to read too early is physiologically impossible and educationally unwise. An early reader is not necessarily a better reader later in life. Other strategies make more sense at this stage—most important, reading to your child.

Reading to your children prepares them for formal education in a number of ways. One benefit of reading to children is that it helps develop and reinforce their *vocabularies*. Through books, children are exposed to complex grammatical structures such as passive sentences—"Peter was warned by his family about the wily fox"—or compound sentences—"Hildie took the rabbit, held it in her arms, and comforted it."

Reading to young children, when combined with face-to-face interaction, also develops children's *thinking skills*. When you read to your child, stop to ask a variety of questions:

Where is Oscar?

What's this?

Why do you think she did that?

How do you think Oscar felt about that?

What color is that?

When is the bird's mommy going to come home?

Remember when Daddy went on vacation? What did you do?

These types of questions encourage children to reflect on what they read, to draw inferences about what has happened, and to understand connections between what they already know and what they're learning. It's important to ask different kinds of questions—questions that have a specific answer (closed-ended questions like "What color is that?"), and questions that do not have specific answers (open-ended questions like "Why do you think he did that?"). It's also helpful to sometimes read the story cover to cover without stopping to ask questions.

Finally, reading also develops children's *fantasy lives*. Books do for children what they do for adults: take them away from their everyday worlds and expose them to new worlds, new thoughts, and new ideas. So, make a regular habit of reading to your children, no matter how young they are. If English is not your native language, read to them in that language; the beauty of reading is that the skills that children learn in one language can be transferred to another.

MAKE READING TIME SPECIAL

We talked earlier about how warm interactions with parents start children on the path to loving books. Make reading with your child a special and fun experience. Sit together in a comfortable place; turn off the TV and other distractions. Sing Dr. Seuss rhymes to whatever tune pops into your head. Use your acting skills to develop distinct voices for different characters; once your child starts reading, encourage her to do the same. (This can also help to relax children who are worried about making reading mistakes.)

CHOOSE BOOKS THAT SUIT YOUR CHILD'S AGE AND INTERESTS

Most big toy stores have a children's book section where the books are divided into age groups: books for toddlers, books for children three to five, and so on. These books are specially designed to hold children's attention and are tailor-made to children's language abilities. The American Library Association is a good source of information on quality children's books (visit their Web site at *http://www.ala.org/parents/index.html*). Encourage your child to browse through the books and try out different ones.

Books, even children's books, can be expensive. Check out your nearest public library; they often have extensive collections for young readers, and may have children's librarians who can offer good advice. Your child's day-care center or preschool may also have a lending library.

CHOOSE BOOKS THAT SHOW A VARIETY OF LIFE EXPERIENCES AND PEOPLE

It's a big wide world out there, and most of us have neither the time nor the money to experience it all firsthand. But through books, you can expose your child to a range of wonders and visions. Choose some books that show life experiences very different from your own. This lets books become a platform from which children can explore the nature of human diversity and human experiences. For example, the American Library Association site above includes lists of books featuring black and Latino viewpoints.

Some Final Words

Here are the points we most want to stress:

- It's never too early to begin reading to your child.

- Read to your child every day.

- Help your child learn her letter names and, if possible, the sounds these letters make.

- When selecting reading material, be sure to include books that are rich in rhyme, even when there are lots of nonsense words.

- If your family is bilingual or speaks a language other than English at home, it's okay to read to your child in your native language; the skills he learns will transfer to English.

- If you suspect that your child is having problems with learning to read, discuss the matter with his teacher. Together, you can devise strategies that might be better suited to his learning needs and style.

It is indeed miraculous that anyone ever learns to read, given how complex and multifaceted the activity is. Unlike children's language development, which follows its course without much explicit intervention, reading only develops when children receive patient, loving, systematic instruction. Almost a century ago, Sir Edmund Huey wrote that reading is "the most remarkable specific performance that civilization has learned in all its history." It is one of the greatest privileges of parenting to bring children into the stream of this marvelous human endeavor.

Suggestions for Further Reading

Mary Ann Hoberman. *You Read to Me, I'll Read to You: Very Short Stories to Read Together.* Little, Brown, 2001.

National Research Council. *Starting Out Right: A Guide to Promoting Children's Reading Success.* National Academy Press, 1999.

Judith Schickedanz. *Much More Than the ABCs: The Early Stages of Reading and Writing.* National Association for the Education of Young Children, 1999.

Jim Trelease. *The Read-Aloud Handbook.* Penguin, 2001.

Photo by Justine Salamone

Electronic Media in Young Children's Lives

Julie Dobrow

> The Levy family had just come home from vacation. Rather than checking their rooms or reconnecting with favorite toys, four-year-old David yelled, "Let's see what's on TV!" and six-year-old Sarah excitedly ran over to turn on the computer. Their dad wonders if they are too attached to electronic entertainment, and whether he ought to push them to go outside or play a board game.

Today's parents grew up in a media-rich environment. Their children are growing up in one that's media-saturated. In the United States, 99 percent of us have televisions (a higher percentage than have telephones), about 97 percent have VCRs, and over three-quarters subscribe to cable or satellite TV. Most of our children have access to computers. And we are exposed to advertising everywhere: it's on TV and radio, it's plastered on everything from billboards to apples, it's on the Internet, it comes before movies and videos—it even comes out with our ATM slips!

The average American preschooler spends about three and a half hours a day involved with media—mostly television. What are they learning from all this? Many parents are concerned about the possible effects on their children's social, emotional, and intellectual development. For example, how do programs and commercials influence what our kids like, want, feel, and do? What kinds of behavior get punished or praised? How do our children handle content they're not ready for?

Parents ponder limiting their children's viewing time and wonder about what other kinds of rules they can make to govern their children's use of media. A few believe that the best thing to do is to purge their homes of televisions or computers; others guiltily pop in a Disney video to get a much-needed break.

In this chapter, we will offer ideas to reduce problems with media use, and to use that media time in positive, educational, and prosocial ways. Researchers have consistently found that adult guidance helps children get greater benefit from watching television and movies and from using computers.

Just as our children need to read and write, they also need to become "media literate." They learn some of the "grammar" of media just by watching, e.g., that a cut from one scene to another means the story has jumped in place and time. But media literacy can also be taught: for example, "Ads are made to sell you things. That's why some toys look more fun on TV than they turn out to be at home." The growing media literacy movement says: "Teach children to become more careful and critical users of media, and they will learn to make good choices in their own selection and evaluation of these ever-present resources."

This chapter will also discuss the *myths and realities of how young children actually view and use television, video, and computers.* We'll offer practical suggestions about how you can help your children use media to promote their social, emotional, and cognitive development, and how you can help make even very young children more critical consumers of media programs of all types.

We'll cover issues such as:

- How children really watch, and learn from, television, and how TV affects learning to read

- How to help your child separate media fantasy and reality—and deal with scary content

- How kids may be affected by exposure to media violence, and how to protect them

- What to tell kids about TV advertising and media stereotyping

- How to handle fights over TV

- Choosing good videos and films, and preparing a child for her first visit to the movies

- What children need to be ready for computers, finding software that's appropriate for them, and an introduction to Internet use

Television and the Preschool Child

HOW PRESCHOOLERS REALLY WATCH TELEVISION

Three-year-old Juana watches television with rapt attention. She stares at the screen, doesn't speak, and seems completely mesmerized by the images she watches. Her mother wonders if there's anything going on behind Juana's seemingly blank gaze.

In a word, yes! Though parents may be alarmed when they glimpse their child sitting riveted to the screen, researchers have found that for young children, television viewing is actually a very active and intellectually engaging activity. Kids look away from the television at least as much as they look at it. One study found that during an hour-long episode of *Sesame Street,* children between the ages of two and a half and five looked away from and back to the screen more than 150 times.

Most children do a lot of other things when they are "watching" TV. They play, sing (how many toddlers can resist singing "I love you, you love me" along with Barney?), talk back to the television ("He's hiding behind the tree!"), and jump around. These behaviors are typical for preschoolers, who are easily distracted from a single focus. Of course, adults do this, too—most of us talk on the phone, fold laundry, pay bills, etc., while the television is on—and we model this for our young children.

We also know from research that children are fairly selective about what they watch. Until around age three, children will only pay real attention to programs, or elements of programs, that they can understand. If a program segment is not clearly understandable to a child, she won't focus on it, though she may look up at the TV if she hears something interesting and familiar. For example, a toddler will not generally pay any attention to the news, unless she hears a child's voice, music, or something else that piques her interest.

> Fourteen-month-old Lexi likes to watch television along with her three-year-old brother, Justin. Sally, their mother, is incredulous: Is it possible that Lexi is really getting anything out of watching TV at her age?

Children show interest very early in pictures and sounds from television. Researchers find that children as young as fourteen months old can remember images from television for a day or more, though they cannot describe them accurately. In the case above, Lexi is also being cued by her older brother that TV is something worth watching.

Two-year-olds are attracted to certain features on television such as animation, strange voices, fast music, rhymes, sound effects and changes in sound, faces or voices of women and children, puppets, and repetition. When you read this list, you can clearly understand the attraction of programs like *Barney, Sesame Street,* or *Blue's Clues,* along with other programs for toddlers.

Recent research suggests that the way children understand and process what they see on TV is akin to the way they learn spoken language: Everything a child sees and hears on TV is a symbol that needs to be translated into something he knows, just as he learns that when you say "applesauce" it means something he likes to eat. The older a child gets, the better he learns to translate and use these symbols, just as he becomes more sophisticated in his comprehension and use of language. In this way, a child learns that when the edges of a picture on TV get fuzzy, this may indicate a dream or fantasy sequence. He learns to translate the visual cues into something he understands, just as he learns that a word represents a real thing.

WHAT CHILDREN LEARN FROM TELEVISION

> After watching a favorite video on Babar the elephant king, four-year-old Devon asked for paper, tape, and crayons. As he built Babar's castle, Devon sang, "B is for Babar, that's good enough for me . . ." to the tune of *Sesame Street*'s "C Is for Cookie."

When we think of children learning from television, educational shows aired on PBS may spring to mind. But a show doesn't need an "educational" label for them to learn from it; learning goes on all the time. There's been a virtual explosion in the number and quality of programs available for children. Shows that expand their understanding of the world and teach prosocial skills and values are found not only on public television, but on a number of other broadcast and cable channels as well.

(Note that commercial broadcast stations are required by the Children's Television Act of 1990 "to serve the educational and informational needs of children both through their overall programming, and through programming that is specifically designed to serve those needs." This translates into at least three hours a week of such programming, or demonstration of "an equivalent level of commitment to educating children." Such programs may be marked "E/I" on the screen. Also, a station's Web site sometimes lists designated "E/I" programs and suggested age ranges.)

Television also has advantages as a teaching tool. In his theory of

"multiple intelligences" (described in chapter 7), Howard Gardner suggested that different children learn best in different ways. Some children
quickly "get" information presented in a written form, others do well
with pictures and diagrams, while still other children might learn best
from information that comes through song or music. Television is well
suited to presenting information in these multiple formats. Many parents note that their children sing, draw, or otherwise repeat things
they've learned from television.

There's been a lot of research about the ways television might bring
positive or prosocial messages to children. We know that television can
be a great way of modeling positive social behavior. For example, a study
of *Barney* found that children who watched the show regularly were more
emotionally aware and likely to share. Other research has found that
preschoolers can learn to be more generous, to cooperate, and to obey
rules such as fire safety rules from television shows.

Perhaps the most researched children's television program is *Sesame
Street*. Hundreds of studies have been conducted all over the world. Most
found that the program has directly helped regular viewers from all
social and economic backgrounds improve letter and number recognition
as well as other cognitive skills.

Many researchers have found that having adult help and reinforcement
is the best way to increase a child's comprehension of television messages.
Some television shows build this into their formats. For example, *Blue's
Clues* has an adult posing questions, offscreen children's voices answering,
and the adult repeating the children's responses—a technique that both
reinforces the message and encourages at-home viewers to respond.

At this writing, other programs (among many) we like for two- and
three year olds include *Bob the Builder, Bear in the Big Blue House, Oswald
the Octopus,* and *Dora the Explorer*. Like *Blue's Clues, Dora* is interactive. It
asks kids to talk back to the TV and gives them time to respond. It also
introduces logic and maps. And, as one of few shows to use Spanish as
much as English, it helps young viewers appreciate and even learn a bit
of a second language.

When choosing programs, it also helps to ask, "Is this something I'd want to watch with my kids?" A clever and well-written show that appeals to you will also continue to appeal to your child as she gets older. Also look for quality music and—especially for younger kids—programs that don't have commercial breaks.

As children get older, they start to enjoy programs about things kids deal with in the real world, such as negotiating differences, competition, and resolving conflicts. Some programs that target elementary-age children, such as *Arthur* or *Hey Arnold,* can also be enjoyed by younger kids.

You can help make watching TV an *active* learning process for your child by watching favorite shows together. Comment on the major actions and themes you see ("Oswald is looking everywhere for his dog. He must be very worried about her.") and ask your child questions about what you're viewing ("Look! What happened to the birthday cake?"). As children get older, the things you select for comment, and the questions you ask, can become more sophisticated. ("Did you hear how Angelica teased her cousin? How do you think he felt?" Or, "Arthur really got frustrated with his sister, D.W. How would you handle a problem like that with your little sister?")

You can think of your young children's media use as a window into their developmental processes. Listen to the way your child describes what is happening on a television program (or what's going on in a computer program) at different stages of development. At two, he might cover basics of the story ("The pipe broke and they got wet"). By five, he'll start to ascribe motives and feelings to characters in the plot ("He needed the wrench to fix the pipe and stop the water, and he got really upset when his friend floated away"). As you watch your child gain a deeper understanding of the content, you'll also see how he's grown intellectually, socially, and emotionally.

THE RELATIONSHIP BETWEEN TELEVISION VIEWING AND READING

Five-year-old Jane Lee knows all of her letters and enjoys being read to. She also likes to watch TV. Her parents worry that watching television will delay her learning to read on her own.

Probably not, though it depends in part on what shows she watches. The widely held belief that television viewing takes away from reading is simply not supported by the research. Most studies from various countries suggest that what television viewing displaces is not reading, but time children might spend with other media activities, such as computer games. Furthermore, some studies show that certain television programs can actually enhance reading readiness. For example, as mentioned earlier, much of the work on *Sesame Street* has shown that television can actually help children gain some of the cognitive skills they'll need to recognize letters and put them together as words.

Several other television shows aired at the time of this writing focus on reading and the written word. In one study, 86 percent of children's librarians polled stated that *Reading Rainbow* was directly responsible for the increased circulation of books featured on the show. The phenomenal success of *Arthur* in the late 1990s boosted huge sales of that book series. (More than 26 million have been sold since the television programs were first shown.) Librarians reported that it was not possible to keep those books on the shelf for any length of time. Many of the show's plots emphasize that reading is fun and important. Finally, some kindergarten teachers even use the program *Between the Lions* for prereaders (ages two to five) because its teaching of vowels, consonants, and combination sounds has been shown to enhance reading skills.

Again, watching with your child will help her make a link between what she sees on the screen and what she will see in print. You can reinforce what she sees on television with books on the same topic. For example, if your toddler watches a segment of *Sesame Street* that deals with pets, read a book about animals. If your kindergartner sees a show about fighting and making up with a friend, you can both ask the children's librarian for books about that. If a favorite show is based on a book, get the book and read it together. Ask, "Why do you think the story is different on TV than it was in the book?"

Also, many programs have ancillary materials (including ones that promote reading skills) that you and your child can use during non-TV time. These include Web sites (e.g., *PBSkids.org* or *Nick.com*), computer or board games, and other educational toys.

TELEVISION MAKE-BELIEVE

> Five-year-old Jeremy was watching a cartoon. He turned to his grand-mother, who was watching with him, and said, "I know that this isn't real."
> "How do you know?" asked his grandmother.
> "Because," he replied, "if it was real, the robots wouldn't have yellow heads, they'd have silver ones!"

So much of what we see on television seems driven by fantasy. How do kids learn that what they see on TV is not the same as what happens in real life? We've all heard cute stories about children who seem to believe that characters or fantasy situations on television are real, or that characters they see on TV are really little puppets that somehow appear in that box. Some think that the actors who portray characters actually have those special powers, or are not actors at all. Researchers have found that indeed, for very young children, television is like a magic window, and children think that there is a literal reality to what they see.

But by age three or four, children start to show a little skepticism and no longer believe that everything they see on television is real. In fact, some researchers in the United States and Great Britain have found that children as young as three are quite aware of the constructed nature of television, identifying some of the techniques used in making the shows or ads they watch, such as close-ups, shifts of camera angle, etc. One mother remarked that when her daughter, age three, heard the voice of James Earl Jones announcing "This is CNN," she proclaimed, "Mommy, it's the same guy who does Mufasa's voice [in *The Lion King*]!"

This is not to say that young children can always identify what is real and what's not. Indeed there are many popular genres of television that aim to blur this distinction for us (think of "reality" programs like *Rescue 911,* or ads that don't look or sound like ads). If it can be confusing for adults, it certainly can be for children. But overall, by the time children are five or six, they can begin to differentiate fairly reliably between reality and fantasy. By the time they enter first or second grade, they are able to understand that even television programs with real people (like ads) don't always have messages that are true.

Help your toddler begin to understand what's real and what's pretend ("Don't you wish people really could fly like birds?"). With older children, assist them in learning to make finer distinctions between fact and fantasy ("Do you think his mom would say that in real life?"). You can also help them understand some of the techniques that television uses; for example, how camera angles and visual effects can make a toy or food in an ad seem really cool, or how music or animation are used to attract them to a particular product.

WHEN TELEVISION GETS SCARY

> While watching a Disney video with his older cousin, four-year-old Hayato was frightened to tears. When his aunt ran over to see what was wrong, Hayato cried, "They took Dumbo's mommy away!"

Children can find certain television images frightening and disturbing, including some that aren't obvious to parents. According to research by Joanne Cantor, there are developmental differences in the ways in which children react to scary things in media. Young children tend to find visual images such as vicious animals, monsters, or deformed characters very frightening. They also can be upset by stories with physical transformations, stories involving the death of a parent, or stories about natural disasters like hurricanes or earthquakes.

Television news can also be a source of fears. The events of September 11, 2001, for example, were so dramatic and so traumatic that even some of the youngest children couldn't help but notice the images of airplanes flying into buildings again and again. Many were confused: some thought that what they saw was a movie, or that each time the frightening images were replayed, another plane was actually crashing—or that a plane was likely to crash into their yard or their school.

When events like this occur, children want most of all to know that they are safe. Parents can help by reassuring them that there will always be someone to take care of them, to answer any questions they have, and help to clear up misperceptions they might have about what they've seen. Follow the child's lead; she doesn't need all the details about a scary news event, just enough to help her understand why adults are upset, and to feel reassured. Finally, try to limit her exposure to news programs by watching them while she's not around.

VIOLENCE AND AGGRESSION

Last week, Duane and LuAnne overheard their five-year-old twins, Leroy and Stevie, trading threats, clearly copied from a favorite TV cartoon. Yesterday, they found the twins engrossed in a live-action show, with one character shaking and punching another. Duane and LuAnne are so disgusted and worried that they're tempted to throw out the television.

While it's certainly your prerogative to throw out your TV set, we wouldn't necessarily recommend it. The important issue is specific program content, not television itself. Television is part of the fabric of our culture. Most children like to watch television, and it becomes part of what they discuss at school and with friends. By the time a child is of school age, if he doesn't get to watch television at home, you can be virtually certain that he will watch it somewhere else.

The issue of TV violence, however, is very important. There is undoubtedly a lot of aggressive behavior and violence on both adult and children's television. It makes sense to think that a child who sees violence might go and try to imitate it. Many of us have seen a child who watches something like *Power Rangers* go outside and try some of the martial arts moves. But this doesn't always happen.

There have been thousands of studies about the possible effects of television violence, conducted over several decades and around the world. While results are mixed, it seems clear that exposure to violent content is linked to increased aggressive behavior *in some children*. This link does not prove causation; in other words, we can't rule out that, for example, children who are more aggressive to start out with are more attracted to viewing aggression on television rather than the other way around. And it may be that other social factors, like poverty or real-life exposure to violence, better account for both what a child might want to view and a proclivity for some kind of violent or aggressive behavior.

Another concern is that television makes aggressive attitudes and behavior appear common and acceptable—at least to those who are exposed the most to such content. Finally, repeated exposure to violent scenes can increase fears of being a victim of violence.

What can you do as a parent to reduce the risk? First, steer children away from violent shows and toward prosocial ones, like the ones described above. Developmentally, younger children are more likely to try to imitate images they see, and need extra protection. While a five-year-old might still want to try out things he sees on television, he is old enough to begin to understand counterbalancing influences ("If I try to cut through this pile of bricks with a karate chop like that cartoon character did, my hand might get hurt"). But older children still need guidance.

If you see your child imitate something you don't like, ask him where he saw it, and make sure he realizes he's copying it from a program. Then you have a golden opportunity to talk about how things we see in TV and movies don't always happen as they do in real life. For example, "See how everyone just got up and walked away after that big fight? Do you think that's true in real life?" With older children, you can point out that violent sequences are carefully planned and carried out by trained stunt people.

One problem with American television programs and movies is that they often don't show us realistic consequences of violence. (Note that Japanese television, which often shows violence, also tends to show its negative consequences, such as blood and the victim lying on the ground.) Talk about how someone would feel after a violent or threatening situation. Also, question if fighting solves the problem. ("Does it solve a problem for you if you punch your brother, or do Mom and Dad just get mad?"). Point out that TV characters have other options ("They could have each given up something and made a compromise; now they just have a big mess"). This also carries over to non-TV play: "Let's think of better ways than grabbing and fighting to work out how to share this toy."

The V-Chip and TV Ratings

Parents now have government help in reducing the negatives of television: the "V-Chip" and the ratings system. Federal Communications Commission rules require all sets (thirteen inches or larger) manufactured after January 1, 2000, to carry V-Chip technology. The V-Chip reads information encoded in rated programs to allow parents to block access to ones they don't want.

Here are the ratings to look for, adapted from the FCC's Web site:

TV-Y (designed to be appropriate for all children). Whether animated or live action, the themes and elements in this program are specifically designed for a very young audience, including children from ages two to six. This program is not expected to frighten younger children.

TV-Y7 (designed for children age seven and above). This may be more appropriate for children who have the developmental skills needed to distinguish between make-believe and reality. Themes and elements may include mild fantasy or comedic violence, or may frighten children under the age of seven.

TV-G (for general audiences). Although this program is not designed specifically for children, most parents may let younger children watch it unattended. It contains little or no violence, no strong language, and little or no sexual dialogue or situations.

> Many stations now add additional information, such as *V* for vio-
> lence, *FV* for fantasy violence, and *L* for language.
>
> In addition to ratings, there are other tools for parents, such as pro-
> grammable "kids' remotes" that let your child choose what to watch
> within a selected range of channels.

DEALING WITH MEDIA STEREOTYPES

While watching a cartoon with four-year-old Nicki, her mom points out,
"Oh, see those scientists in the laboratory? Your aunt Diane is a scientist;
she works in a lab like that."

"Mom," says Nicki with scorn. "Scientists have glasses and sticky-up
white hair!"

Just as we don't know the whole story of how TV violence affects
children, we also don't know exactly how much stereotypes on TV affect
their ideas or attitudes about gender, race, and jobs—to name a few. But
if you watch television carefully, you'll soon notice that grandmothers
usually have gray hair and glasses, scientists are mostly old men, and fat
people are rarely around.

African-Americans, Latinos, Native Americans, and—most recently—
Arab-Americans have protested the way they are portrayed in cartoons
and movies. Far fewer Hispanics (and other minorities) are seen on television than in real life. What's more, male characters are the norm, out-
numbering female ones by three or four to one (until recently, this was
even true of *Sesame Street*).

Some researchers believe that the formation of attitudes about gender
and race have more to do with what children are exposed to in real life
than what they see on television. Others insist that the highly inequitable
world of televised images plays a major contributing, if not leading, role
in what children learn about the world outside their own home.

Intentionally or not, advertising also carries social messages. Researchers studying advertising targeted at children see a clear gender divide: ads directed at girls use pale pastel colors, soft music, and female voice-overs; ads directed at boys feature only male characters, bold and primary colors, fast and loud music, fast cuts, and male voice-overs. In the few ads for products treated as gender neutral (for example, games or cereal), boys tend to be featured more prominently than girls.

When you see a stereotype that bothers you, talk to your children about how different it is from real life. For example, you can point out that not all police officers are male, or that their own pediatrician is female, so we know that sometimes doctors can be women even though we don't always see this on television. Even very young children can be taught to recognize stereotypes. One parent said her four-year-old son had wondered aloud why there were no girls featured in the LEGO ads he saw—when he knew for a fact that his sister liked to play with LEGOs!

Television Viewing and Imagination

Franco and Owen, age six, are debating what to play. "Let's play Jackie Chan," says Owen, mimicking a martial-arts move.

"No, I want to play James Bond," counters Franco. "You can be the bad guy trying to take over the world!"

Some parents are concerned that television and movies may limit children's imaginations. Imagination is hard to study and measure. What we do know, from both research and parent observations, is that children regularly incorporate television shows, plots, and characters into their imaginative play. On the one hand, TV and movies might limit imaginative options (as when a child fan of the Harry Potter books finds, to her disappointment, that in the movie version, Hermione is nothing like she'd imagined). On the other hand, television can expand the scope of a children's imagination, providing ideas and images that they couldn't have thought up themselves.

Make use of what you have, and encourage imaginative play that comes from television viewing. Engage in pretend dialogues between a television character and your child. Tell bedtime stories that incorporate some of the characters you like most from your child's television viewing. Encourage older children to write or tell stories that use ideas or characters from television. Talk with your child about ways in which television images are the same as or different from ones we see in real life.

TELEVISION ADVERTISING

After days of whining and pleading, Delia gave in and bought her five-year-old the pudding that looked so sparkly and delicious on TV. But when little Mandy finally tried some, she made a face. "Mom, what's wrong with it? Your pudding tastes way better!"

Most television in this country is supported by advertising. Children have become an increasingly important target for advertisers. Corporations spend a billion dollars each week advertising to them. The average American child sees up to twenty-thousand commercials each year on television alone. Of course, television isn't the only medium that exposes children to advertising. By some estimates, including ads in electronic media of all sorts, and those logos, labels, and announcements children can see in other places, hundreds of advertising messages of one sort or another flicker across their consciousness each day! Most of the ads targeted at children are for fast foods or snack foods, followed by ads for toys. (Experts believe that junk-food ads, along with too much sitting, share some blame for the increase in childhood weight problems.)

We know from the research that children as young as three can recall the visuals and some of the audio from ads—and as any parent, teacher, or child-care provider can tell you, most children love to parrot the ads to which they are exposed. Many of the elements that attract children to television shows attract them to ads: colors, sound effects, fast cuts, close-ups of people's faces, and catchy music. By age four or five, children also like ads that feature gimmicks, humor, and familiar celebrities.

Try to limit children's exposure to ads when you can. You can also make a rule (or a game) of muting the television when commercials come on. In addition, help your child become a careful and critical viewer of ads. You can start with children as young as three. Point out the techniques advertisers use to make products look more attractive: "They make the toy look so much bigger than it really is," or "You have that truck; does it make sounds like it does in the commercial?"

With children five and older, you can begin to point out more subtle things: "This ad makes it seem that if you buy this toy, all these kids will want to play with you. Does that make sense?" You can also explain that advertising pays for programming, and that advertising's only purpose is to get you to buy. Finally, educating children about advertising also has a side benefit: less begging for advertised goodies.

SQUABBLES OVER TELEVISION

Eight-year-old Aaron likes to commandeer the remote and decide what everyone will watch. But his choices often elicit howls of protest from five-year-old Elana and two-year-old Gus, both of whom have other favorite programs they want to see.

Living with children who are at different developmental stages can be challenging when each is clamoring to see his or her own favorite program. Such conflicts are inevitable. Furthermore, they may be about more than simply who gets to watch his or her favorite program. Some researchers have suggested that it might be easier for siblings to fight about who gets to select which program to watch or who holds the remote than it is to fight about who feels she or he is getting more attention from Mom and Dad. (For more on sibling fights, see chapter 2.) Television viewing can be a way for a family to get together, or it can be a source of conflict and a way to isolate from one another. What's more, there are some interesting findings that when families watch TV together, the experience can influence what kinds of behavior children think are appropriate and desirable in a family. Families watching TV together have an opportunity to talk about appropriate and inappropriate ways of dealing with issues that are modeled on TV, like sibling rivalry. This reinforces the importance of coviewing with children, and of selecting programs that reflect your family's values.

Establish family rules for what gets viewed. Include a mix of programs appropriate for children at different developmental stages. Younger siblings benefit from viewing with older ones in the same way that all children benefit from viewing with adults. Avoid the temptation to put a television set in a child's room. Televisions should be placed in public spaces, like a living or family room. This will encourage viewing things together, as well as taking turns.

Sometimes you might need to record programs appropriate for older children, and let them watch them while younger ones are sleeping. Make sure you explain to older children why some shows that do not frighten them (such as shows on wild animals or ghosts) might frighten their little siblings.

Movies, Videos, and Preschoolers

AT THE MOVIES

Reyhan, age four, spent much of her first visit to a movie theater turned around in her seat: she was fascinated by the projector, and kept looking up at its beam of light. Later, she was very frightened when a whale swallowed Pinocchio, and she could see the whale's insides.

At what age is it appropriate to bring a child to a movie theater for the first time? There's no hard-and-fast rule; you need to gauge this based on her attention span, interest level, toilet-training stage, and personality. Keep in mind that a movie theater will expose a child to darkness, crowds, unusual seats, and to very loud sounds. If she is fearful of these things, be sure to consider them, and prepare her. You should also keep in mind that watching a full-length movie in a theater is a different experience from seeing one at home; a child cannot get up and walk around, make loud comments, or push a pause button as she can when watching a video.

The decision to go to a movie also depends on the movie's content. Read reviews in newspapers and family magazines, look carefully at ratings, and talk to other parents who have seen the film before deciding whether it would be an appropriate experience for your child. As in the story above, even something rated "G" might contain images that would be scary.

THE HOME MOVIE THEATER: VIDEOS

Videos can be wonderful for preschool children because they feed their love of repetition. Some researchers have found that even older children enjoy seeing the same thing over and over again because it is familiar, because they can introduce friends or younger siblings to something they've enjoyed, or because they get different things out of a tape after multiple viewings. (How many times have you watched *Casablanca* for similar reasons?)

Videos can also be great teaching devices since you have the ability to be very selective about what you show, and to stop the tape when you want or need to. This allows you to view with specific educational goals in mind (such as pointing out particular shapes for younger kids, or how foreshadowing is used in the plot of dramatic fare for older children). Use rewind, replay, and the slow-motion feature to help young children understand aspects of a story on video. If you are not viewing with your child, be sure that the television is tuned to a channel or program you approve of so she's not surprised by an inappropriate program when the tape or DVD ends.

Many newspapers and parenting magazines run columns that discuss and rate children's videos. Sometimes video stores have summaries or reviews of children's tapes that you can read before renting them. Also check the Web; for example, the American Library Association at *http://www.ala.org/parentspage/greatsites/* lists good books and videos for children.

Should you feel guilty about popping a tape in the VCR while you make dinner? No. We don't encourage using the VCR as a baby-sitter, or as a substitute for parental involvement with a child's viewing, but there is nothing wrong with allowing children to watch a tape now and then while you're doing something else. Video gives you much more control than unsupervised television watching. And if you build up a library of tapes or disks (movies and TV shows) for your child, there will always be something "good" to watch.

Computers and Preschoolers

IS YOUR CHILD READY FOR A COMPUTER?

> Two-year-old Kishana seems very interested every time her mother turns on the computer. Her mom wonders whether it is too early to get her daughter started on using this technology.

If she shows interest, it's probably not too early. Many children crave a chance to imitate their parents and try this exciting tool. Making pictures, typing letters, or solving problems in computer games can give children a sense of mastery and control. Parents are responding to this desire (and perhaps to the hype about computers); recent surveys show that the fastest growing segment of the home computer market is families with children between the ages of two and seventeen. There's a wide array of software available for children; there are even "kids' laptops" featuring programs designed for toddlers on up.

What is the best age to start your child on the computer? While there's little research yet on this, we do know that there are certain skills children must have to be able to use one successfully: hand-eye coordination, the ability to follow simple directions, and the ability to sit still for a period of time. Children develop these skills at different ages. One parent reported that her second and third sons each became interested in computers at age two, but one was able to use the mouse at age two and a half, while the other was just over three before his coordination was advanced enough.

Do computers give young children an educational boost? While more research is also needed on possible benefits and drawbacks of computers (and specific software) for children, there is support for the idea that computer use helps them develop their visual-spatial and visual attention skills. But ignore the hype; there's no reason to rush. Remember that computers supplement, not replace, other play and art materials. Take the cue from your child about when he seems ready to start with a computer. (It helps to realize that each new medium—film, radio, comic books, and television—has raised excitement about its potential for education, and fears about its effects on the young.)

As with television, your child needs your guidance with computer use. Many games for young children work best when parents play along. As your child gets older, she can move beyond clicking on hidden animation and doing simple navigation to solve more problems on her own (e.g., how can Putt-Putt the car lower the bridge to rescue the baby giraffe?). As your child becomes more skilled, establish rules and limits for use, as you do with other media. A timer or alarm clock is helpful, since it's easy for children to lose track of time.

CHOOSING SOFTWARE

Marcia wandered through the children's software aisle. *Freddi Fish, Backyard Baseball, 102 Dalmatians, Barbie Fashion Designer, KidPix, Blue's ABC Time*—there were so many titles for young children. Given the cost, she wanted something that her kids would use a lot, that she would have fun using with them, and that would teach them a few things.

Every day more software for children appears on the market. The same types of guidelines that we mentioned for selection of TV programs and videos apply in the selection of software. While marketers know that putting phrases such as "educational" or "teaches reasoning and memory skills" on the box of a program tends to attract parents, simply having the words there doesn't necessarily make it so.

When selecting software for a young child, in general, you want to make sure it's right for her stage of development. For example, are the directions clear and understandable to your child? Do the games teach useful skills that would be appropriate for her (e.g., sorting colors or shapes for two- or three-year-olds, selecting words with similar sounds for four- or five-year-olds, or using logic to solve a problem)? Are there characters, music, and graphics that your child would find attractive? Is there content that goes against your values (e.g., characters fighting)?

There was a lot of concern that boys were becoming more interested in and skilled with computers than girls. But with the wider selection of software now available, including some geared especially to girls, this gap is closing. To get a better idea of what's out there, check software reviews and rankings in books, newsletters, and parent and family magazines; also search the Web for the many children's and educational software review sites (e.g., *http://school.discovery.com/parents/reviewcorner* and *www.thereviewzone.com*).

If you'd like to try before you buy: some libraries have software for children that you can preview and discuss with librarians. Stores that sell toys or specialize in educational products may have display copies of software available for preview. There are even outlets in some communities in which parents can exchange software with one another; local parenting Web sites or papers might help you identify these.

YOUNG CHILDREN AND THE INTERNET

Children under the age of ten should not be using the Internet alone. But there are a number of good Web sites designed for young children to use with their parents. For a start, there are nonprofit sites, such as those based on PBS programs. Sesame Workshop (formerly Children's Television Workshop) has a Web site for preschoolers with educational games and stories (*sesameworkshop.org*). The library-sponsored site *www.Story-*

place.org has animated stories in English and Spanish, with related activities and reading lists. There are also university-sponsored sites such as Parents and Children Together Online, an on-line magazine with original stories for parents and kids to read together (*www.indiana.edu/%7Eeric_rec/www/indexwr.html*).

The U.S. Department of Education maintains a full listing of federal Web sites for children at *www.kids.gov*. They also offer free stuff for kids at *www.ed.gov/free/kids.html*.

Finally, there are some commercial Web sites that are highly rated by children, parents, and educators. One such site is MaMaMedia, which includes shared parent-child activities for ages four and up (*www.MaMa-Media.com*). Also check sites for favorite television programs and cable channels (such as Nickelodeon) for fun activities. Be aware, though, that these sites will contain advertising.

Media-literacy advocates point out that advertising to children on the Internet raises new concerns. While print and TV advertising is subject to regulations that prohibit the most deceptive and manipulative types of advertising, no such regulations yet exist for the Web. In the cyberworld, it's not always clear what constitutes an ad. Many ads appear as banners along the top or side of a page, with confusing buttons that can transfer a child to the advertiser's Web site with a simple click—and possibly connect her to chat rooms, gambling sites, contests, and other inappropriate content.

What's more, while so-called program-length commercials are prohibited on television for children, ads on the Internet may blend content with commercial advertising, creating cyber-infomercials. An entire Web site might constitute one large ad for a particular product.

Let your children know early that some things on the Internet may not be safe. Teach children old enough to read and write how to spot on-line ads; by learning the conventions of advertising, they will become less vulnerable to it. (Be aware, though, that new types of ads appear frequently, as advertisers struggle to gain attention and clicks.) Children (and adults) should ask themselves: "Who created this site I'm in, and why was it created? How credible is the information on this site—and its source? Is someone benefiting from me believing in it?"

Make sure your child understands that she should *never* type her name, address, or any other personal identifying information while on-line without asking you first. While Web sites are legally required to obtain parental consent before collecting personal identifying information from children aged twelve or under, this is not easily enforced.

In addition, you can buy software that lets you block access to Web sites you deem inappropriate for your children (e.g., NetNanny, McAfee Privacy Service). Some software will also allow you to check to see which Web sites your children have visited. The children's on-line safety organization, GetNetWise, offers excellent suggestions (*www.getnetwise.org*). Blocking software such as AOL Parental Controls or many others currently available can be useful.

Although some of these suggestions are more geared toward parents with older children, it's important to begin training children to be media-literate consumers of computers as early as possible—just as we would have them become more media literate consumers of television or other electronic media.

Some Final Words

In this chapter, we have looked at how children's use of and reactions to electronic media create a window into their cognitive, social, and emotional development. We've also suggested ways for parents to use the energy and attention that children give to media in ways that will foster and encourage their development.

We encourage you to watch TV and use software along with your child. (A survey by the Kaiser Family Foundation found that parents watch along with young kids less than 20 percent of the time.) If you are there, you can reinforce messages you believe are important, answer questions your child has—and, by posing questions of your own, encourage him to keep on asking.

It is also important to *set limits* on what young children watch, and on how much time they spend at the screen. Become an informed viewer yourself; read descriptions of shows and software, and observe the ratings posted on them. Tape unfamiliar shows and preview them before allowing your child to watch. When children are present, break the habit of leaving the set on as background noise.

By providing your children with clear and consistent guidelines about their media use, and giving them tools to evaluate the media to which they are exposed, you empower them to make good choices about their media.

Suggestions for Further Reading

There are abundant resources available to parents regarding children and media use. What follows is a partial listing of books, organizations, and on-line sources that may be helpful.

Adults

Cary Bazalgette and David Buckingham (eds.). *In Front of the Children: Screen Entertainment and Young Audiences.* British Film Institute, 1995.

Gordon Berry and Joy Keiko Asamen. *Children and Television: Images in a Changing Sociocultural World.* Sage, 1993.

Virginia Boyle (ed.) *Facets Non-Violent, Non-Sexist Children's Video Guide.* Facets, 1996.

Joanne Cantor. *Mommy, I'm Scared: How TV and Movies Frighten Children and What We Can Do to Protect Them.* Harcourt Brace, 1998.

Justine Cassell and Henry Jenkins (eds.). *From Barbie to Mortal Kombat: Gender and Computer Games.* MIT Press, 1998.

Milton Chen and Andy Bricky. *The Smart Parent's Guide to Kids' TV.* Bay Books, 1994.

Children's Partnership. *The Parents' Guide to the Information Superhighway.* National PTA and Urban League, 1998. Order from *www.pta.org/programs/guide.htm.*

Gloria DeGaetano and Kathleen Bander. *Screen Smarts: A Family Guide to Media Literacy.* Houghton Mifflin, 1996.

Gene Del Vecchio. *Creating Ever-Cool: A Marketer's Guide to a Kid's Heart.* Pelican, 1997.

Educators for Social Responsibility. *Changing Channels: Preschoolers, Television and Media Violence.* 1996. Order from *www.esrnational.org.*

Aletha Huston, et al. *Big World, Small Screen.* University of Nebraska Press, 1993.

Addie Jurs. *TV: Becoming Unglued.* Robert Erdmann Publishing, 1992.

Diane E. Levin. *Remote Control Childhood?* National Association for the Education of Young Children,1998.

Kathleen McDonnell. *Kid Culture: Children and Adults and Popular Culture.* Second Story Press, 1994.

W. James Potter. *Media Literacy.* Sage, 2001.

Robert Schrag. *Taming the Wild Tube: A Family's Guide to Television and Video.* University of North Carolina Press, 1990.

Ellen Seiter. *Sold Separately: Children and Parents in Consumer Culture.* Rutgers University Press, 1993.

Dorothy and Jerome Singer, and Diana Zuckerman. *The Parent's Guide: Use TV to Your Child's Advantage.* Acropolis Books, 1990.

Children's Books

Berenstain, Stan and Jan. *The Berenstain Bears and Too Much TV.* Random House, 1984.

Brown, Marc. *Arthur's Computer Disaster.* Little, Brown, 1999.

White, Nancy. *The Magic School Bus Gets Programmed: A Book About Computers.* Scholastic, 1999.

Christine Winn and David Walsh. *Box-Head Boy.* Fairview Press, 1996.

Harriet Ziefert. *When the TV Broke.* Puffin Books, 1993.

Web Sites

Annenberg Public Policy Center, *www.appcpenn.org/mediainhome/* (research on children's media).

Center for Media Education, *www.cme.org/children/index=_chld.html* (research and advocacy).

Children Now, *www.childrennow.org/media/index.html* (research and advocacy on kids' media).

GetNetWise, *www.getnetwise.org* (Internet safety guide and help finding Internet safety tools, child-safe search engines).

Media Literacy Review (formerly Media Literacy Online Project), *www.interact.uoregon.edu/MediaLit/mlr/home/index.html.*

National Institute on Media and the Family, *www.mediaandthefamily.org* (rates games and TV shows).

Safe Kids, *www.safekids.com* (Internet safety for older kids).

Organizations

Better Business Bureau, Children's Advertising Review Unit, 845 Third Ave., New York, NY 10022. Web site: *www.caru.org/* (good information on explaining advertising to children).

Classification and Rating Administration, Motion Picture Association of America, Inc., 15503 Ventura Blvd., Encino, CA 91436-3103. Web site: *www.mpaa.org.*

Coalition for Quality Children's Media, 535 Cordova Rd., Suite 456, Santa Fe, NM 87501. Web site: *www.cqcm.org/kidsfirst* (reviews films, videos, software, and television shows).

Cultural Environmental Movement, 3508 Market St., Philadelphia, PA 19104.

Families Against Violence Advocacy Network, 4144 Lindell Blvd., Suite 408, St. Louis, MO 63108.

Federal Communications Commission, 1919 M St. NW, Washington, D.C. 20554. Web site: *www.fcc.gov/vchip* (information about the rating system and how the V-Chip can be used to block programming that parents find objectionable).

KIDSNET, 6856 Eastern Ave. NW, Suite 208, Washington, D.C. 10012. Web site: *www.kidsnet.org*

Lion and Lamb Project, 4300 Montgomery Ave., Suite 104, Bethesda, MD 20814. Web site: *www.lionlamb.org* (advocacy to reduce violence in games and entertainment media).

National Coalition Against TV Violence, 5132 Newport Ave., Bethesda, MD 20816.

Parents Television Council, 333 S. Grand Ave., Suite 2900, Los Angeles, CA 90071. Web site: *www.parentstv.org/* (monitors the television industry).

TV Parental Guidelines Monitoring Board, P.O. Box 14097, Washington, D.C. 20004. Web site: *www.TVguidelines.org* (industry-sponsored monitoring board).

Photo by Shirley Scarlett

C H A P T E R   T W E L V E

Sending Your Child to School:
The Home/School Partnership

Deborah LeeKeenan and Betty Nolden Allen

Svetlana and Vitalyi spent months on research, questions, and worry over finding the right school for little Anya. They finally felt comfortable with their choice. When the first day arrived, Anya was proud and ready in her new red dress and tights. But as her father tried to say good-bye at the classroom door, she clung to his leg, crying, "Don't leave me here!"

For many parents, sending their "baby" off to child care, preschool, or kindergarten for the first time is harder than they ever expected it would be. You feel horrible seeing your child cry, but you have a schedule to keep—and your child seemed so eager and ready before. The teacher says, "Don't worry, she'll be fine!"

You start to second-guess all your previous decisions. Did I make the right choice sending her to school now? How do I know this is a good school? Is my child really ready? What if the teacher doesn't like my child? What if she doesn't like the school? (You may feel this way even if your child, to your amazement—and slight hurt—simply says, "Bye!" and runs to join the group.)

Our goal in this chapter is to help you sort through and answer these questions and more as you prepare to entrust your child's care and education to a group outside the family for the first time. This is a very emotional experience because, just as you make a careful assessment of the school, you feel that you and your child are now open to judgment. "To touch the child is to touch the parent. To praise the child is to praise the parent. To criticize the child is to hit at the parent. The two are two, but the two are one."*

Our goal in this chapter is to help you choose a school or program that's right for your child, get her ready for school, and deal with the inevitable problems and concerns—and ultimately create a good experience that will prepare her to meet later social and educational challenges.

We'll cover:

- Making a match: tools for finding a good early childhood program or school

- Transitions: sending your child to school, including the impact of that first day

- Advocating for your child: communication between school and parent

- Ingredients for an effective home/school partnership

Here, we define the term "school" broadly to include the various types of early childhood programs for young children (center-based, family day care, nursery school, kindergarten), whether on a full- or part-time basis. The word "parent" can also refer to all caregivers of the child.

---

*J. Hymes, "Effective Home School Relations," talk at Sierra Madre: Southern California Association for the Education of Young Children, 1974.

Making a Match

THE "RIGHT" SCHOOL

> "If my child doesn't get into_____Preschool, then she won't be prepared
> for_____Elementary School, or_____High School, and she certainly
> won't get into_____College!"

In some communities, there's tremendous pressure to get into the almost panicked mind-set above. This type of thinking concerns us greatly for several reasons. First of all, what is best for one child may not be best for another. Second, as children grow and develop, the types of school or environments they will do best in may change.

> Neighbors Allen and Claudia run into each other at the Laundromat. "We're thinking of sending Miranda to preschool," says Allen. "I looked in the Yellow Pages at the list of child care centers . . . but I don't know how to tell which ones are good."
>
> "I heard that Mary Lou is sending her daughter to the Children's Choice Center in September," Claudia replies. "I've been thinking about that for Teddy . . . but he can't sit still for as long as she can. I don't know how they deal with kids who need to move."
>
> "My worry is that Miranda is so small and quiet, she could get lost in the shuffle. Is she really ready? I don't want her to start off with a bad experience."

Sending your child off to school is a little scary, whether there are many choices or few. Some choices won't match your logistical needs: not open the right hours, or too hard to get to. Some choices are complicated by your needs as a family, by the personality of your child, and by the expectations of the program. For instance, does the school expect all children to be toilet-trained? What's their approach with a slow-to-warm-up or very active child? Will your child be the only one of her ethnic, racial, or religious group? Do they make efforts to accommodate children with special needs? This section will help demystify the process of choosing an early childhood program and will offer a list of considerations involved in the decision-making process.

In the story above, Allen wonders if his child is *ready* for school. The real question should be, is the *school* ready for the child? There is no one quality or skill that children need in order to do well in school; a combination of factors contributes to success. According to the National Association for the Education of Young Children (NAEYC), the organization that accredits early childhood programs nationwide, school success depends largely on the "match" between children's skills and knowledge and the school's expectations. More children succeed when the school's expectations reflect knowledge of child development and early learning.

The Meaning of Success

> Margo and Izabel are watching their children at the sandbox in the local playground. "I wish Eddie wouldn't grab things from other kids," sighs Izabel.
>
> "I've learned a lot from Tracie's preschool teacher," says Margo. "Tracie used to barge right in and take things without asking. The teacher worked with her on that, and we've practiced trading toys and taking turns at home."

When planning any new project, it helps to ask yourself, "How will I know if it's been a success? What would have to happen?" This approach also helps in choosing the right school for your child. What kind of experience do you want him to have? What would success in preschool look like?

Research suggests that real success in preschool has little to do with learning the alphabet or other "academics." Success has to do with social and emotional well-being: your child looks forward to school; while there, she is engaged and involved with people and activities. Success is also a process: learning to engage in give-and-take with children and adults, to negotiate, and to start and maintain social relationships. Your

Making the Most of Family Child Care

The best (or only) child care option for you may be a grandparent, uncle, aunt, or neighbor. With planning, your child can get some of the same benefits (including intellectual stimulation and social interaction) she would get in a good preschool setting.

Safety is the primary concern; be sure the home is appropriately childproofed for your child's age. Also, tell the caregiver about your child's usual eating and sleeping habits, other routines, and any health issues.

Work with the caregiver to develop a daily schedule for your child; this reduces the chance that he will end up in front of the TV all day. For a toddler, a sample schedule might include a morning snack, activity time, lunch, a story, and rest time.

Toddlers need to be able to move around and do a lot of physical exploration, so try to arrange some active play every day. If a safe park is available, that also gives your child a chance to practice socializing with other children.

Language stimulation is important; ideally, your caregiver should speak the same language as your child, and be available to talk to and read to her. Some of this might also come from one or two quality television programs. Ask to limit TV exposure to channels that don't run commercials (at least during shows) such as PBS and Nickelodeon. (See chapter 11 for more on this.)

As far as play materials, bring some favorite things from home—stuffed animals, toys, a blanket—to promote security, as well as books (cloth or board ones for very young children). You don't need elaborate toys: young children can get a lot out of pots and pans, a sifter and flour, and water play at a sink with plastic dishes. For more ideas, see chapter 7.

child gains confidence in handling transitions and adjusting to new people and places—she can "step up to the plate" and take a risk. Your child starts to have a life away from home. Ultimately, she is ready to socially and emotionally handle elementary school—and through that, more prepared for academic success.

REVIEWING THE AVAILABLE CHOICES

Before you begin looking at different programs, it is critical to think about what is important for the child and what is important for the parent/family. A decision about schooling cannot be based on philosophical priorities alone. Many practical needs must also be met. You must identify your own family's requirements.

There are a variety of early childhood programs available today. Not all communities have all varieties, but it is helpful to know what the differences are in the various programs. Programs may offer full-time or part-time care.

Home-based family day care
In these programs, the child is cared for in a private residence in a family atmosphere. Many states regulate and license family day care settings just as they must do for any school or other center-based care. For example, in Massachusetts, the Office of Child Care Services is the state licensing organization. In that state, care may be given in a provider's own home for a maximum of six children, including the provider's own children.

Preschool programs
The traditional "nursery school" program falls under this category. These programs are often part-time and are housed in schools, churches, temples, or community buildings. They may be public programs that have separate funding, or private programs that charge tuition.

Head Start programs, which began in 1965, were among the first federally funded early childhood programs. They offer free full- and part-time care for children ages two to five from income-eligible families, and for children with disabilities. Another option is parent cooperative preschools ("co-ops"), in which every parent is required to volunteer his or her services on a regular basis to the school. Volunteer jobs range from teacher assistant in the classroom to computer helper, carpenter, or window washer.

Group child care

These are center-based programs that usually provide a full day of care for young children. Children are generally separated into groups based on age. Centers may serve children of various ages from birth to age six. They're usually open longer hours than preschool programs in order to accommodate working families (although nowadays some preschool programs offer extended hours as well).

Kindergarten

Kindergarten programs are generally for five- and six-year-olds; age cut-off dates vary from community to community. There are public kindergartens in most public schools; there are also private kindergartens, which tend to have a little more flexibility in their entrance age. Kindergarten programs may be full- or part-time.

Most states have their own licensing agency, which regulates all of the above programs. They can be of enormous help to parents who are just beginning to find out what's available in their community for child care. The National Association for the Education of Young Children has a national listing of accredited early childhood programs. (Their contact information is listed in the resource section at the end of the chapter.)

KNOW YOUR CHILD

To make a good match between child and school, you need to think first about your child. What are his strengths? What comes easily for him, and what things take work? What does he like to do, and are there tasks or situations he avoids?

How does she like to spend her time? Does she like to play outdoors, or look at books, or do pretend play? Does your child spend a long time doing one thing, or does she prefer to do lots of different things in a short amount of time?

Does he prefer the company of adults or other children? Has he had caregivers other than a parent? Who are they? How does your child respond to competition for toys, or for adult attention?

How does your child learn? Does she need to move around and explore, or does she do better with closer supervision and a great deal of structure? Would this child thrive in a large, busy atmosphere, or would a smaller, intimate learning environment serve her better?

KNOW THE SCHOOL: GATHERING BASIC INFORMATION

Parent-teacher relationships are built in slow steps. They form in subtle ways from the very beginnings of enrollment as you ask your first questions about a child-care center or nursery school for your child (usually by telephone) and then arrange a visit to see the program and meet the staff. Consider not just the questions and answers, but also the tone and bearing of the staff who respond. Is there respectful and careful attention paid to your concerns, no matter what those concerns may be?

There are several ways to get information about a specific school or program. Read the school's information packet or brochure. Ask questions of the director, teachers, or other school personnel. Finally, talk to other parents whose children attend these schools or programs. Some schools may have a parent advisory board you can access.

Here are the basics, which can help you decide whether the school is worth a visit:

• *What is the school philosophy, and what are its educational objectives?* Is there a current philosophy of education about which you feel strongly? A particular child may do well in more than one kind of program—and in fact, most programs use a mixture of philosophies and methods. Most child-care facilities and preschools have a handbook that describes their approach. But the handbook is no substitute for observation. Regardless of the labeled philosophy, what's most important is finding a school that is *flexible* in responding to individual children's needs—and that makes you feel comfortable and welcome.

• *Does the center meet local, state, and national accreditation guidelines?* The National Association for the Education of Young Children (NAEYC) will certify that a child care center, preschool, or kindergarten meets certain standards. They also post a searchable list of accredited programs on their Web site (*www.naeyc.org*).

• *Is the facility safe?* For example, are there rules about who is allowed to pick up your child? Do teachers have first aid/CPR certification? What is the school health policy? What happens if your child gets injured?

• *What is the average class size/teacher-student ratio?* Your state may have regulations on this, e.g., a minimum of one teacher for five toddlers or ten preschoolers. (You can look this up at the National Resource Center for Health and Safety in Child Care Web site: *http://nrc.uchsc.edu/states.html*.) But you can also check how the school compares with others in your area. Ask the director about staff turnover. Stability can be a good indicator of quality.

• *What are the teachers' educational backgrounds and experience?* The senior staff should have a good grounding in child development. A university affiliation—with student teachers from a major university present—can be another sign of quality.

• *Is the staff diverse ethnically, racially, and/or culturally?* Is this highlighted as an important value in school materials? You can also ask about the kinds of families they look for: Are they trying for an ethnically diverse population, or seeking to include children with disabilities?

• *Is the school flexible in meeting the needs of a wide range of learners?* By this, we mean children with special needs, and children whose primary language is not English—as well as special resources for gifted and talented children. Even if this is not a concern for you now, this kind of flexible and responsive approach shows that staff are aware of children's individual differences and needs, and that they strive to keep all children appropriately challenged. Remember, at some point, most children will have some kind of difficulty that needs extra attention.

• *What are the assessment and evaluation procedures for children?* The school should have a process in place for setting goals and checking on progress. (See the section on goal setting later in the chapter.)

• *What kind of parent involvement is encouraged?* Parents should be welcomed, and their involvement encouraged (more on this later). Staff should be available for conferences at times that suit the schedules of working parents.

VISITING THE SCHOOL: A LOOK IS WORTH A THOUSAND WORDS

"As I walked into the classroom, there were small groups of children doing different things. The teacher was playing with puppets with three children on a rug. Another group of children was building with blocks; several others were at a water table, and some were painting at an easel. If a child needed something, she would ask another child for it. From time to time, the teacher would shift her position and comment on what different children were doing in the room. The atmosphere was active and calm at the same time."

Once you've decided to take the next step and visit a school, find out what their procedure is for visiting and observation. Some schools (especially private ones) prefer that parents come on set visiting days. If they seem reluctant to allow visitors, even if you explain your goals, that could be a "red flag."

When you go to observe, bring a pad, pencil, and list of questions so that you won't forget to ask anything important. When observing, be respectful of the school's guidelines and procedures and remember that you are only seeing a small slice of the school on a particular day. Keep an open mind, and don't judge too quickly.

Observing people

- Observe the *teacher-child ratio* and *class size*. Are volunteers, student teachers, and parents active in the room?

- How *diverse* are the staff, students, and parents? Are cultural differences celebrated or just tolerated? For example, take a look at the school's artwork, books, and toys. Do all pictures and dolls represent one ethnic/racial group?

- Is there a generally pleasant and friendly *atmosphere*? For example, do children welcome newcomers to join in their games? Do adults approach and talk to you (as appropriate)?

- Who is doing most of the *talking*—children or adults? Ideally, it's the children. Where young children are busy exploring and developing skills, they should not have to be quiet.

Observing classroom management

- What types of *questions* does the teacher ask, and how does he or she respond to the children? For example, there are several ways a teacher could respond to a child's drawing: (1) "What is that?" sends the message, "Your drawing should look like something I can recognize." (2) "Tell me about your drawing" is more open-ended, and acknowledges that the child has ideas to share. (3) "I noticed all the colors you used, especially the red and blue" says that the teacher is observing closely but doesn't judge, or push the child in a narrow direction. His goal is to help build the child's awareness and observation skills.

• Are the teachers *listening* to children's needs, and *flexible* in responding to them? Are they appropriately patient? Notice both verbal and nonverbal responses, as well as tone of voice. Here's an example of how a teacher might respond to a disruptive child, and what it suggests about that teacher's philosophy:

It's circle time, where children are sitting on the floor together while a teacher reads them a story. One child fidgets and starts wandering around, distracting the other children. How might the teacher respond? *Option 1:* The teacher says, "Come back and sit down; you need to be part of the group and hear the story." Message: I expect everyone to be doing the same thing. *Option 2:* An assistant or student teacher helps bring the wanderer back, and perhaps puts him on her lap. Message: You need to come back; everyone should be part of group—but we'll provide extra support for you. *Option 3:* The child wanders to the book corner, a basket with some Koosh balls, or the crayons in the art corner, and engages in a quiet activity. Message: Even though others are at circle time, if it's hard for you to be there right now, there's another (planned) option for you if you can't sit that long. It's okay for children to do different things, within limits.

It's not a bad thing for everyone to be part of the meeting—in fact, that's the long-term goal—but in the short term, some kids may need extra flexibility or support. This last response shows that teachers understand that no two children are exactly the same or developing at the same rate. (Parents need to do this at home, too, since no two sibs or playmates are the same!)

Another example would be a child who takes her shoes off during group singing time. Does the teacher ignore it unless the child throws her shoe? Does she keep singing while helping the child put her shoes back on? Or does she say, "We all stop singing until Janine's shoes are back on"? The way she talks to the child (e.g., through gritted teeth) is just as important as how she acts.

- How do teachers *handle children's conflicts?* Here is an example:

Leilani and Frannie are involved in a game on the playground. Malika comes over and asks to join in. They say no, and Malika starts crying. A teacher comes over.

   Option 1: *She says, "In this school we're all friends and everyone has to play together." Message: The rule is, everyone's included. But we won't give you strategies to help you do that.*

   Option 2: *She redirects and involves all three children in something they can play together, e.g., a wagon, swings, or climber. Message: You need to include Malika, and here's a way to do it.*

   Option 3: *She says, "There seems to be a problem here. Let's talk about this. Can you tell me what's going on?" Message: This is an occasion for problem solving. The teacher will provide the support (but not take over) while the children come up with possible solutions.*

As a parent, which option are you most comfortable with? It is always important to ask questions after you observe, if there is something you don't understand or agree with.

While observing parents might be upset to see children excluding others, this is normal behavior at this stage of development. Learning social skills is part of the work of preschool.

Observing the physical environment

- What is on the *walls?* Look for child-centered decor, especially child-created artworks hung at kids' eye level.

- Are there *activity centers* and display tables? For example, there may be an art area, a block area, a sand-and-water table, a pretend-play area with costumes, props, and dolls (and perhaps toy kitchen or fire-station equipment), and/or a science area. The point is that there are different spaces for different types of activities, and children know what kinds of things happen there without always being told by a teacher. Spaces should also be set up so that children can easily find things to play with, and later put them away in their proper places.

• Are there a *variety of materials* accessible in the room? Look for small building toys, clay, paints, art materials, blocks, and hands-on science projects.

• What type of *outdoor play space* is available? It's important to have an outdoor space—and one that's not just asphalt. Look for a variety of places to play, climb, and move, such as a place for riding toys, a sandbox, and swings. A creative climbing structure that can be used in multiple ways (including pretend play) is ideal. You also want to have some shady space with shelter from the sun. (One of the most popular areas on our lab schools' playgrounds is the bushes, which children turn into all kinds of imaginary environments.)

• Is the classroom generally *bright* and *clean?*

• Are there a *variety of places* for children to work: at desks, on the floor, in soft chairs, at tables?

Observing the curriculum (what's going on in the environment)

• How is the *daily schedule structured?* Look for a variety of times when children can make their own choices, interspersed with some large- and small-group time. There should be opportunities to work independently and cooperatively. There should be times outside and inside, snack times, and quiet times. Schools use different names for these activities (e.g., work time, project time, choice time, circle time); ask if the terms aren't clear to you.

• Are words, letters, numbers, and drawings included in *displays?* This is a useful clue to the school's educational approach. For example, a child's painting of a tulip may have a label written (or dictated) by the child, noting that it's based on something the child saw on a school field trip. There might even be a photo from the trip, or one of the child making the painting, placed next to it. The goal is to create something that a parent or teacher can use to understand the child's process, and that a child can interact with and continue to learn from.

• Is there opportunity to try out *new ideas?* Are different ideas accepted or viewed as disruptive? For example, are parents or guests welcome to come in and talk about their customs or occupations, or to work with children on projects?

• Look at *transitions* between activities; what do children do when they are finished with an assignment?

> For example: When she finishes a project, four-year-old Alyce sits and waits, looking bored. *Message:* Children are passive and must wait for the teacher to show them what to do step by step.
>
> Alyce puts her art materials away in marked places on the shelf, washes her hands, and goes to the block area. *Message:* Children are taught what to do when they are done, and have some choices to make. The environment becomes another teacher (e.g., through labels showing where markers and scissors go, or a sign that says PUT YOUR PROJECTS HERE with appropriate stickers on it), and the child gradually becomes more self-sufficient. This routine would be taught to children over the first weeks of school.

• Does the curriculum include *reading* for pleasure, *music,* art, and dance?

• Do children seem *challenged?* Do they seem productive and happy?

• Do the children have *jobs or responsibilities* in the classroom? Children should have jobs from the very beginning, starting with simple ones such as hanging up their jackets and putting their lunch boxes away. (Jobs also provide a clue to the staff's expectations of children and beliefs about their abilities.)

Here's a cleanup-time example: One child rings the bell to signal the start of cleanup; two are assigned to clean up each activity area, and a final two set the table for snack. Children who need extra structure especially enjoy having jobs. They're also useful for kids who need to burn off energy; for example, their job might be to fill up heavy water jugs and carry them to the snack table. (These are examples of teachers taking individual temperaments and needs into account.) Jobs also give a feeling of accomplishment that boosts children's self-esteem.

- Do you feel a *sense of community* in the classroom or school?

MAKING A DECISION

Making a decision is a complicated process. Choosing a good school is a very personal matter. It may come down to a gut feeling of what's right for your child and your family, and your philosophies and values. You may find your views change after you've seen the various possibilities. While it's useful to gather information by talking to neighbors and acquaintances with children in different programs, each family will have different needs and experiences; that's why you need to visit the programs yourself. We hope that the information we've given will make you more comfortable with your decision.

Transitions: Sending Your Child to School

PREPARING YOUR CHILD, AND YOURSELF, FOR SCHOOL

Your feelings about change are contagious. If you feel excited and confident about your child starting school, she'll likely feel the same. To help your child prepare, read books together about starting school. That's also a natural opportunity to answer her questions and let her know what to expect. (See the end of the chapter for some recommended books.) Children who haven't spent much time away from home before are especially likely to have unrealistic worries, such as "Will they have a bathroom?"

It also helps if your child can see at least one familiar face on her first day. Try to set up playdates with a future classmate or two. If you can arrange a visit to her new classroom before school starts, your child can get acquainted with the space and have a mental image of it. Good teachers understand that all children and their families are different, and need tailored support in making transitions. Many teachers will visit a child and family at home before the program starts; this can be a great way for all to feel reassured. (See chapter 6 for additional suggestions on helping your child make the transition to school.)

Three-year-old Anya (from our opening story) has spent very little time away from home without her mom or dad. Her mother, Svetlana, had arranged in advance to spend extra time with Anya on her first day at preschool—and was very glad she did that first morning. The girl buried her head in her mother's skirt, looking tentatively and only occasionally at the other children, who were playing with dolls or building walls out of wooden blocks.

Anya's mother and the teacher talk and develop a plan. Svetlana will arrange to stay at preschool with Anya in the mornings for as long as she's able (say, fifteen minutes to read a story or do a puzzle with her), with parts of that time spent away from Anya in the hall. After two weeks of these extended farewells, Anya is getting used to making the transition. Within a minute or two, she now goes to the painting area or the "house" corner and starts playing with friends.

Svetlana is surprised to find herself missing their long good-byes. It's nice to feel needed, after all.

Many parents follow a progression like Svetlana used when leaving their child at school: they start by playing one-on-one with their child, then move back a little bit, spend a minute out of the room, and finally leave the room for the whole day. Be sure to let your child know, through words and attitude, that you feel comfortable about leaving her at school. "What a great school this is. It looks like a lot of fun to me. Let's go over to the clay table for a while. I can make a snowman with you, but then I'll have to go. I'll see you again after lunch."

Follow through on the plan, and don't forget to say good-bye. Some parents try to sneak out when their child is having a good time, but that can backfire. When your child realizes you're not there, she will be less trustful of you and the new surroundings. If your child cries when you say good-bye, most likely it's for a short amount of time; she'll soon be involved in play.

Many parents, caught up in the details of preparing to send their child to school, are surprised by the emotional impact when the moment actually arrives. Frequently, parents feel like crying themselves. Just as it is a milestone for your child to go off to school, it's a milestone for you as well. You may feel a sense of loss when school starts, particularly if you're sending off your first or last child into this world outside the family. And the younger the child, the more vulnerable and sensitive you can feel. Add to this feeling of loss the feeling of guilt. If your child doesn't want you to leave (a reasonable response when she's in an unknown place), sending her to school can feel like a huge mistake.

Sometimes the transition is made even harder by parents finding themselves being overly critical of the teachers. Often parents can't explain why they take a dislike to a teacher. At times, the reason may be that parents have bad memories of their own school experiences, memories that color their interactions with teachers. Teachers are human, too, and will make mistakes. But if parents and teachers can keep the focus on the child and what she needs, the transition will be easier. Children do better if they see that important adults in their lives are working together. It can also help to talk your feelings over with other parents who are going through this stage, or have been through it already.

Handling Difficult Transitions

Four-year-old Kathy entered the classroom each morning clutching her blanket and crying. Her parents were worried about whether she was ready for preschool. The teachers tried to figure out a way to distract her and get her engaged. With one hand clutching her blanket and the other hand in her mouth, she didn't have any hands free to explore.

To get around this, the adults decided to give Kathy a job. At home before leaving for school, she and her parents picked out a tasty morsel for the classroom guinea pig; Kathy's job was to feed him as soon as she arrived. This tiny change helped her make the transition and start her day on a positive note. Caring for the pet gave Kathy a sense of importance, and helped her feel cared for.

If your child cries every morning long after you've left, and cannot be consoled or distracted, he is having a difficult time. A child who's not adjusting well may also be unwilling or unable to get involved with play materials, teachers, or other children, or be increasingly hard to get out of the house in the morning. Sometimes the child won't show these signs, but instead will refuse to eat, sleep, or use the bathroom at school.

What can you do? First, try not to worry about what other parents might think. (Odds are that they've been in a similar situation with their own children at some point.) Given extra support, your child will successfully make this transition. Work with the teacher to create a plan for establishing a predictable morning routine that will help both you and your child feel more relaxed. You may have to adjust your work schedule for a few days, but it will be worthwhile in the long run.

For some children, leaving school to go home at the end of the day is the more difficult time—as indicated in the following example.

Susan showed her displeasure at her mother by running away from her when it was time to go home. Her mother, Danielle, always arrived with Susan's new baby brother in her arms, and couldn't chase after Susan even if inclined to do so.

To stop this habit, the teacher agrees to take the baby for a few minutes after Danielle arrives. This lets her spend a little time focused just on Susan—allowing them all to leave in a better mood.

Separations and transitions are an issue throughout childhood. At some point during the year, the typical child will show some reluctance to go to school: if not at the start of the year, then perhaps after a holiday break or a family vacation. With some preparation, you can minimize the problem.

Nathan didn't want to go back to school after the December winter break. A couple of days before the return to school, his dad called the parents of two of Nathan's classmates and arranged for the families to meet at the local children's museum. Just seeing his friends again made Nathan feel more excited about returning to school.

Advocating for Your Child in Schools

Thomas, age four, can be challenging at times. He makes big messes in play areas, and doesn't often put his toys away. He has also hit playmates more than once.

DeAnne, his mom, cringes when she hears the preschool teacher's voice on her answering machine. Her first thought is, "Oh, no. What did he do now?" She puts off returning the call.

Why is DeAnne afraid to call the teacher back? The teacher may be partly responsible. Does he call only when there's a problem, or also when there's positive news to share? Teachers should also have regular communication with families, calling just to check in and keep parents informed of what their child is up to: whom he's playing with this week, and favorite or new activities. Parents want to feel that the teacher knows their child, and likes and cares about him.

If a problem does need discussion, the teacher can frame it in terms of brainstorming solutions that the school and home can work on together—such as using the same toy storage methods and following a consistent cleanup routine at both locations. The key thing is to keep the lines of communication open between parent and teacher.

One of the most important responsibilities a parent has is advocating for her child in schools—in a constructive way. The goal is simply to be able to have the home and school work together to benefit the child. While this may seem simple, it can become complicated very quickly, even adversarial. This section will provide some concrete suggestions on how to make the home/school partnership one of reciprocity, mutual respect, and support.

GET THE FACTS FIRST

When he picks her up from preschool, Marcia's dad asks, "What did you do today?"

"Nothing," she says.

"I think Marcia is bored with preschool," he tells his wife later that day. "She never seems excited about what she's doing. I wonder if we should talk to the teacher—but I don't know what to say without sounding insulting."

It's not unusual for young children to respond as Marcia did, even if their day was very full. Also, some children bring all kinds of projects home, while others leave them stuffed in their cubby—or enjoy the process and lose interest once they're done with the project. This can mean that parents (especially those who can't visit the classroom because of work hours) feel out of touch with what their child is doing, and may feel uncomfortable talking to the teacher. Try not to jump to conclusions or make assumptions about how teachers will respond.

In this case, Marcia's parents can describe the facts (what she says, what they see) and ask the teacher for her interpretation and ideas. If her parents want to see more of what she's doing in school, the adults can work out ways for that to happen, such as sitting in on class for an hour now and then, looking at art and photos on the school wall, or getting update phone calls from the teacher on a regular basis.

KEEPING IN TOUCH WITH THE SCHOOL

"As a new teacher, it has taken me a long time to recognize that even though parents know their own children very well, they know much less about children in general. Yet in the beginning of the school year, I am in the opposite situation. I know a lot about children in general, but very little about the individuals.

"I realized that I need to spend more time sharing what I know about children and child development with parents, but also that parents have a responsibility to share what they know about their child with me."

Many of the conflicts that arise between parents and schools are related to communication. Sometimes it is a misunderstanding of intent; sometimes it's a difference in styles. Many schools highly value the uniqueness of each child, and give a lot of thought to uncovering individual learning styles. But too often, schools don't recognize the uniqueness of parents and their cultural styles and histories. These histories and styles are very relevant to the classroom work with children. Meaningful home/school partnerships require both sides to be open-minded and strive to respect each other's feelings and methods. It is the parent's role to educate the teacher about her child by sharing the family's culture, history, and style. Participating in classroom activities is a great way to share family recipes, traditions, hobbies, etc. For instance, one class had parents come in to share their bedtime rituals.

If parents need to be prepared to participate in their children's education, schools must be prepared to facilitate that participation. As parents, you need to provide pertinent information to the school and classroom, and the school needs to provide assurance that this information will be held in confidence. The teacher needs to invite you to participate, but you need to be willing to trust and be open and honest about your feelings and thoughts. Teachers also need to make it clear to parents how they can participate in the classroom, and how they can reach and stay in touch with the teachers. Some teachers are taught to talk rather than to listen to parents. In some settings, parents feel they are back in the role of child when communicating with teachers and principals. Some teachers see parents as the people who undo all their good work. The initiative for establishing the communication and setting the positive tone rests with the school, but parents can be proactive by taking initiative in communicating with and making suggestions to the school.

Types of Home/School Communication

Formal: newsletters, parent conferences, family handbooks, memos, letters to the whole community, class letters, parent meetings, parent workshops, PTA/PTO meetings, home visits, class breakfasts, curriculum nights, school projects/journal, progress reports/report cards, daily journals.

Informal: spontaneous notes, phone calls, postcards/letters from the teacher, neighborhood walks, drop-in chats with school personnel, community social events, potluck suppers, chats in the hallway or on the playground.

The school needs to give you a variety of ways to stay in touch. For example: Is there a regular newsletter that comes home? Is there a parent bulletin board with daily messages you should check? Is there a weekly call-in time? Can you leave the teacher a written message and ask her to call you back? Does the school use E-mail? Is information available in languages other than English? Finding answers to these questions will increase the odds that you'll stay in touch and work in partnership with the school.

Parents of children with special needs may need more frequent contact through a daily journal, a weekly phone call, or some kind of curriculum participation log so that you know what is going on in greater detail and can both participate and communicate with the teacher and the child about it.

Another concern is finding ways to provide parents with informal access to the school. Parents can make their needs known to schools, use other parents as resources, and consult other community agencies for some of their needs. At Eliot-Pearson, we have monthly parent groups to discuss common issues such as sibling rivalry, stress management, choosing quality enrichment activities for children, eating and sleeping problems, and discipline questions. These kinds of groups create a much-needed sense of community, and reassure parents they are not alone in their problems or their feelings.

WHEN HOME AND SCHOOL DISAGREE: WHAT TO DO

It's lunchtime at preschool; the children have gotten their lunch boxes out of their cubbies and are opening them up at the lunch table. Dun Wu, three and a half, quietly sits and waits for someone to help him open his box.

When the teacher talks to his mother about this, she says, "We don't expect him to get out his food at home. Sometimes we even feed him because otherwise he won't eat."

In this situation, listening and mutual respect for differences were key. Dun Wu's family, in part because of their Korean cultural background, expected to do more for him, and saw this as an act of caring. Their expectations of what a child of his age was ready to do on his own were different from those applied at the preschool.

Once Dun Wu's teacher understood the reasons behind his behavior, she explained the school's typical expectations to his mother, noting that one of the goals at their school was to develop children's self-help skills. She asked his mother if she was comfortable with the school taking this different approach, and working toward that goal over time. "What we'll do is provide extra support for him, showing him how to do it, and doing it together, so home and school don't feel so separate."

Every child and family is unique. All families have their strengths, and all need support at one time or another. When home and school are very similar, roles are clearer and school feels like an extension of home. When home and school have different expectations or routines, the possibilities for misunderstanding are much greater, and trusting relationships require more time and nurturing to develop. The first step is for both sides to be aware that cultural values and child-rearing philosophies will differ, and will need at times to be explained and discussed, without rushing to judgment.

Common Areas of Cultural Differences and Misunderstandings

- discipline and child guidance techniques

- how children respond to authority

- autonomy (dependence/ independence)

- school achievement/family obligations

- cooperation/competition

- handling confrontation (direct/indirect ways)

- individual vs. group emphasis

- age-related expectations of children

- sleep patterns and routines

- child's role and responsibility in the family

- toilet training: methods and timetable

- diet and mealtime behavior

- how parents talk to children

- how parents show affection

- how children address adults

- importance of gender identity and traditional sex roles

- dress and hair care

- illness and use of medicines, folk cures, and remedies

- use of supplementary child care

- acceptance, meaning of, and response to crying

- child's attachment to adults, separation from adults

- cleanliness

Most of us were not brought up to see conflict and disagreement as a normal part of the communication process. Thus, when slights or conflict arise, they are taken personally. The ability to remain calm, to listen to each other, to try to see the other point of view, and to compromise in order to benefit the child is essential to being an effective advocate.

Soo-Yung comes to school in party dresses. Her mother complains that she gets so dirty at school, and has asked the teacher to make sure she doesn't get paint all over her clean clothes. The teacher believes that messy art experiences are essential for creative and sensory development, and refuses to discourage a child from participating in these key activities, no matter what parents say. They work out a compromise: the parents bring in an extra set of clothing that Soo-Yung can wear for painting.

Child rearing is a very personal matter, and the "experts" don't know everything. However, we can make the basic assumption that all parents want their children to be healthy and successful in life. From there, we can work out shared understandings about helping children grow up well.

In a useful book, *Developing Cross-Cultural Competence,* the authors compare culture to looking through a one-way mirror; everything we see is from our own perspective. Achieving cross-cultural competence involves taking risks and being willing to accept other perspectives. It also means not just being aware of the different perspectives, but willing to change our own behavior to become more culturally responsive.

When teachers discipline a child, parents are often upset, worried, even angry. Parents and teachers can have quite different styles of discipline:

Parent: I don't want Julia scolded in front of other children. It makes her ashamed. If she does something wrong, okay. But I want her spoken to in private.

Teacher: If you have one or two children at home, you have the option of private discussions of right and wrong. That's not true on the playground. All the children understand it. They will see it happen to everyone.

Here are some suggestions for handling disagreements and misunderstandings between home and school:

• Try to remain calm and get accurate information. Separate the person from the problem/conflict. Understand your emotions and their emotions. Acknowledge emotions as legitimate, but separate them from the issue.

• Talk directly to the person involved, taking a problem-solving approach (instead of accusing or blaming). Look for common goals and values in the situation. (For example, a parent says to the teacher, "Billy tells me every morning he doesn't want to go to school because no one pays attention to him. Can we find a minute to talk about this, and figure out some ways to make the morning transition go better for him?")

• A good program will have a handbook in which many policies and procedures are spelled out. Make sure you know the relevant policies.

• Listen carefully to other points of view in a nonjudgmental manner. Summarize what you hear, and ask for clarification. ("I can see that you're feeling frustrated that George has difficulty sitting with the other children for more than a few minutes during group time. Is that right? Let's see what we can both do to help him settle down.")

• Brainstorm several possible solutions together. Develop a temporary plan and then set a time to meet again to assess the situation.

• Work with the teacher first. If you're not satisfied with the response you receive, or don't see any progress toward a solution, then involve the school's director. A family-friendly program will attempt to make appropriate adjustments if that is required.

BEING AN ACTIVE PARTICIPANT IN THE GOAL-SETTING PROCESS

"I notice that Jilly seems comfortable playing alongside one other child, but she seems to just hang back and watch if there's a group. Maybe one thing she could work on at school is practicing ways to join the play of two or three other kids."

Near the start of this chapter, we talked about setting appropriate goals for preschool success. Goal setting is a mutual process: teachers may have goals they feel are appropriate for a particular child, while his parents may have others. The main developmental goal at this age is to learn how to play with others. Teachers work toward this, for example, by having children work with a partner on some activities, and by helping children learn to resolve their conflicts. From the parent's perspective, it's also important for their child to have playdates, and for the teacher to alert them to potential friendships.

The first step in the goal-setting process is to think about your child's strengths and needs. Think about specific examples, and jot down notes about what he likes to do, what frustrates or upsets him, what kinds of things he learns quickly and what things take more time, and so on. (Look back to on page 318 at the questions in the "know your child" section under "Making a Match.")

The next step is explaining your child's strengths and needs to the school. At the beginning of the year, some teachers invite parents to tell them about their child. In other programs you often meet with a director or staff member at this time. Parent and teacher should reach agreement on goals, and define each of their roles in helping the child meet them. This means that parents have their own "to dos" to support their child's goals.

At the Eliot-Pearson Children's School, parents are given a "parent goal form" to write down things they want teachers to know about their child, as well as their dreams, goals, and hopes for their child each year. This does not guarantee that the child will accomplish those goals, but it does help the teacher understand the parents' thinking, and what's most important to the child and parents. It also gives parents a chance to step back emotionally and begin to think of their child as a separate individual who has needs outside the family.

A sample benchmark for socialization might look like this: "Ellen is able to play comfortably alongside another child, and at times move on to sharing materials or ideas with that child, without adult facilitation." The teacher would look for signs of progress. For example, if a child says

"Let's pretend that . . ." and Ellen usually says no, or only wants others to share *her* fantasies, that would be an area to work on.

Most schools have parent conferences a couple of times during the year. This is another opportunity to share information about your child that will help the school better understand his needs and strengths. Parents of children with special needs who have an IEP (individualized educational plan) participate in team goal setting for their child each year through an annual review process. If your child has a disability, this is your right under federal law, through the Individuals with Disabilities Education Act.

No Place Is Perfect . . . and the Benefits of Bumps

Over the years we've noticed increased concern among parents about protecting their children from experiences that are less than ideal. Every year is different for every child. Having different types of teachers and settings can be a good thing for your child. Children are resilient—and if they are not, we want them to develop this quality. Life is full of ups and downs, and we want our children to be prepared for this. One of the best ways to prepare them is to let them fail in safe ways where there's appropriate support to help them recover, and to learn that they can move on. A bumpy school year can often be a blessing in disguise. If we as parents can see the pros and cons of a situation, and focus on the positive, it helps our children develop the inner strengths and skills to do the same.

Defining the Home/School Partnership

"If you don't believe everything you hear about the school, I won't believe everything I hear about the home. But let's talk if you hear things that worry you, and I will do the same."

What does it mean to partner with the school? The essential ingredients for an effective partnership are respect and trust—feelings that children also need if they are to thrive in school. Since most of us only begin a relationship with a school when our child enters it, that trust must be built from scratch. Partnership can mean one thing to teachers and something else to parents. There's the traditional role of "room mother" (now "room parent"), who helps with class trips, bakes cookies, or brings a dish to the potluck supper. And then there are parent-teacher group meetings. But do these really amount to a partnership?

Recall that until recently, parents and other community members were the primary or only teachers. Children learned the family business by working alongside the adults, or were apprenticed to a community member to learn a trade. Formal schooling was only for the select few.

Gradually, as schooling became expected and mandatory, questions arose on the best roles for home and school in children's education—and on how schools might serve the needs of parents as well as children. Back in 1935, the Pennsylvania Department of Public Instruction, stated in their Parent Education Bulletin number 86:

> The job of the school is only half done when it has educated the children of the nation. Since it has been demonstrated beyond doubt that the home environment and the role played by understanding parents are paramount in the determination of what the child is to become, it follows that helping the parent to feel more adequate for this task is as important from the view of public education and the welfare of society as is the education of the children themselves. Moreover, an educated parenthood facilitates the task of the schools and insures the success of its educational program with the child.

By the 1950s, parents' major form of involvement was through PTAs and PTOs (Parent Teacher Associations/Organizations). While the role of parents was limited, it was generally positive and complementary. More recently, parents began to question the authority of the schools; alternative and parent-run schools cropped up around the country. There was vigorous debate about the role of parents in the schools. And, as a result of their education and experiences, today's parents often have a lot to contribute.

Because they increasingly serve families who have different backgrounds, cultures, and lifestyles, schools need to work harder at finding innovative ways for parents to participate so that all parents can be effective members of the community. Parents, in turn, need to be open with the schools and communicate their questions, concerns, wishes, and dreams for their child with their teachers. They also need to appreciate the difficulty of the task at hand. Remember the teacher has to think about fifteen to twenty children on a daily basis, not just your one child. Your child is best supported when you and the teacher have common goals for him or her, as well as respect and appreciation for the well-being and development of the whole group.

Here is one example of how a school partnered with parents to address a concern.

Several parents noticed that more and more, boys in the kindergarten were shutting girls out of their play—and vice versa. The parents pointed this out to one of the teachers. Knowing that it's common for kids this age to want friends of the same gender, and not realizing how strongly they felt about this issue, she told the parents, "Well, that's just how kindergarten kids are." The group felt their concerns were not taken seriously.

The parents asked for a meeting to discuss the issues with the teachers. Everyone shared specific incidents they'd noticed in the classroom. Then they thought up activities that would help bring boys and girls together.

One day, the teachers had pairs of boys and girls create little posters together, using interlocking circles (Ven diagrams) with drawings, stickers, photos from magazines, and words, showing how they're the same and how they're different. The posters were put on display in the hall so parents could see what was done.

A week later, the teachers said, "Find your poster-making partner and play with them outside today." With gentle nudges from teachers as needed, boys and girls took turns pulling one another in wagons, played on the climbing structure, and pretended they were different ani-

Sending Your Child to School: The Home/School Partnership   *343*

mals and chased one another. One teacher took a few photos for a later display, to remind the children of their fun.

Another school had a similar problem: Kids had gotten into an argument about sports, saying, "Girls can't play football!" Working with a teacher, one parent arranged to have a friend who played on a women's football team visit the class. She also showed a video of the team playing. This opened the eyes of many adults as well as children.

A good teacher is open to such opportunities and responsive to parent concerns. Parents should feel their ideas and thoughts are welcome. While parent and teacher may not always agree, both should be open to talking about it.

In sum, what is an effective home/school partnership?

- collaborative, flexible ongoing relationship between home and school

- Recognition, acceptance, and understanding of cultural and familial complexities

- Appreciation and respect of the school structure, philosophy, and values

- An understanding that children, families, and teachers all need support

- A community resource, both material and personal

Some Final Thoughts

Good parent-teacher partnerships take thoughtfulness and an ability to communicate clearly, without blame or defensiveness. Since children's growth is never even, an effective working relationship will sustain both you and the teacher through the inevitable ups and downs, and help create the best situation possible for your child. We end with a quote from Irene Hannigan, a kindergarten mother who kept a journal of her feelings during her son's kindergarten year. In reflecting on the newsletters that the teacher, Ms. Yardley, sent out, she speaks of a parent-teacher relationship that worked well:

As it turned out, Ms. Yardley's messages provided more than just answers to "what happened at school today." Strategically placed passages informed parents about her goals, what she valued, what was important, and how the year was progressing. I eagerly looked forward to them on Friday afternoons and read each and every word. She became someone I trusted and admired, and she also became someone who educated me. In fact, as the year progressed I found myself writing letters to her in my journal! In these letters Ms. Yardley was my confidante, my mentor, my friend. (Irene Hannigan, *Off to School*, 1998)

We hope that you, too, will have a positive experience with your child's teachers and school and that the points we've covered here will help make that possible. Open hearts and minds are key tools for a rewarding relationship. An effective partnership between home and school is greater than the sum of its parts.

Suggestions for Further Reading

Parents and Teachers

Nancy Balaban. *Starting School, from Separation to Independence: A Guide for Early Childhood Teachers.* Teachers College Press, 1985.

Eugenia Berger. *Parents as Partners in Education: The School and Home Working Together.* Prentice Hall, 1999.

Irene Hannigan. *Off to School: A Parent's Eye View of the Kindergarten Year.* NAEYC, 1998.

Eleanor Lynch and Marci Hanson. *Developing Cross-Cultural Competence: A Guide for Working with Children and Their Families.* Paul H. Brookes Publishing Co., 1998.

Douglas Powell. *Families and Early Childhood Programs.* NAEYC, 1989.

Susan Swap. *Developing Home-School Partnerships: From Concepts to Practice.* Teachers College Press, 1993.

Young Children is the professional peer-reviewed journal of the National Association for the Education of Young Children. It contains readable articles on the latest developments in early childhood education (NAEYC, Washington, D.C., 800-424-2460).

Children's Books

Edith Baer. *This Is the Way We Go to School: A Book About Children Around the World.* Scott Foresman, 1992.

Margaret Wise Brown. *The Runaway Bunny.* HarperFestival, 1991.

Nancy Carlson. *Look Out Kindergarten, Here I Come!* Viking, 1999.

Miriam Cohen. *Will I Have a Friend?* Aladdin, 1989.

P. K. Hallinan. *My Teacher's My Friend.* Ideals, 2001.

————. *A Rainbow of Friends.* Ideals, 2001.

————. *My First Day of School.* Ideals, 2001.

James Howe. *When You Go to Kindergarten.* Mulberry, 1995.

Jonathan London. *Froggy Goes to School.* Viking, 1996.

Jean Marzollo. *I Spy School Days: A Book of Picture Riddles.* Cartwheel Books, 1995.

Jacqueline Rogers. *Tiptoe into Kindergarten.* Cartwheel Books, 1999.

Amy Schwartz. *Annabelle Swift, Kindergartner.* Orchard Books, 1991.

Joseph Slate. *Miss Bindergarten Gets Ready for Kindergarten.* Puffin, 2001.

Jean Van Leeuwen. *Oliver Pig at School.* Puffin, 1994.

Rosemary Wells. *Timothy Goes to School.* Viking, 2000.

Tano Yashima. *Umbrella.* Scott Foresman, 1985.

Support Organizations

Child Care Action Campaign, New York, NY, 212-239-0138. *www.childcareaction.org* (advocates and helps parents lobby for quality and affordable child care).

Child Care Aware, Washington, D.C., 800-424-2246; *www.childcareaware.org* (directs parents to local child-care resource agencies).

Council for Exceptional Children (CEC), 888-CEC-SPED; *www.cec.sped.org* (provides information to teachers, administrators, and others concerned with the education of gifted children and children with disabilities).

Children's Defense Fund, 1-800-233-1200; *www.childrensdefense.org* (provides information about legislation in health care, child welfare, and special education).

Disabilities Rights Education and Defense Fund, 510-644-2555; *http://www.dredf.org* (law and policy center to protect the rights of people with disabilities; referral and information is offered).

Federation for Children with Special Needs, Boston, MA, (617) 236-7210; *www.fcsn.org* (offers parent training and information).

Parent Educational Advocacy Training Center. Springfield, VA, 703-923-0010; *www.peatc.org* (professionally staffed organization that helps parents to become effective advocates for their children with school personnel and the educational system).

National Association for the Education of Young Children, Washington, D.C., 800-424-2460; *www.naeyc.org* (the nation's largest organization of early education professionals of children from birth to age eight; has excellent resources— books, brochures, videos, *Young Children* journal; accredits early childhood programs nationwide).

National Association for Family Childcare, Salt Lake City, UT, 801-269-9338; *www.nafcc.org* (dedicated to the support and accreditation of family day care).

National Information Center for Children and Youth with Disabilities, 1-800-695-0285; *www.nichcy.org* (information clearinghouse on children with special needs and services).

Parents United for Child Care, Boston, MA, 617-426-8288; *www.pucc.com.* (advocates for affordable child care, assists parents in setting up care for school-age children).

Zero to Three: The National Center for Infants, Toddlers and Families, Washington D.C., 212-638-1144; *www.zerotothree.org* (an organization of child development professionals promoting research and awareness of a child's first three years of life).

Web Sites

readyweb.crc.uiuc.edu. Readyweb is an electronic collection of resources on school readiness sponsored by the ERIC Clearinghouse on Elementary and Early Childhood Education.

www.machildcare.com. The on-line resources for child care in Connecticut, Maine, Massachusetts, New Hampshire, Rhode Island, and Vermont. Information for parents seeking child-care and providers. Generic information on child care programs also available.

www.floridasmart.com/education/orginfo_child.htm. Offers a wide range of early childhood education resources for parents, educators, caregivers.

CONCLUDING REMARKS: PARENTING IN THE TWENTY-FIRST CENTURY

W. George Scarlett and Ann Easterbrooks

Three, it's a nice age. Children at this age, being especially devoted to their parents are easy to lead.

Benjamin Spock, *Baby and Child Care* (1946)

Four presents an interesting combination of independence and sociability.

Arnold Gesell, *The First Five Years of Life* (1940)

These two quotations by the leading parenting gurus of mid-twentieth-century America have one thing in common, namely, a remarkable faith that a child's age tells us most if not everything we need to know about a child. Twos are "terrible"; threes are "nice"; fours are somewhere in between. There is, then, no mention of individual differences owing to temperament, gender, disability, culture, or whatever. But in truth, each of these, and more, should influence how a parent responds to a child.

From their focus on age as the defining factor, Spock and Gesell rein-forced the notion that what most concerns parents are simply phases that children go through. As a result, that generation's pediatricians often gave the calming nonadvice, "He'll grow out of it."

What exactly were the concerns that Spock and Gesell discussed at length only to dismiss or treat lightly? Were they concerns about divorce and problematic family life? About growing up in a bilingual family? About the effects of TV? About finding good out-of-home care? Not at all. The concerns that they discussed were quite different from those discussed in this book as the main concerns of today's parents.

So, what has changed for there to be a new set of concerns? The nature of children has not changed. But what has changed is our society and the new demands placed on families. What has changed are the new problems and opportunities that present new challenges and new satisfactions for parenting in the twenty-first century.

Today, we are much more aware of the reality of *diversity,* not just as revealed in discussions of temperament, but also in discussions of life situations and family structure. Parents today are concerned to know if diversity and being different might also mean being deficient. In mid-twentieth-century America, professionals wrote as if they thought families should happen in one stereotypic way—fostering this concern that differing from the norm might be harmful for children. For example, single, working mothers were said to be not simply raising children, but raising them in broken homes and depriving them of being home with their mother.

We know better now. We know that parenting is not about living out one cultural norm within one kind of family structure. We know that old parents, young parents, single parents, gay parents, black, white, Asian parents—all kinds of parents in all kinds of life situations and family structures can do a wonderful job parenting if they do the same old jobs of tucking children in at night, keeping them safe, supporting their interests, and challenging them when they need to be challenged. In short, we know that nurturing children in ways that children have always needed to be nurtured is what matters. Therefore, our concern today must be about what it takes to support children in a variety of life situations and family structures. This leads to a second and related concern among today's parents.

Today, we are much more aware that if we are to nurture children well, we must nurture those environments that support children. We can't simply "run" households. We need to create homes—homes that are stimulating and positive in their overall climate. The home is something created, not given. With more women in the workforce, more homes with a single parent, more "blended" families—in short, more life situations and family structures that make parenting more demanding and complex—creating a stimulating home with a positive climate can be a remarkable challenge indeed. Furthermore, parents are concerned about how to create and maintain a home environment that will support the positive development of not just one child, but everyone in the family.

Another environment needing to be nurtured is the environment where young children receive out-of-home care. With the exception of nursery school, Spock and Gesell said little about out-of-home care because few parents then sent their children for such care. In contrast, today's working parents have many questions about out-of-home care and how nonparental care can be a positive, rewarding experience for their children.

Third, there are changes in technology that have brought new parenting concerns—television and the Internet being the most obvious. One of the concerns around technology has to do with the ease with which it takes adult problems in the outside world and brings them into the home. No longer is it possible to raise children in a protective bubble—as it was in Spock and Gesell's day. Back then, parents and professionals worried about children peeking into their parents' bedroom. Now we worry about children peeking into virtually every room around the globe and observing every sordid event imaginable.

The wisdom of Spock and Gesell, then, is not wisdom enough for today. Their wisdom was for parenting in the middle of the twentieth century. In contrast, this book's wisdom is for parenting at the beginning of the twenty-first century. In particular, it has outlined how you can create and maintain a home that is both nurturing and stimulating regardless of whether your life situation and family structure fits someone else's definition of what is or should be the norm.

However, the main wisdom of this book lies in its helping you to parent proactively. That is, it is meant to help you be more "planful" and smarter—to draw upon the common sense within you, but also to draw upon the uncommon sense of those with a good deal of experience observing and caring for young children. In so doing, you can come to see the world as your child sees it, and act accordingly; you can come to balance short-term needs with your child's long-term needs for growth and development. And you can come to support your child and family in ways that prevent problems from occurring in the first place. This is what we mean by parenting proactively. In saying this, we do not mean that successful parenting requires formal education. It doesn't. What we do mean is that the challenges and opportunities facing today's parents require parents today to be smarter, more clever, more proactive.

ABOUT THE CONTRIBUTORS

Coming together to write *Proactive Parenting* is a group of authors who are collectively responsible for over two hundred books and innumerable articles, geared for both academic and lay audiences, on child development, early childhood education, family-support programming, parenting, and family development. This book has profited from the extensive resources and excellent reputation of the Eliot-Pearson Department of Child Development at Tufts University. Several names in this book will be instantly recognizable both to parents and to professionals who work in this field.

An important feature of this book is that it is written by individuals with considerable expertise in their own areas, in a collaborative editorial process that brings the knowledge and experience of others to bear on each topic. In addition to the authors of specific chapters, the book has benefited from the input of the larger group of colleagues that make up the Eliot-Pearson community. As researchers, teachers, practitioners, and parents themselves, each member of this community has had insight and information to share that enriched each author's work.

Betty Nolden Allen, M.Ed., received her master's degree in early childhood special education from Lesley College. She has been a preschool teacher and special education specialist for many years, joining the Eliot-

Pearson community in 1997 as a preschool and kindergarten teacher, later taking on the additional role of special needs resource teacher at the Eliot-Pearson Children's School. She is currently a lecturer in the Department of Child Development and the coordinator of student teaching and field placements. Ms. Allen's professional work has been focused on inclusive education, diversity and developmentally appropriate practice, collaboration between regular and special educators, and parent education. She is a consultant to preschools and teachers on anti-bias issues, inclusion, behavior management, and developing parent groups. She has a son and a daughter of her own who have successfully left the nest.

Julie Dobrow, Ph.D., is a lecturer and the coordinator of Initiatives on Children and Media at Tufts University. She teaches courses on media in Tufts's Experimental College and courses on children and media in the Eliot-Pearson Department. Dr. Dobrow received her Ph.D. in media studies from the University of Pennsylvania in 1987. Her research focuses on the effects of media on children, ethnic and gender representation in media and its effects on different groups, and cross-cultural communication. The mother of four young children, Dr. Dobrow devotes much of her time to reviewing and critiquing children's media.

Ann Easterbrooks, Ph.D., is associate professor and chair of the Eliot-Pearson Department of Child Development. A developmental psychologist, Dr. Easterbrooks received her Ph.D. from the University of Michigan in 1982. Her research and teaching focuses on social and emotional development of young children, developmental psychopathology, attachment and family relationships, and infancy. She is also interested in adolescent pregnancy and parenting, and is the co-principal investigator of the evaluation of the Massachusetts Healthy Families home-visiting program for parenting teens. Dr. Easterbrooks also serves on the advisory board of the Boston Institute for the Development of Infants and Parents and is a consultant to the Better Homes Foundation on families and children who are homeless.

David Elkind, Ph.D., is professor of child development at Tufts and has been a member of the Eliot-Pearson faculty for over twenty years. He is an internationally known expert on cognitive and social development in children and adolescents and has published widely on the application of Piagetian theory to education. His most recent work has focused on the effects of stress on children, youth, and families. Dr. Elkind's many books include *The Hurried Child, The Child & Society, Miseducation, Reinventing Childhood,* and *Ties That Stress: The New Family Imbalance.* He is a sought-after speaker on family development and parenting. In addition to his academic teaching and research and his popular writing, Dr. Elkind is a board member of the National Parenting Association and Institute for Family Values, and a member of the National Forum on Leadership in Early Childhood Education. He is the co-host of *Kids These Days* on the Lifetime cable channel, and is a frequent commentator on television and radio.

Calvin Gidney, Ph.D., associate professor of child development, holds a doctorate in linguistics from Georgetown University and joined the Eliot-Pearson faculty in 1995. Prior to coming to Tufts, Dr. Gidney was a lecturer in the University of the District of Columbia's Department of Speech-Language Pathology and Audiology and a consultant at the Center for Applied Linguistics in Washington, D.C. Dr. Gidney's teaching and research interests are focused on linguistic development, sociolinguistic difference, and language and social interaction. He is currently involved in research projects related to children's name-calling behavior, the use of language in children's cartoons, and the language development of African-American English-speaking children. Dr. Gidney consults to schools and teachers on topics of language development, bilingualism, and education. Dr. Gidney has spent several years teaching and studying abroad. He speaks six languages and is now working on his seventh.

Deborah LeeKeenan, M.A., is a lecturer and the director of the Eliot-Pearson Children's School, the laboratory school for the Eliot-Pearson

Department of Child Development. The Eliot-Pearson School serves approximately seventy-five children and families from preschool through grade two. It is a model facility used as both a training and observation site and a research facility for faculty and students. Developing parent education and parent advocacy is a major emphasis of the lab school program. Ms. LeeKeenan received her master's degree from the University of New Mexico in early childhood and special education. Past professional experience includes over twenty-five years of teaching in diverse university, public schools, and early childhood settings. She has consulted and led parenting workshops in many schools and programs throughout the New England area. Her professional interests and specialties include anti-bias/multicultural education, developmental curriculum, teacher education, and developing partnerships with schools. Ms. LeeKeenan has written articles for various journals and newsletters on parenting issues and curriculum development. Ms. LeeKeenan is a parent of two young adults, ages sixteen and eighteen, and has been a consumer of parenting books herself over the years.

Richard M. Lerner, Ph.D., is the Bergstrom Professor of Applied Developmental Science at Tufts University. A developmental psychologist, Dr. Lerner received a Ph.D. in 1971 from the City University of New York. He has been a fellow at the Center for Advanced Study in the Behavioral Sciences and is a fellow of the American Association for the Advancement of Science, the American Psychological Association, the American Psychological Society, and the American Association of Applied and Preventive Psychology. Prior to joining Tufts University, he was on the faculty and held administrative posts at Michigan State University, Pennsylvania State University, and Boston College, where he was the Anita L. Brennan Professor of Education and the director of the Center for Child, Family, and Community Partnerships. During the 1994–95 academic year, Dr. Lerner held the Tyner Eminent Scholar Chair in the Human Sciences at Florida State University. Dr. Lerner is the author or editor of 40 books and more than 275 scholarly articles and chapters, including his 1995 book, *America's Youth in Crisis: Challenges and Options* *for Programs and Policies.* He edited volume 1, on "Theoretical models of human development," for the fifth edition of the *Handbook of Child Psychology.* He is known for his theory of, and research about, relations between life-span human development and contextual or ecological change. He is the founding editor of the *Journal of Research on Adolescence* and of the new journal, *Applied Developmental Science.*

Fred Rothbaum, Ph.D., is a professor in the Department of Child Development. A developmental and clinical psychologist by training. Dr. Rothbaum received his Ph.D. from Yale University in 1976 and has been a member of the Tufts Faculty since 1979. His research on parent–child relationships and parents' and children's perceptions of control has been widely published. Dr. Rothbaum's recent research has focused on children's sexuality, cultural differences in family closeness, and parental caregiving practices that are antecedents to aggressive problems in children. In addition to his teaching and research interests, Dr. Rothbaum provides counseling for parents and families. At Tufts, he is also the co-founder and science director of Child and Family News (CFN), a web-based resource for sharing current information about child development research and innovative programming with journalists throughout the country to promote improved coverage of child and family issues in the media.

W. George Scarlett, Ph.D., received his doctorate in psychology from Clark University in 1978. He joined the faculty of the Eliot-Pearson Department of Child Development in 1990 and is currently an assistant professor and deputy chair. Dr. Scarlett has written numerous articles on children's play and on behavior problems for scholarly publications as well as for parent audiences. He is the editor of the book *Trouble in the Classroom: Managing the Behavior Problems of Young Children.* He has also co-edited two books on children's religious and spiritual development. In addition to his writing and teaching, Dr. Scarlett has directed a residential camp for children with serious emotional problems; consulted for Head Start programs on classroom management, early childhood education, and program development; and served as a research associate on the Harvard Project Zero study of young children's play. He has two young children of his own who have done their best to prepare him for contributing to this book.

Susan Steinsieck, M.A., is currently the kindergarten teacher at the Eliot-Pearson Children's School at Tufts and lecturer in the Department of Child Development University, teaching child art. She has a B.F.A. from the Rhode Island School of Design and an M.A. from Columbia University Teacher's College. She has been teaching in lab schools since 1988, and has taught materials and curriculum courses at Parson's School of Design, Mount Ida College, and Leslie College. Before beginning her teaching career, Ms. Steinsieck was a professional vocalist for more than a decade, working in the United States and Europe with jazz greats such as Benny Goodman and Scott Hamilton. Her most recent publication is a chapter in *Trouble in the Classroom: Managing the Behavior Problems of Young Children* entitled "Curriculum as a Tool for Managing Behavior."

Elaine Dyer Tarquinio received her bachelor's degree in child study from Tufts University. She was a preschool teacher at the Eliot-Pearson Children's School for five years and a teacher at the Concord Early Intervention Program for several years. She is currently a full-time parent of two daughters ages seven and fifteen. She is a published author who focuses on the integration of developmental, parenting, and special education issues.

Maryanne Wolf, Ed.D., received her doctorate in education from Harvard University in 1979. She is associate professor of child development in the Eliot-Pearson Department of Child Development at Tufts University and is the director of the Center for Reading and Language Research (CRLR). CRLR is part of a large, three-city reading intervention grant from the National Institute for Child Health and Human Development (NICHD). Across the three funded sites, Dr. Wolf and her colleagues are investigating the efficacy of state-of-the-art reading intervention treatments with different groups of reading-disabled children. For over two decades, Dr. Wolf has been engaged in cross-sectional, longitudinal, and cross-linguistic research on the application of theoretical research to the diagnosis and intervention of developmental dyslexia. Her current theoretical work involves projects in the cognitive neurosciences, socio- and psycholinguistics, clinical (e.g., risk and resiliency factors), and educational fields. She has published widely on the topic of reading development and reading disabilities. In addition to her theoretical work, Dr. Wolf is also involved in an extensive range of applied projects through the Center for Reading and Language Research, including several tutoring and after-school reading programs.

Janet Zeller, Ph.D., has been the director of Tufts Educational Day Care Center, and a member of the Eliot-Pearson faculty, for seventeen years. Her practice and teaching is focused on the inclusion of underrepresented populations, particularly children with special needs, in the mainstream of education. Dr. Zeller received her doctorate in 1985 from Harvard University where she worked with Dr. Sheldon White on research related to changes occurring in children between the ages of five and seven years. While at Harvard, she was the manuscript editor of the *Harvard Educational Review* and taught several undergraduate courses on child development. Prior to coming to Tufts, Dr. Zeller directed the graduate special education program at Wheelock College, and was instrumental in forging both state and federal legislation related to the educational rights of children with special needs and of their parents. She is a frequent consultant to school systems and early childhood programs that are implementing improvements in their services to children with special needs, and is a popular speaker on matters of inclusion. This year, Dr. Zeller is the recipient of the Teacher of the Year Award from the Massachusetts Arc (the largest state organization serving people with special needs and their families).

Cheryl K. Olson, M.P.H., S.D., (editor) is associate director for production and research at the Harvard Medical School Center for Mental

Health and Media. She holds a doctorate in health and social behavior from the Harvard School of Public Health, and is a clinical instructor in the Department of Psychiatry at Harvard Medical School. Dr. Olson previously worked in Basel, Switzerland, as a strategic communications consultant for Hoffmann-La Roche, focusing on health-related behavior change. She is an award-winning documentary writer/producer on health, psychology, and youth topics, and the ghostwriter of two *New York Times* bestselling books on healthy living. She is also a former columnist for *Parents* magazine.

INDEX